Advance Praise for *Writing about Patients*

"Kantrowitz's important book marks a turning point in the clinical and ethical culture of psychotherapy and psychoanalysis. Whereas twenty-five years ago there was a consensus that clinicians who publish case studies must disguise the patient's identity, today analysts more regularly believe they should obtain informed consent from patients and that therapeutic benefit may even result from participating in the writing process. Although this represents a change in our ethical understanding and in our attitudes toward authority, it even more significantly results from a dramatic change in how psychoanalysts understand the nature of the therapeutic process. As always, Kantrowitz conveys the wisdom of a seasoned clinician, the scientific spirit of an empirical investigator, and the moral sensitivity of an ethicist and humanist. She considers general observations and principles as well as the uniqueness of each patient, analyst, and clinical dyad."

—Lewis Aron, Ph.D., director, New York University
postdoctoral program in psychotherapy and psychoanalysis

"This book represents one of the most comprehensive and thoughtful research projects ever conducted about an important aspect of psychoanalytic life. It is remarkably attentive to the emotional nuances involved in writing about analytic patients, both in the analyst's experience and from the patient's point of view. It is clear that Kantrowitz has no wish to attack the profession or to defend it, but rather attempts to reach a truthful and open assessment of both benefits and dangers in this kind of writing, as well as in the divergent approaches to the dilemmas of disguise, consent, showing written material to patients, and related ethical conflicts. Of particular value is the in-depth exploration of the way numerous analysands, both within the profession and outside it, actually experienced being written about, and at times discovering this on their own. In our literature, in which analyst accounts by far outnumber patient accounts (including analysts' rare accounts of their experiences as analysands), this is a refreshing and valuable exception, and I hope many authors will follow in these footsteps."

—Emanuel Berman, Ph.D., professor of psychology,
University of Haifa; Training analyst, Israel Psychoanalytic
Institute; chief international editor, *Psychoanalytic Dialogues*

"One of the most important and difficult tasks in psychoanalysis today is to provide the core clinical data that is vital for the field to continue to evolve and progress. Increasingly, we demand that theories be backed by clinical evidence, and this, in turn, requires the publication of the experience of the patient–analyst dyad. This definitive volume explores the intrinsic difficulties that analysts confront in attempting to share their experiences in a scientific publication. Kantrowitz has assembled an international sample of analysts who describe their very varied experiences in attempting to write, or deciding not to write, about their patients. All the possible conflicts and their solutions, or impossibility of resolution, are described. Questions of whether to disguise the material, to ask the patient for permission in advance, to discuss with the patient the possibility of writing about the analysis, asking for approval of a draft, etc., are all discussed with sensitivity and depth. This important book is essential reading for anyone contemplating publication of patient material."

—Arnold M. Cooper, M.D., professor emeritus in consultation-liaison psychiatry, Cornell University Medical College; former editor of *The International Journal of Psychoanalysis*

"In the last two decades pressure has mounted to potentiate valid psychoanalytic research. *Writing about Patients* was written by an author who is both a very well-trained researcher with numerous publications and a highly experienced analyst. It is the definitive text about the formidable problem and evolving challenge of using clinical data in professional communications. It is an interesting, thorough, sensible, timely, and very clearly written book, with theorizations closely connected to an impressive amount of data. It is illustrated with an enormous array of patients' responses to the reading of their own 'contribution' to the literature. I hope this intelligent, wonderfully documented, and very helpful book will be widely read."

—Cecilio Paniagua, M.D., Sc.D., honorary professor, department of psychiatry, Madrid University

"Dr. Kantrowitz takes on the singlemost important issue for the survival of psychoanalytic literature, seeking out facts about the experience of writing and being written about. Taking us behind the scenes into the private thoughts of both analyst and patient, she opens a window into aspects of the analytic relationship that do not easily fit into the usual analytic categories. It is a fresh, challenging, and sometimes troubling view. This is fascinating reading for everyone in the field."

—Henry F. Smith, M.D., editor in chief, *The Psychoanalytic Quarterly*

Writing about Patients

Responsibilities, Risks, and Ramifications

Judy Leopold Kantrowitz

OTHER

Other Press
New York

Production Editor: Mira S. Park

This book was set in 11 pt. Apollo MT by Alpha Graphics of Pittsfield, NH.

10 9 8 7 6 5 4 3 2 1

Library of Congress Cataloging-in-Publication Data

Kantrowitz, Judy Leopold, 1958-
    Writing about patients : responsibilities, risks, and ramifications /
by Judy Leopold Kantrowitz.
        p. ; cm.
    Includes bibliographical references.
    ISBN-13: 978-1-59051-144-2
    ISBN-10: 1-59051-144-1
    1. Psychotherapist and patient—Moral and ethical aspects. 2. Confidential
communications—Physicians. 3. Psychoanalysts—Professional ethics. 4. Medical
records—Access control. 5. Privacy, Right of. 6. Medical writing. 7. Medical ethics.
    [DNLM: 1. Psychoanalytic Therapy—ethics. 2. Publishing—ethics.
3. Confidentiality—ethics. 4. Informed Consent—ethics. 5. Professional-Patient
Relations—ethics. WM 460.6 K165w 2006] I. Title.

    RC480.8.K36 2006
    616.89'14—dc22

                                                            2006000755

To Steve, Amy, and the memory of Jeff

Contents

Acknowledgments

Many people have contributed in various ways to this book. I wish to thank them all and apologize in advance if I neglect to mention some specifically by name.

My first thanks go to the analysts and patients who generously gave their time by participating in interviews. Obviously, without them I could never have written this book. They were willing to discuss a very controversial topic with candor. Sometimes the situations described were painful and distressing. I am grateful for their openness and hope that they can derive some satisfaction from knowing how much other clinicians will learn from their ideas about preserving confidentiality and their experiences in relation to it.

Glen Gabbard is the next person I wish to thank since it was his article on this topic that initially stimulated my interest in exploring analysts' attitudes and practices. During the course of this study, he has on several occasions been a discussant of my work when I presented at psychoanalytic meetings. His contributions were consistently helpful and it was a pleasure to work together. I am also grateful to Paul Stepansky for suggesting that I interview analysts who would enable me to make generational and theoretical comparisons. This information has broadened and enriched this study. I am deeply appreciative of Natalie Bluestone's introducing me to the ideas of W. K. Clifford. She immediately grasped the kind of philosophical underpinning I was seeking and unhesitatingly sent me to it. As always I am also grateful to her for discussing ideas and challenging my thinking. I am grateful to Ellen Golding for asking questions about my deeper motivation for undertaking this project. She facilitated my realization that in taking the role of an investigative reporter, not passionately committed to a particular point of view, I was unconsciously identifying with my journalist son who had died shortly before I began this study. This insight led me to understand why the project has been satisfying to me in a different way than other projects I have undertaken.

Many people have read parts of this book along the way and offered useful ideas. My writing group—Steve Bernstein, Dan Jacobs, Malkah Notman, and Judy Yanof—provided ideas about both substance and style that I believe greatly improved the quality of this work. Richard Bernstein offered cogent and helpful comments in relation to philosophy and ethical decision making in Chapter 14. His ideas and writing helped me appreciate broader philosophic principles underlying my own views. Ernest Wallwork also read Chapters 14 and provided useful ideas in relation to ethical principles. I am also grateful to the readers and Editors of *JAPA*, *IJP*, and *Psychoanalytic Quarterly* for their suggestions on earlier drafts of papers that appear in somewhat different form as part of this book; they sharpened my thinking. The editors of these journals also gave me permission to reprint the material contained in papers they published; I am very grateful for their willingness to share this content. The material from these papers appears in this book in slightly different form in Chapters 2, 3, 7, 8, 9, 11, and 12. Participants in workshops, discussion groups, scientific meetings, and panels where I have presented parts of this study have all offered ideas that have helped to refine my own. CAPS (Center for Advanced Psychoanalytic Studies) Group VI was especially helpful since I presented to them after I completed the first draft of the book and they were responding to more fully formulated ideas. I am especially grateful to Bill Grossman for his suggestions in relation to the last chapter.

Allanah Furlong, Dan Jacobs, and Tony Kris each read and critiqued the entire book. They were extremely generous with the time and care they took, and their suggestions helped me in reworking the final version. Allanah Furlong, whom I met first as the discussant of the material contained in Chapter 7, not only exchanged a long email correspondence with me in relation to this topic but also edited the manuscript. My appreciation of her efforts on my behalf is beyond words.

I also offer thanks to Judith Feher-Gurewich and Stacy Hague as editors of this book. Their support has been greatly appreciated. My thanks also go to Elaine Lindenblatt for her copyediting and Mira Park for production editing.

I have been working on this project for over three years. I am thankful to friends and family for their support, interest, and patience with me through this process. They listened as people outside the field and provided different and useful perspectives.

In giving acknowledgments, I want to express thanks to my family. In addition to support and love, my father's focus, hard work, and optimism despite obstacles and my mother's creativity, acceptance of loss, and grace in aging have provided me with models that have helped the development of my professional self. My husband Paul has supported and encouraged me throughout every step in my professional life and has been understanding and generous about the time writing takes. His care and devotion enable me to freely pursue my work.

This book is dedicated to our children. All three have had a commitment to social justice and the betterment of members of society less fortunate than themselves—to not only learning, but also giving back to others. The form this commitment took has been different for each. Steve is a historian who teaches and writes about the struggles, triumphs, and defeats of nineteenth-century African Americans and abolitionists, including issues of class and gender. Amy is an educational administrator who works creatively to improve public education and make opportunities available for those who cannot yet do so for themselves. Jeff was a journalist who wrote about immigrant communities, their art, and their food, and vividly captured the courage and joy of these people who had ventured to come to America. Models come not only from elders. I admire my children's paths and they serve as an inspiration to me. In writing this book, I hope in some small way I too am contributing to raising social consciousness of the effect of what we do and of our responsibility to our patients as well as to our professional community.

Introduction

When I began writing for psychoanalytic publications in the mid 1970s and early 1980s, my first papers were based on clinical research. The patients had all given a written informed consent. Most of the material was presented as group findings. Individual examples were confined to a few sentences with no specific information about the particular patient. Under these circumstances, writing about patients posed no conflict. But although I have done clinical research throughout my career, my primary identification has always been as a clinician. As such, I have wanted to make research findings clearly relevant to clinical work and to illustrate their applicability with my own patients. So like all clinicians who write, I have had to struggle with making decisions about using disguise alone or also asking for consent. My decisions have varied on the basis of many different factors. I was never satisfied with any solution. At times I would feel relieved when what I was writing about was not my own clinical work and I was not faced with this dilemma. But then I would begin to feel that I was skirting a problem.

I believe that it is necessary for clinicians to expose their work and their thinking about it—for themselves as well as for other clinicians and for psychoanalysis as a field. Since I believe that, I believe I should be doing it too. When I read Glen Gabbard's paper "Disguise or Consent? Problems and Recommendations Concerning the Publication and Presentation of Clinical Material" (2000), I was impressed by his reflections on the nature of problems related to publication of clinical material. I found myself wondering what most analysts thought about this issue and how they went about making their decisions. I thought other analysts might also find it useful to know the attitudes and practices of their colleagues.

Other issues dominated my personal and professional life at that time, so it was nearly a year later before I returned to this topic. I read everything that I could find on the subject. In 2000, there were not a great number of articles to read, though some about methods of preserving confidentiality were beginning to increase (Gabbard 2000). The papers that did exist all emphasized the difficulty posed by writing about patients.

I wanted to know not only about analysts' attitudes and practices but what they perceived as the clinical reverberations when their patients read about themselves. I assumed the decisions clinicians made when writing about patients would be informed by the clinical consequences they had encountered. If an analyst never had a patient discover an article about him or her, disguise alone might seem more acceptable and less risky than for an analyst who had a patient, or patients, who had discovered a paper in which their clinical material had appeared. I wondered how analysts dealt with patients' discovering they had been written about. I also wondered to what extent opinions and approaches were actually influenced by experience or whether other factors like changing cultural attitudes and changing analytic theory primarily influenced beliefs. I decided to do a study to try to answer these questions. Though analysts rarely talked publicly about these matters, I thought if the sample were large enough, and if they could be assured that their confidentiality would be preserved, they might be willing to talk with me. Certainly, an overview of the ideas, approaches, and experiences of a large number of analysts would provide a useful background for other clinicians faced with similar dilemmas.

I decided I would begin my inquiry on this topic by asking my United States colleagues about their thoughts and experiences when writing about patients. I selected authors who had published clinical material in the *Journal of the American Psychoanalytic Association*

(*JAPA*) between 1995 and 2000. I chose this group because I thought they would represent the ideas and practices of most analysts trained in the American Psychoanalytic Association. In addition, they were the colleagues with whom I had the most contact and, therefore, would be the ones most likely to be willing to talk to me about this subject. I wanted to interview analysts, rather than therapists, because I assumed that they would be able to offer the most in-depth exploration of the meaning to the patient and the long-term ramifications of the experience. However, I also assumed that what I would learn would be of use to all clinicians, therapists as well as psychoanalysts, who write about patients.

I selected the analysts in a randomized but systematic fashion so that at least one analyst-author was chosen from each issue of *JAPA*. Many of my colleagues, especially those I knew less well, were at first quite hesitant to discuss this subject. They assumed that there was a presumptive "correct" way to proceed and that they would be judged for not adhering to it. They also wanted to be assured that they could not be identified. A number of analysts wanted to read what I would quote from them. I always complied with these requests. Some analysts did not respond to my call and others refused to participate. The topic seemed much more emotionally loaded than I had anticipated. My database was large enough that I was able to find thirty analysts who were willing to be interviewed. The diversity of their responses, both in terms of how they thought about the issue and what they chose to do, was considerable. It made me wonder whether analytic colleagues around the world would be similarly diverse and if there were any generalizations I would be able to make from the material I was gathering.

I e-mailed or wrote letters to all the international analysts who published clinical material in the *International Journal of Psychoanalysis* (*IJP*) between 1995 and 2001. I knew far fewer of these analysts and thought I would have fewer responses. Although that turned out to be correct, those analysts who did respond were far less hesitant to express their views and state their practices. Perhaps this was because most of their answers were written, allowing more time for reflection before they responded. It may also be that since they did not know me as well, or in many cases not at all, they were less concerned with how I would view them based on their attitudes and practices. The number of responses, even when I added an extra year to the sample, was insufficient; therefore, I broadened my base and included authors who provided clinical material in papers published in the *Canadian Journal of Psychoanalysis* and *Revista Argentina de Psicoanalisis* and *Revista Brasiliera de Psicanalise* during the same time period.

The responses from these international analysts were similar to their United States colleagues in their increased concerns about the preservation of confidentiality and about patients' rights. Their attitudes and practices were more similar to United States analysts than I had imagined they would be. This led me to wonder how analysts who had published in these journals had thought about and approached matters of confidentiality before they had become attuned to the two-person nature of analytic engagement and aware of patients' rights to autonomy. To answer this question, I then interviewed all the analysts I could locate who had published clinical material in *IJP* and *JAPA* between 1977 and 1981.

The time frame of 1977–1981 was selected because James T. Mclaughlin's paper "Transference, Psychic Reality, and Countertransference" was published in 1981. This paper, I think, was the first publication by a mainstream United States analyst in a mainstream analytic journal that privileged the role of the analyst's countertransference as central to analytic work. As such, it brought the idea of the two-person nature of analytic work to the consciousness of many North American analysts and began to change how they thought about psychoanalysis. Perhaps this new sensibility might have led to different reflections about the concept of ownership of clinical material and raised questions about publishing without obtaining patients' permission among analysts who might previously have viewed clinical material as theirs alone and its publication as no different from publications in medical journals.

In the course of all these interviews, I learned that many analysts had been written about by their own analysts. Their reactions to this experience had notable variation. As I continued these interviews I realized I wanted to hear more patients' first-person accounts. To this end, I posted a notice on the Internet Psychoanalytic Bulletin Board asking for volunteers. Meanwhile, I was presenting the preliminary findings of this study at scientific meetings of local and national psychoanalytic groups. After these meetings, former patients, who had been in the audience or who had friends attending the meeting, would volunteer to discuss their reactions to having been written about by their analysts. Almost all of these former patients had been analyzed by analysts trained in institutes sponsored by the American Psychoanalytic Association.

While informal discussions with colleagues, discourse at scientific meetings, and the psychoanalytic literature all began to reflect changes in how analysts both thought and worked, it seemed that the literature had lagged behind. My curiosity was piqued as to whether analysts identifying with a relational perspective—where patients and analysts are viewed as co-creators of the analytic process—adopted a different stance when writing about patients. To explore this additional question, I interviewed American analysts publishing articles with clinical material in *Psychoanalytic Dialogues* between 1995 and 2003.

It was only after I had completed all these interviews and written the first draft of this book that one of my colleagues called to my attention the fact that there had been an IJPA discussion group of Glen Gabbard's paper on the International Psychoanalytic Internet Bulletin Board. The opinions of analysts contributing to this forum varied from the belief that all clinical papers include an addendum by the patient to the possibility of not publishing case material at all. One patient who volunteered to have material published stated that the motivation for doing so was to give something back to the field. The patient did not want that motive to be analyzed and wanted to be allowed to just have the joy of giving back. Other patients were furious about not being asked for their consent, and many analysts joined in their strongly expressed sentiment that analysts must ask permission. Someone proposed that if an analyst published clinical material without using the analyst's name as author, it would be very unlikely for patients to find the article or recognize themselves if they did. While it was acknowledged that this approach would be a way to provide material for colleagues, future patients, and science, it would eliminate the more personal motives for publishing, and it was unlikely many analysts would accept this solution. However, one of its editors stated that the *Journal of Clinical Psychoanalysis* had in fact, at times, published clinical papers without authors' names.

Despite intense disagreement about how to approach confidentiality, there was overall agreement that psychoanalysts have to communicate clinical material with each other in order to remain a "thoughtful profession open to new ways of seeing and understanding human emotional distress." To view the desire to publish as purely narcissistic was seen as singling out psychoanalysts unfairly since all professional fields require publication.

This brief summary of ideas presented in the Internet discussion of Gabbard's paper "Disguise or Consent?" provides an introduction to this book in which I will present the attitudes and practices of 141 analysts and the effect on thirty-seven patients when they read about themselves. While analysts were selected for the sample, the implications of the findings apply to every clinician who writes about clinical material. The impact on patients in psychotherapy who read about themselves is unlikely to be different from patients in psychoanalysis. The difference is only that they may be less likely to explore it as intensively and extensively. Of course, in any given instance, this assumption of a restriction in exploration may be incorrect. Many therapists are as aware as analysts about the effect of writing on patients; as you will see, not all analysts remained attuned to the impact.

In this book, I will report what analysts actually do to ensure their patients' confidentiality when they write, how they think about the choices they make, and, when the data permit, what effect these decisions have had on their patients and the treatment. I will examine the practice and ideas of psychoanalysts who have published articles using clinical illustrations from their practices. Eighteen of the 141 analysts who were interviewed had also been written about when they were patients. Another nineteen former patients, eight of whom are also analysts, volunteered to discuss their experiences of reading about themselves.

When I quote the analysts' responses to me, both oral and written, I have made minor changes, a light editing, in order to make the person's ideas come across more clearly. In these instances, I have done so without drawing attention to my changes in the text. As a result, there are slight differences in these quotes from those that appeared in published articles. In addition, when I thought the original phrase was ambiguous or that I needed to interpolate meaning to help the reader to understand, I included these ideas in square brackets.

The material collected in this study has made me more conscious of the enormous difficulties posed when writing about patients. I remain in agreement with Gabbard (2000) that there is no simple solution to the problem. Strict guidelines that apply to all situations do not appear to make clinical sense—though as you will see, many analysts strongly believe that they should be established and adhered to. Nonetheless, the study has sensitized me to the nature of difficulties that can occur, thereby permitting me to offer some general recommendations about this issue. While I know my conclusions fall far short of the kind of advice many clinicians wish for, I hope I will have provided some basis for their reflections about the decision to write about a patient and about the manner in which they write if they conclude it is desirable to do so.

In the first section of this book, I review the literature on confidentiality when publishing clinical work and present the attitudes and practices on this topic of the 141 analysts interviewed in this study. I report the thoughts of these analysts about why they write, how they think about preserving confidentiality, contemplate patients' reactions, and how conscious they are of struggles set off in themselves. Stimulated by their communications, I also offer some of my thoughts about motives and conflicts related to writing about patients. Pursuing the same questions, I compare international analysts with United States analysts. I also compare the views of an earlier generation of analysts with the practices and ideas of contemporary analysts who have published articles using clinical illustrations during the last decade. In addition to this generational comparison, I consider the impact of theory on decisions in relation to writing by comparing the attitudes and practices of more classically oriented analysts with a group of relational analysts.

The second section presents the literature on analysts' perceptions of patients' reactions to reading about themselves and the perceptions of analysts I interviewed of their own patients' reactions to reading about themselves. Patients read about themselves in two different situations: they discovered articles written by their analysts or their analysts asked permission to use this material and showed it to them. The analysts' accounts of the clinical ramifications are discussed. I also present the perspective of relational analysts some of whom believe that discussing their papers with their patients can act as a vehicle for analytic work.

In the third section, I present patients' own descriptions of the effect of reading what their analysts wrote about them. The section begins with a summary of the only fully elaborated written account I could find outside of the psychoanalytic literature, that is, of Phillip Roth's experience. It is followed by the reactions of other patients who are also not analysts. The last chapter in the section contains accounts by patients who are themselves analysts, or were analytic candidates at the time they were written about. The unique aspects of writing about analysts and candidates are examined.

The fourth section explores analysts' use of themselves for clinical examples when they present themselves in disguise. These illustrations are discussed in relation to other examples in the psychoanalytic literature where it has been presumed that analysts have presented material in this fashion. Another chapter considers ethics in relation to clinical writing. In a final chapter, I summarize my understanding of why analysts write, the possible clinical ramifications of analysts' decisions in relation to publications, and some implications about the effect of analysts' choices on readers of psychoanalytic publications and psychoanalytic literature itself in influencing conceptions about psychoanalysis as a field.

I
ANALYSTS' ATTITUDES AND PRACTICES

I
Background Literature

Psychoanalysis is a theory of psychic organization, a clinical technique, and a method of research. Research requires data; for that reason, Freud (1905) maintained that analysts have a duty to publish what they learn from treating patients. This knowledge advances psychoanalysis as a field; it also may help future patients. Yet most analysts identify themselves primarily as clinicians, not as researchers or theorists. Most analysts do not write.

Supervision, peer groups, and other mutual sharing of clinical work with colleagues provide opportunities for continued professional growth; however, only a relatively small number of analysts participate in such activities and the majority of these are likely to have been trained in the same places, often at the same time. Analytic literature, by contrast, exposes analysts to diverse ideas and experiences and stimulates them to reflect on new, strange, and even "dangerous" ideas. Because clinical material published in psychoanalytic journals has been peer-reviewed, readers are assured that the ideas presented have been evaluated in terms of their merit for consideration. Analysts who contribute to the literature, in a sense, have dual careers. Like their colleagues, their first allegiance is to their patients; but they are also, in Freud's sense, researchers who are studying the nature and process of

3

analytic work and the phenomena they discover in this process (Freud 1905, Goldberg 1997, Michels 2000, Reiser 2000, Szecsody 2000, Tuckett 2000a,b).

Psychoanalysis is not a hard science; nonetheless, its method, while shaped by the art of individual clinicians, has a structure and certain shared principles. When analysts write they are often developing variations on themes, but sometimes they are also challenging, even disproving previously held beliefs—for example, our gradually discarding the value, or even the possibility, of the analyst as a "blank screen." Such challenges may change long-held assumptions or may redress imbalances in emphasis; at times these new ideas may be only of passing interest and are ultimately discarded.

Everyone agrees that it is essential to the development of psychoanalytic ideas and clinical work that at least some analysts engage in the enterprise of writing. But analysts who write about their patients are inevitably placed in a conflict of allegiances. They must protect the confidentiality of their patients while simultaneously providing accurate enough clinical data to support their ideas.

Debate about how best to ensure protection of patients' privacy is not new, but recently it has become a topic of increased attention as concerns about patients' rights have become prominent. Should analysts simply disguise clinical material or should they ask patients' consent as well (Aron 2000, Gabbard 2000)? What are the consequences of either choice? Authors who have written about publication of clinical material have often noted how few examples there are in the literature of the effect these choices have on individual patients or analytic work in general.

Articles that use first-hand observations from the analytic situation as the basis for drawing conclusions are relatively rare (Stein 1988a). Of the sixty most quoted psychoanalytic articles from 1969–1982, only fifteen of them presented clinical reports (Klumpner and Frank 1991).

The problems posed in writing articles containing clinical illustrations are multifold. Freud (1905) believed that no patients would have spoken freely if they had thought their material would be published, nor would they ever have granted permission had they been asked. In discussing the case of Dora, Freud enumerated the precautions he took to ensure her confidentiality. The patient he wrote about was not from Vienna; no one knew he was treating her; he waited four years from the end of her treatment to write and learned of changes in her life that led him to think she would no longer be interested in the events he reported; he used no names that would be recognizable, and he published the case in a scientific journal, which made it highly unlikely that the non-medical reader would come across this article. Further, he believed that if Dora herself were to see the publication, she would learn nothing she did not already know and would realize that no one besides herself could have recognized her.

Contemporary analysts' concerns are similar, but the ease in finding published material makes them feel less confident than Freud that these methods for preserving confidentiality will be effective, even if they were feasible. As it turns out, unfortunately, the identity of Freud's patients was not always as adequately disguised as he had assumed (Mahony 1984, 1986).

Recent articles (Aron 2000, Gabbard 2000) have explored and summarized the nature of current debates about how best to maintain confidentiality. I will review the highlights. There is no disagreement among analysts that patients' confidentiality needs to be protected; what is debated is how to do this with the fewest possible negative consequences for the patient. Should analysts simply disguise material and count on no one, including the patient, recognizing the patient, or should the analyst also ask the patient's consent? Many analysts believe that changing identifying features, though not the dynamics or contents of process, preserves both the integrity of the presentation and the patient's confidentiality (Aron 2000, Freud 1905, Gabbard 1997, 2000, Goldberg 1997, Renik 1994, Shapiro 1994, Stein 1988a). There is the lingering concern that disguise may mislead as the details become distant from the actual facts (Klumpner and Frank 1991, Lipton 1991). Other analysts propose removing material that is not essential to the understanding of the case or illustration (Clifft 1986, Galatzer-Levy 2003). Composites are another solution, but they may seem too much like fiction (Gabbard 2000, Goldberg 1997). Having another analyst write the examples is proposed as an alternative (Gabbard 2000), but not many analysts are offered this opportunity and analysts often want to express their own ideas regarding their patients.

Still other analysts argue that it is wrong not to obtain the patients consent (Michels 2000, Reiser 2000, Smith 1995, Stoller 1988). And even when permission is obtained, it may be asked whether informed consent can ever be a meaningful concept in relation to clinical material; unconscious factors stemming from the transference inevitably influence the patient's decision (Aron 2000, Gabbard 2000, Goldberg 1997, Stoller 1988, Tuckett 2000a).

Granting consent itself may or may not be preceded by the patient's reading what the analyst has written. When patients read material about themselves there is a danger that the process may become intellectualized (Aron 2000, Lafarge 2000); extra-analytic information about the analyst contained in papers may inhibit associations because of guilt over knowing "secrets" about the analyst (Berman 1995); the patient may become aware of the analyst's professional self and the professional community and experience them as intruders on the analysis (Crastnopol 1999); or the very act of the writing may itself serve as a transference–countertransference enactment that ruptures the analytic frame (Feiner 1996). The specific aspect of treatment that the analyst selects to write about provides an inevitably incomplete picture of the patient that potentially may "freeze" the patient's process of exploration. The patient may also consciously or unconsciously discern previously unrecognized aspects of the analyst's personality or internal life that may affect the patient's self-image in light of the revised relational place the patient then imagines he or she may have had for the analyst. It may concretize intersubjective fantasies of the patient (Furlong 1998). In addition, the patient's feelings about the publication of personal material may change over time (Crastnopol 1999, Stoller 1988).

On the other hand, some analysts who individualize their decisions, selecting only certain patients to whom they show their examples, believe that a collaborative approach in discussing their clinical material may have therapeutic benefit for certain patients (Aron 2000, Crastnopol 1999, Lafarge 2000, Scharff 2000, Schwaber 1997). Stoller (1988) believed that a patient–analyst collaboration around written material was almost always to the patient's benefit. Some specific advantages may be that it provides an opportunity to clarify what may have been misunderstood by either patient or analyst or initiate a piece of working through in de-idealization of the analyst (LaFarge 2000, Pizer 1992). Gerson (2000) maintains that patients' knowledge of their analysts' writing about them both disrupts and contains the intensity and insularity of the patient–analyst dyad. But many analysts do not agree.

Levin (2003) argues that no matter how useful or therapeutically beneficial it may be in individual instances, soliciting patients' views on what their analysts have written about them imperils the credibility of the work. If clinical reporting requires universal patient approval, what is published may be assumed to be censored in accordance with patients' narcissistic needs. The result will be a discrediting of the reliability or full veracity of the clinical material and of the authors' conclusions. Clearly, there are diverse and conflicting views about the effect of patients' reading their analysts' accounts of their material; they range from potential facilitation of the analytic process to potential interference of the process (Scharff 2000) and of the literature itself.

The timing of requests for permission is another controversial issue. To ask during treatment introduces the analyst's extra-analytic agenda into the process; to ask after termination intrudes on the patient's life and may rekindle issues put to rest, possibly leading to a need for more analysis (Lipton 1991). For these reasons, some analysts believe that to make a general request at the start of treatment is the best option (Goldberg 1997, Lipton 1991, Michels 2000). Others, however, have found that this solution does not work since beginning patients do not know the analyst well enough to have developed a trusting, working relationship, or a knowledge that their therapeutic needs will be met by the analyst (Aron 2000). Writing about patients still in treatment poses the potential problem that analysts may begin to fit patients into a theory they have formed about them (Michels 2000). Many analysts join Freud (1905) in maintaining that analysts should neither ask for permission to use patients' material nor write about an analysis until it is over (Gabbard 1997, 2000). But in addition to drawbacks already cited to this approach, there is the objection that it leaves analysts no chance to get a sense of their patients' reactions and patients no opportunity to analyze them unless after termination they return to their analysts (Aron 2000). While exploration of these reactions might be beneficial to a former patient, it is problematic if the need has been stimulated by the analyst's request. Whatever time the analyst chooses to write, the effect of the analyst's subjectivity must also be taken into account when reading any presentation of patient material (Tuckett 1993).

The multiplicity of difficulties involved in protecting both patients' confidentiality and treatment amply explains why clinical examples have been relatively scarce in psychoanalytic literature. Stein (1988a) believes that when analysts decide to write they not only have an intensified interest in a subject but also wish to attain some distance from it. When work with an analytic patient leaves the analyst with unresolved and painful questions about what was not accomplished, analysts may use writing to reduce their tension about these problems. Writing a paper may decrease the painful affect by gaining a greater perspective on what occurred. If the conceptualizations and use of data are presented effectively, they may contribute something to the field. Stein's implication is that the scientific contribution may be a way to make up for feeling badly about a clinical failure. Stein notes that in the process of writing, the analyst may be able to explore his or her own conflicts about the case, even if these reflections do not accompany the publication. Alternatively, when analysts are not aware of intense and uncomfortable feelings in relation to analytic work, their unacknowledged presence may be a factor in the analyst's not writing. He seems to suggest here that the wish for distance can be so great that the analyst does not want to bring to consciousness disquieting feelings or thoughts stirred by the analytic work.

Other reasons Stein cites for analysts' reluctance to write include anxiety about the reception of their papers by colleagues and concern about the added complications to transferences in ongoing analyses when patients read analysts' papers. He grants that there are also real-world considerations that may prevent analysts from writing. Some analysts who are skilled in talking to patients experience difficulties in putting their ideas and interpretations in written form. Analysts may also be too busy with other things that take a priority. Family life and long work hours to support a family may leave little time left over. Reflections on analysts' motives for writing are rarely introduced in the literature. Stein's contribution is unique in addressing this topic.

Stein suggests that papers would be better if the process by which attention was focused and explanations formulated was revealed in addition to their observations and conclusions. Such candid description of thought processes would require more self-revelation than analysts have been accustomed to offering. He elaborates that while there is good reason for analysts to be reluctant about revealing their private lives to their patients, there is no reason to conceal the process by which they have observed and come to conclusions. The ideas put forward by Stein anticipated a trend toward greater self-exposure of analysts' thoughts. Over the next decade and a half after his paper, analysts not only revealed their own feelings and countertransference reactions more fully, but this transparency in analysts' thoughts and feelings came to be expected in analytic writing.

Despite all the problems involved in writing about patients' material, there is agreement that analysts have a responsibility to write for psychoanalysis as a field, for its advancement as a science (Freud 1905, Goldberg 1997, Michels 2000, Reiser 2000, Szecsody 2000, Tuckett 2000a,b). It is necessary that analysts exchange ideas (Reiser 2000), put thoughts into words that confront understanding (Michels 2000), and share cases for research, interdisciplinary dialogue, the community (Goldberg 1997), and for the benefit of future patients (Schwaber 1997, Tuckett 2000a).

Having provided the background for my topic, I will next report what I learned about the attitudes and practices of analysts trained in American Psychoanalytic Association-sponsored institutes who published clinical examples in the journal sponsored by this organization.

2
Journal of the American Psychoanalytic Association (JAPA) Authors[1]

As I stated at the beginning of this book, writing about patients poses a conflict of values for analysts. They believe it is vital for the health and growth of psychoanalysis that clinical material be presented to analytic colleagues and other academic scholars. In addition, without such accounts there would be no history of changes in ideas and techniques. On the other hand, the value of the integrity of the patient–analyst relationship and its confidentiality is foremost in the minds of most analysts. Finding ways to assure patients' privacy and their trust in their analysts' intentions to keep their welfare foremost is essential.

In previous decades most, but by no means all, analysts believed well-considered disguises would prevent others from recognizing patients and was all that was necessary; however, most analysts were also aware that they could not disguise the material from the patients themselves. As a result, they generally chose not to write about patients who were in the

1. Material in this chapter has previously appeared in slightly different form in the *Journal of the American Psychoanalytic Association* (2004) 52:69–99, © 2004 American Psychoanalytic Association. All rights reserved. I am grateful to the editor for granting permission for the material to be reprinted in this book. The permission was conveyed through the Copyright Clearance Center, Inc.

mental field or had relatives in it. If they decided to write about these patients, most often they sought the patients' permission. Sometimes these precautions were not adhered to and frequently enough, as you will learn in the second section of this book, there were untoward outcomes. At the present time, the Internet makes access to information about others, including what they write, easily attainable. As a result, there is an increasing concern among analysts about both confidentiality and the impact of what they write on their patients; potentially, any patient who wishes to may discover and read what his or her analyst publishes.

In this chapter, I will report on the attitudes and practices of thirty analysts residing in the United States who published clinical material in *JAPA* between 1995 and 2000.[2] Each analyst-author was interviewed by telephone for thirty minutes to an hour. The interviews were transcribed immediately on completion. The authors were asked how they decided to write about a given patient. Once they decided to write, did they ask for consent? Did they show the patient what they had written? At what time in relation to the analytic work did this conversation occur? What were the ramifications? Had they ever had a patient refuse permission? Give permission and then rescind it? If they disguised the material, how did they do this? When in the course of treatment did they write or begin to write? Did a patient not asked for permission ever discover that he or she had been written about? What were the ramifications? What were their ideas about the benefits and

---

2. A systematically random selection of papers including clinical illustrations (for example, selecting the last example with clinical material in the first volume, the next-to-last article in the second volume, the third-from-last article in the third volume, etc.) was made using the *Journal of the American Psychoanalytic Association*. At least one article was selected from each issue in the period 1995–1999, including a supplement, and from the first issue of 2000. Thirty-six authors were called to be interviewed. Two analysts indicated that their example was not from their own material; two declined to participate in the study, and two who were left messages did not return my phone call. The sample then comprised thirty authors who agreed to be interviewed. All were graduate analysts, twenty-seven of whom have graduated from institutes affiliated with the American Psychoanalytic Association. They ranged in age from their early forties to their eighties, the majority being in their fifties or sixties. Twenty-three are male. Twenty-four were psychiatrists, five were psychologists, and one had an academic Ph.D. Most of these analyst-authors identified themselves as modern Freudians with an essentially ego psychological orientation, though two spoke of a shift toward relational theory and another of the influence of intersubjectivity.

problems of the approach they chose? Did they think differently in regard to writing about patients who worked in the mental health field? Had their views about using disguise or consent in relation to clinical examples changed? If they had, what factors were responsible? Had they ever written about themselves in disguise?

Reasons for Case Selection

Why did analysts choose to write about the patients they did? Almost all the analyst-authors stated some variation on the theme that a patient's material stimulated a new idea or illustrated an idea already in focus. Manifestly, the analysts' choices of patients to ask for consent were based on a belief that these patients would not be identifiable to readers and that their conflicts would not become inextricably entangled with the request. Latently, no doubt, these choices were multiply determined. Interdigitation of the psychological issues of patient and analyst may consciously or unconsciously have stimulated the analyst to explore and try to master these shared issues in displacement through the writing process. The specific meaning of any manifest topic or particular patient, of course, cannot be known without the analyst's associations and elaboration and a majority of the sample did not provide this material.

Three analysts spoke of writing as a kind of self-supervision. They were aware that they used writing, which included intellectualization, as a way of managing countertransference reactions. These analysts seemed conscious of these latent issues, though they did not explicate them in detail. Here are their remarks:

> I usually write about a patient because something in the work is troubling me. I seek a consultation and I work on it in the writing about it.

> When I write I'm trying to work out a problem through a kind of self-supervision. I try to understand certain issues that pose transference/countertransference reactions and writing helps me keep on an even level. I think I write to understand why I did what I did. I wait till an issue is resolved to publish it.

> I came to the view that writing about a patient for me is a countertransference enactment. I could say it's an interesting clinical or

theoretical problem. But really I think the papers arose from the treatment rather than some intellectual interest. Writing helps me to shake off an excess quanta of stimulation coming off the case and to channel it into the writing. Patients make me interested in something that gets stirred up in me—probably not the way it works for many others. They may have intellectual interests and scan for cases. But for me writing gets me to reflect; it gets me to master what is stirring me up. I try to bring intellectual leverage to a puzzling or disconcerting experience.

Reasons for Not Selecting Patients

All the analysts in this study made it clear that they would never write about certain patients. The reasons for this decision were always presented in terms of the patient's welfare. There were some patients who could not be disguised adequately; usually, this was because they, or their relatives, were in the mental health field. Some other patients were thought likely to read the psychoanalytic literature and eventually recognize themselves; the analysts of these patients were concerned about negative consequences to the patient or the treatment process if permission were asked. Since for these patients disguise seemed inadequate, they chose not to write about them.

All the analysts also agreed that there were clinical indications in certain patients that mitigated against requesting permission or writing about them without it. These indications related primarily to character structure. Patients with masochistic or paranoid characters and patients eager to please were among those whom analysts thought might respond in a manner detrimental to their treatment. Some analysts also made a distinction between writing a case in on-going analysis and a case written after termination; the assumption was that after termination the impact on the patient would not have negative ramifications while it might during the course of the treatment.

CONFIDENTIALITY

Once analysts decided to use a patient's material, their methods for dealing with confidentiality had several variations.

Disguise Alone versus Disguise and Consent

Almost twice as many analysts (15) chose to disguise material as regularly asked for permission (8). Seven analysts varied their approaches to confidentiality, at times using disguise alone and at others asking consent as well, depending on the circumstances. The small number of authors (3) who wrote about patients in the mental health field always asked the patient's consent. They also obtained the patient's assurance that the material was sufficiently disguised by having the patient read the vignette in question.

Twelve analysts showed their patients what they had written about them. Half of these stated that they wanted to be certain about the adequacy of the disguise. Other reasons for showing patients material about themselves included the analysts' wish for reassurance that what they had written, and how they had written it, was acceptable to the patient. Two analysts who showed their patients clinical material did so with the express intention of making it part of the analytic work; in one of these instances, the analyst did not consider the work formally analytic, due to the severity of the patient's pathology.

It might have been anticipated that the older analysts in the sample, trained at a time when analysts were not as sensitized to issues of patients' rights, as is the case today, would be more likely to employ disguise alone when writing clinical examples. However, age was not a factor that discriminated among the analysts in terms of their method of preserving confidentiality. Nor did gender differentiate between the groups.

Methods of Disguise

All these analysts, whether or not they asked consent, disguised the clinical material. They did so in a variety of ways. They changed names and other identifying data, such as, profession, geographic location, age or number of siblings, religion, and in a few cases, gender. Most analysts who changed a patient's gender worried that readers might draw incorrect inferences from this alteration, but they did not consider gender relevant to the point they were trying to illustrate and believed that the change ensured the patient's privacy. Some analysts disguised their patients by omitting demographic details. This approach was often used when a paper was illustrating an aspect of technique or analytic process. Other analysts disguised their patients by introducing "red herrings." They altered or added details that bore no relevance to the central issues being illustrated, for example, adding extra siblings or making siblings cousins. One analyst elaborated this strategy, giving a nuanced sense of how details can contribute to disguise.

> I change locations. I put the patient in a different climate, for example Alaska rather than Mexico and say something about the weather, for example snow delayed the patient whereas the patient was really late but for another external reason.

The analyst-authors were all clear that they would not change the dynamics or alter verbatim material. Some, however, disagreed with the "red herring" solution, believing that such disguises might well affect the depiction of dynamics.

Consent

Eighteen of the thirty analysts had on at least one occasion asked a patient's permission to use his or her clinical material for publication. All eighteen analysts had at least one patient who consented to material about them being published. Many of these eighteen analysts had several patients who had given this consent.

In this sample, three patients are reported to have denied permission to have their material used for publication. In most instances in which a request was made, unless the analyst pursued a patient's reaction or addressed related material in displacements, the topic ended without questions or exploration. Some analysts reported pursuing the issue; others did not.

Two analysts focused on the meaning and motives of patients' consent.

> Sometimes a patient may want to be exhibitionistic; sometimes patients may want you to write about them, even as an attack on relatives. It's complicated because the motive may be self-ridicule or ridicule of their family. So even the patient's consent is not the whole issue.

I've never had a patient refuse permission. I've had patients give permission where later it turns out not to have been good for them and there could have been a masochistic component. Permission plays out characterological orientations. Sometimes there are reverberations, where issues keep coming back, sometimes for years. With one patient the reality negotiation about giving me permission was central; she felt that she had given me something and so had become part of my life outside the office; it felt meaningful to have a role in my life. For others giving permission doesn't seem to make a lot of difference one way or the other; they metabolize it and move on.

The latter analyst's description indicated that he explored the meaning of consent with at least some of his patients. Other analysts may also have done so, but they did not indicate this in their accounts. When analysts accept patients' consent without further exploration, it can seem pragmatic on the surface. It is reasonable to suppose that consent relieves analysts from the worry that the patient might refuse or that their request might iatrogenically stir conflict. The fact that no one in this sample expressed feelings of relief may reflect the latent conflict experienced by analysts when using patient material. At the end of this chapter, I will discuss this issue and some possible reasons why analysts avoid exploring these conflicts.

While some analysts were quite reflective about the meanings and motives of their patients' consent and reactions to written material, neither they, nor most other analysts in this sample, discussed the analytic meaning of their choice of patient to write about nor their reactions to their patients' responses when permission was easily granted. The absence of this self-exploration may be an artifact of the interviews not having specifically included this question. Or perhaps, knowing that I would be publishing this material, these analysts might have been showing a preconscious reluctance to expose this more personal dimension— even though they also knew that their anonymity would be ensured by virtue of the size of the sample and the absence of identifying details.

There were, however, some notable exceptions to this trend toward non-reflection. One such counter example was offered by an analyst, who wished it had been possible to withdraw a paper already published, because of later reactions from the patient.

A patient in the mental health field had said fine, no problem, good for the field, but then there was a problem. The patient felt embarrassed about some of the material. I recognized this in a derivative form. It was not in overt feelings. Looking back on what I wrote I see that the patient saw himself as quite regressed; this was the patient's view, not mine. In retrospect, I did not feel comfortable with the patient's feeling this. I wished I'd never published it. I feel I should have waited longer for reactions from him. If I had had the full force of the patient's reactions, I probably would not have rushed it. I wouldn't do that again. I don't know about the long-term consequences because the analysis was interrupted for reality reasons. That left a lot unclear. Part of me would like to talk to the patient about it even now but I don't want to intrude on his life or interfere with his current treatment.

The fear of intruding on a patient's analysis or life was a factor that influenced many analysts in regard to the timing of their requests for permission.

TIMING OF REQUESTS FOR CONSENT

Requests at the Beginning of Analysis

Four analyst-authors introduced a request at the beginning of analysis for a general permission to use clinical material. The request was presented in the context of a discussion of other working arrangements, such as fees, vacations, and policies about missed hours. These analysts explained to the patient that they taught and wrote and that analysts involved in these activities used illustrative patient material by disguising any identifying data. The analyst asked the patient to think about how he or she would feel about giving permission to use their analytic material in this fashion; if this were not acceptable to the patient, the analyst would not do so. One of these analysts added that he had many vignettes from patients over the years, and that a patient might read something he wrote and assume it was about him or her when in fact it was not. This analyst reviewed his arrangements once a year so that patients could reconsider how they felt about them. Two of these four analysts no longer believed that this generalized consent was necessary. Here is what one of them said:

> I used to tell all my patients at the start of treatment that I did at times write about patients after the treatment. I never write about a

patient until treatment is over and then I wait at least a year. I would send them a copy of what I wrote and ask for their permission. I'd disguise it. The patient would then write back giving me permission. I used to do this because I was a full-time academic and I'd be publishing. It was a clearing the way. There were never any objections or strong reactions so after a time I just stopped making that initial statement but I always asked permission afterwards.

Request in the Middle of Analysis

The five analysts who requested permission in the middle of analysis stated that they encountered no strong reactions and did not believe the request interfered with ongoing work. They chose to ask for permission when clinical material captured their interest because, in the words of one analyst, "the material [at such points] has a vividness and freshness that it lacks after the fact." This alive, affective engagement with the material was also the reason given by those analyst-authors who used only disguises and wrote while the treatment was ongoing. For this group of analysts, ongoing material held their interest in a way that was more gripping than when they were no longer treating the patient. One of these analysts, who used disguises but did not request permission, stated that writing even earlier would not feel problematic, but it was unlikely until the middle phase of analysis that she could know her patient well enough to clearly formulate an understanding.

Two other analysts made similar points:

> Originally I was swayed by people who said not to write until the treatment is over. It makes sense because you don't know whether your conclusions are true or false. But for me I found and I find that I want only to write during the treatment because that's when the iron is hot and grabs me. I do bear in mind the scientific limitations of doing it that way. But writing gets you to reflect and read about similar problems that have been reported in the literature. It helps the treatment.

> Although many feel that writing during treatment is a problem, I think it gives an opportunity to work with the patient on what has been written about and the reactions to it. To ask at the start of treatment in a blanket way seems to be asking a lot to negotiate at the start.

If I were the patient I'd want to know what the analyst would write about, when it was being written, and I'd want to see it. Initially, it would likely feel invasive, a use of power and control, and seems destructive to the initial sense of safety. After a while, you have a whole set of understandings that have created a sense of trust. It's usually in the middle or late phase and I only do it in a treatment where I think it will be tolerable.

Requests in the Termination Phase

The five analyst-authors who chose to ask the patient's permission during the termination phase believed that this allowed the patient's reactions to become part of the treatment process which would not have been possible in the same way after termination. One of these analysts offered this view:

> I prefer to wait until the patient is in the termination phase to ask about writing. There are pros and cons about any way. If you wait until after termination, they don't have the opportunity to get to the unconscious meaning of giving or not giving consent. If you ask earlier, it's introducing a parameter and the patient may not yet be ready to understand why they are agreeing or not. But by the end the patient is psychologically stronger. It seems like the best compromise.

Requests after Termination

Only one analyst in this sample always waited until after termination to request the patient's permission. Two other analysts frequently, but not routinely, waited until after termination to ask patients for consent. Five analysts ask permission during treatment but choose not to write until afterward because of the effect on the analyst's listening. One analyst's explanation follows:

> I don't like to write while I do the work. The nature of writing pushes me for closure. I don't mean what I write isn't honest but the actual writing changes the way I feel about the patient and the analysis. So I don't write while I see a patient. When I write it becomes something I'm invested in. It forecloses openness to their material in my mind. When I work I want to be open to wherever it may go.

APPROACHES TO PRESERVING CONFIDENTIALITY

Analysts Committed to a Method

The five analyst-authors who have always asked for patients' permission have worked in academic settings where asking and granting consent are a commonplace occurrence and often a requirement. These analysts extended this assumption or rule to their analytic work. Two of these authors are not themselves directly involved in academic work but have been mentored by those who are. None of these analysts reported any awareness of negative effects from asking patients for their consent.

In contrast, ten analysts who always employ disguise believed that their patients would be affected negatively by a request. These ten analysts never asked permission. Some of their reasons were as follows:

> The point about writing about a patient is never about him or her but about the possibility that the dynamics described would apply to many patients. I wouldn't want to emphasize the importance the patient has for the analyst in terms of scientific interest. I would not want the patient's satisfaction or dissatisfaction with what I wrote or the fact I was writing to be a factor in the analysis.

> I'm not comfortable asking patients for permission. If treatment has been going on for a long time, I worry patients would wonder what I've been interested in all along, whether they would think I was using them, whether it would take away the feeling treatment has for them. Patients are under pressure to say they agree because of the transference, to comply, a lot doesn't get talked about. If the patient doesn't give permission, there's a countertransference response, a tension. The patient's response gets talked about, but I'm not sure it all really gets resolved.

> I always disguise. I feel strongly that patients shouldn't be told. I heavily disguise. Patients I can't disguise well enough, I can't write about. I think it's a transgression to ask a patient. I feel a level of betrayal to use a patient for myself, to be writing about them. I don't know when you could ask during the treatment or call someone back. Informed consent is a pseudo notion. I don't think it can be worked through: being special, being used, and paying for the time. I hate the whole thing because I love to write. I not only worry about the

writing but also about how it affects the treatment—that I'm doing it—that the idea in the patient's material becomes what I'm listening for and then the patient may try to deliver it.

I never inform the patient. I try to disguise it, try to choose someone who won't read the literature, and I worry. I don't ask because I think it corrupts everything in the treatment. It's a narcissistic gratification, a seduction, and a gratification. I'd be using them and it couldn't be analyzed.

I don't see it as a free choice. Is it conceivable that someone as a result of analysis and a time lapse could and might be asked? Maybe. It would have to do with my view about the resolution of the transference and the characterological structure of the patient: dependent, masochistic, paranoid would disincline me. Someone quite autonomous, post-analysis, on the healthy end of neurosis might be able to give permission, but even then it may not be pure although maybe it wouldn't hurt them. The way asking might be harmful is that something necessary to analyze might become less available. If the patient felt special or that I had special regard for them or that I was tied to them, love them, [was] dependent on them in their fantasy . . . this extra analytic thing could get in the way of bringing that to analysis because it would seem confirmed by my request. Or maybe that they would have to suppress their aggression, their wish to say no, to submit to me, feeling it as my dominance. So the hurt would be in the sense of limitation on the work.

Ambivalent Views

Other analysts were more conflicted about how to deal with confidentiality. Regardless of the decision they have made to disguise or ask consent, they worried and viewed it as a serious dilemma for which they have not found a satisfactory solution. Several analysts described their conflicted feelings about using patient material.

I've been writing about clinical work for fifteen to twenty years. I've become more inclined to ask permission, to show patients what I write and at the same time be more protective if I feel I can't show it to them, more concerned that for some it might be harmful. I feel less inclined to write about patients. It takes a toll of anxiety, guilt; it's tiring to have to deal with the self-serving component in it. Yet it's essential to write about treatment in a truthful way but I'm less optimistic that you can do it. You can learn from how someone thinks and works, but it can also seem exhibitionistic. It happened to me. In [a particular paper] I wrote about things in a very self-exposing way. I wouldn't do that again. Many saw it as exhibitionistic. Is there a way to remove that quality? Virtually impossible to do. If we write with all of our fantasies and feelings, communicating what we show and see, it stimulates voyeurism. One can experience analysis from the couch and one can describe it from the analyst's perspective, but to try to take on describing the process, that's something else.

The first issue is responsibility to the patient. A patient I wrote about had finished and came back. . . . She was a writer and I wanted to show her I'm a writer too, look what I did, what we did together. There was that feeling of competition. I didn't do it, but I couldn't get over the intensity of the wish. The excitement, pleasure at the idea of sharing it. What do you do with that? Would she have liked it? Probably. It's stimulating, provocative, but unfair. It ties you to the analyst, a narcissistic tie and idealization not worked through since you are chosen and there it is in print forever. It makes it real, concrete forever—saying the patient's words. The patient thinks of the analyst writing about them alone. It's charged; it's a burden. I think people [analysts] who tell patients are rationalizing other things; it isn't in the patient's interest. There's a deprivation in the work; maybe because the analyst uses the self so minimally, writing helps. It's an expression of the analyst that isn't in the treatment. On the other hand, analysis isn't that fragile. I don't know if it's so different from other issues that have to be worked through. There's no reason patients couldn't come to tolerate and work through all that is stimulated when they know their analysts have written about them.

I'm not sure it's ever helpful for a patient to read about themselves with the full complexity spelled out. If you can get permission without seeing it, it's a different issue. But if the patient is going to read it, it inhibits what you'll want to say. You can't say everything you want to say about your own feelings and everything you think about the patient. The way I write is with a lot of detail that an adult wouldn't want shared no matter how nice it was about them. I have adult patients who were written up as children who have a distance on it and find it kind of interesting. But you don't know how they'll feel reading it later. But if you don't write, that's not that good either. We have to write because we can't learn if we don't. So we have to weigh it.

I worry that patients reading about themselves may promote an overly intellectual part of their experience; patients have a more fluid and evolving conception of themselves. I think of it as being a post-termination request, but a lot of work goes on after termination. Reading about themselves from their analyst's perspective might put their ideas into a static form that could be an impediment to further working through. My concern is that the analyst's view, my view, might be substituted for the patient's own and lead to a petrification of the patient's insights, a stunting of the post-termination process. I imagine the longer one waits after termination the better, but old cases are probably not as compelling to write about. But I worry that all my justifications for not asking are covers for cowardice. I wonder if my concerns are a rationalization of my apprehension, yet I do think there is reason for concern.

One of the concerns of this analyst was that the written words of the analyst could usurp the patient's experience. This subsuming of the patient's experience would occur seemingly because the patient would accept the analyst's view as truer or more valid than the patient's own. Concern about the influence of the analyst, due to the power of the transference, was a theme that occurred repeatedly.

Changes in Views

Nine analysts have changed their views; eight of them concluded they should now ask for consent; they were divided in their reasons. Four believed they needed to ask consent because they have become more worried about patients coming upon their material and feeling betrayed. One analyst described this concern.

With all the easy access to articles on the Internet, it's a different world. I'm going to try a new policy and see how it works. In the introduction and arrangements at the beginning of treatment, I am going to say that in the course of our work I may find it useful to consult with someone about a particular problem and sometimes I find it useful to convey something in writing and if I do either of these things with total anonymity, how would they feel about that. I'll bring this up, get their reaction, see how it feels. Would I show the article? Probably not. If the patient asked to see it, I'd say yes. Not comfortable entirely but at least it would be out front. I wouldn't offer it. The downside is that to ask suggests I have an interest outside of the patients themselves. They could view me mostly as a scientist. It sets a different agenda. The worst outcome though is to find something written about you or someone you know. I found something written about my father and another close relative. I never told them. I know they weren't asked. That's got to be a betrayal. I've taken that risk for thirty years. It's never safe, but now it seems too easy to look up papers.

Four other analysts, initially hesitant to ask for permission, believed, based on their experiences, that asking consent had posed no problems for the treatments when they had requested it. Three of the four did not believe they had seen any derivatives that suggested interference with the analytic work. Their views are expressed in the words of one analyst:

> I told one patient in the mid-phase of a six- or seven-year analysis that I'd like to write about him. He gave permission. There were some exhibitionistic dreams that related to the homoerotic transference but I think that would have come up anyway. This man was obsessive so there wasn't that much affect anyway. He thought it was important for the field to have things written and didn't feel exposed or betrayed. I don't think it had an adverse effect; but that is my inference. I never offered to show him the written material and he didn't ask. There was nothing in it that the patient didn't know. I didn't see any derivative effects of asking permission to use material with him or others I've asked, but my own defenses may keep me from seeing the effect on the treatment.

Two of these analysts' views about analytic work as well as about asking consent have changed.

> My views and ways of dealing with writing about patients have changed. In previous papers, I did not ask for consent. I concealed heavily. Afterwards, I felt I had done the wrong thing, not because I thought the patient would see it but because I became aware that transference continued even after termination. I had gone back to see my own analyst and patients of mine came back to see me. Transference issues were still active. It made me think that I would be uncomfortable having a secret from a patient if the patient were to come back. Actually one patient I had disguised in writing and not asked did come back and I was not so uncomfortable. So I had anticipated an interfering countertransference that did not occur. But my model of treatment

had also changed. Before I had been constructing what was occurring in words from the patient but I'd begun to see that what I was constructing also had my own stamp on it, that there was a constructing coming from me that was part of it. This changed my view to more of a two-person model of analysis. So writing a vignette changed. Whatever I thought was not true, unless the patient thought part of it, and the patient had to contribute to it. [The analyst means that only if both analyst and patient report their views can the report be considered valid.] So I decided to try to discuss this with some of my patients . . . but not patients in the mental health profession where I thought it would become intellectualized. I thought that this would not be such an intrusion into the analysis to ask and to bring the material I was thinking about since it was the patient's material.

I think more about whether to inform patients now. I was trained to maintain anonymity. Initially I was less likely to ask permission. Something that has always bothered me is how contemptuously people wrote about their patients. In principle, I'd never do that. I'd never write anything about a patient that I would feel funny about their seeing, even when not asking their permission. I had that guideline. I want to write so they would feel okay if they read it but now I feel a greater sense of wanting them to see it. I feel more comfortable with self-disclosure and the relational impact. Writing about patients has instilled a certain kind of conscience that means making sure whatever a patient reads has to not be destructive to them or their treatment. Generally I write about issues that the patient and I have sufficiently analyzed together. There is nothing new or surprising to the patient in what I write.

In contrast, one analyst expressed increased concern about asking consent because of the effect he believed it had on the treatment.

It complicates things to ask. The two experiences I had when I asked I didn't feel good about . . . I feel it was an interference to bring things in. I think I wouldn't write about a patient in the field again. The way I like to do treatment and think is best for the patient is for the patient to unfold his story at his own pace and let it remain the patient's treatment. I think I work best when I have no purpose other than understanding the patient. Things inadvertently break through the frame, like countertransference. But this [the asking] is a preventable intrusion. It introduces something you want.

OTHER ISSUES

Patients' Discovering Articles about Them

Patients and their friends and relatives do find and read articles about them. Eight analysts reported their patients unexpectedly learning about or finding articles about themselves. Seven other analysts had themselves been written about when they were patients; four of these analysts, in treatment at the time of publication, had not been asked for permission. The ramifications of these discoveries will be presented in the second and third sections of this book.

Negative Consequences

Other complications in relation to writing about patients include the countertransference stirred when patients refuse permission, which three patients did. But more devastating were lawsuits filed by patients who felt betrayed and sought redress. Two analysts reported having been sued by former patients who discovered they had been written about. Neither patient won the suit, but the analysts experienced considerable distress in the process.

Three analysts withdrew clinical material based on their patients' responses. They did so despite the fact that the patients had given them permission. In each instance they did not believe it was in the interest of the patient's treatment to have the material published. These examples will also be illustrated and discussed in a subsequent chapter in the second section of the book.

Self as an Example

One solution to the problem of using clinical material without struggling with issues of patient confidentiality is for analysts to write about themselves in disguise. Most analysts rejected this solution. They thought it could not be objective or valid. In this sample, no analyst wrote an entire case about himself or herself. The nine analysts who did employ this method used some material, most often from their own analysis, to illustrate a particular point; they did so on only a few occasions. Using oneself as an example without identifying the material as being about oneself will be discussed in the third section of the book in a chapter on the self in disguise.

DISCUSSION

If the views of the thirty analysts in this study are representative of North American analysts who write using clinical material, then contemporary ideas about how best to maintain patient confidentiality seem to be divided between emphasizing the benefits of only disguising versus asking for consent as well. Lipton (1991) reports a similar finding from his informal survey of analysts. Another finding similar to Lipton's is that the majority of analysts in this project did not request permission from patients who they assumed were unlikely to read the psychoanalytic literature; these patients most often did not work in the mental health field.

Writing about Mental Health Professionals

Almost all of the analysts expressed considerable concerns about the risk of loss of confidentiality for patients who work in the mental health field or whose relatives are mental health professionals. Most analysts in this sample made a point of requesting permission from patients in the mental health field. But a few analysts viewed such patients as no different from any other and when writing about them did not alter their policy of only using disguises. While some analysts are strongly committed to each position, the greater number, whichever method they chose, view neither strategy as being without some hazard, especially when writing about patients in the mental health field.

Informed Consent

The current cultural climate has sensitized analysts to the potential for abusing power. They are aware the material they wish to publish may not be considered only theirs. Patients are also more aware of their rights and the potential for having them violated. Concomitantly, analysts are also more conscious that the power of the transference may make it impossible for patients to not grant permission. This change in attitude accompanies the analytic community's increased sensitivity to the role and influence of authority in general, as well as its specific relevance in analytic work.

Another change in attitude has come from a new understanding of the nature of transference itself. Since transference is no longer thought of as a phenomenon that ends with termination of treatment, but rather as persisting over time—though in diminished form—it no longer seems a solution to the problem of influence to request permission after termination. This change in thinking about the persistence of transferences may be one of the reasons why only one analyst in this study routinely waited until after termination to request permission. Analysts who favor asking consent after termination argue that it is not only a question of the persistence of transferences but whether the patient depends on the good will of the analyst at the time of the request. If the request comes after a "decent interval," the patient does not have this added burden.

Patients' Gratifications: Enacted and Therapeutic

Although they valued having patients' conscious consent, most analysts indicated an awareness of many characterological traits that might have led patients to grant permission that may have reflected enactments of the patients' problems. Exhibitionism, masochism, compliance, the wish to please or to be special are some of the motives analysts believed to have been behind consent. A few analysts believed that for some patients reading the analyst's account of their work together could be a validation of the work that was done, of the relationship with the analyst, or be a confirmation that the analyst shares the patient's understanding of his or her difficulties and the process of their work. When patients experience reading the material in any of these ways, it could also be therapeutically beneficial in addition to being gratifying.

Analysts' Gratifications: Professional and Personal

Most analysts did not believe that patients benefit from being written about. The benefit they see from publishing clinical material accrues to their colleagues, to the psychoanalytic community, and the science of psychoanalysis. All of the analysts in this sample also knew that they obtained personal benefit from writing.

Some analysts are clear that they use writing to work out counter-transference issues. In that respect, their writing may also have been of benefit to their patients. Most analysts, however, think of their writing as primarily an intellectual endeavor. This would seem a manifest, and at best a partial, explanation of their motives. Choice of topic, patient, and time of writing each are undoubtedly multiply determined. Intellectual interest represents only the conscious, surface layer. But certainly most analysts know themselves and their complexity better than to stop there. Possibly these analysts just did not want to reveal more in the interview.

Many analysts wrote out of the belief that authorship brings professional advancement or, at least, greater recognition and sometimes greater regard among their colleagues. Recognition of self-interest may have been a major reason for analysts' reluctance and ambivalence about asking a patient's permission; it introduces the analyst's agenda into a situation that, apart from payment, is meant to be solely for the patient.

Analysts, of course, are likely to derive other satisfactions from the work, but these benefits remain a private matter; they are not usually something about which the patient has direct information. Analysts have their own personal and characterological reasons for having chosen their profession, including often a wish to master their own psychological issues. Doing analysis may provide a way for analysts to continue learning about themselves (Kantrowitz 1996). Whether these private benefits to the analyst adversely affect patients is not an either/or matter. It depends on how the analyst's gratifications and frustrations interdigitate with those of the patient. Analysts try to monitor themselves, keeping these potential interferences in mind. Every analyst interviewed was clear that if a piece of writing could be perceived as interfering with the patient's treatment, the material should not be used even if consent has been given. But this, of course, means that the analyst had to have been aware that the writing about the patient posed a problem for the patient. Examples and discussion of analysts' perceptions of the effect of writing on their patients will be presented in a subsequent chapter in the second section of the book.

FURTHER THOUGHTS ABOUT DISGUISE

Gabbard (2000), Aron (2000), Tuckett (1998, 2000b), and Goldberg (1997) have provided excellent summaries of the issues and dilemmas in deciding between disguise alone versus disguise with consent as a method of preserving confidentiality. The discussion that follows builds on their ideas and extends them based on the results of my interviews with these thirty analyst-authors.

The greatest drawback in choosing to disguise clinical material and publish it without obtaining patients' permission for its use is that patients may come across it, recognize themselves, and feel betrayed. The worst outcome is seen when such a discovery negatively affects a patient's feelings and alters what was otherwise a positive analytic experience (Person 1983). The discovery may adversely affect the patient's feelings about their analyst as well as about the treatment itself; it may then erode psychological gains. In the current litigious climate, some patients may even sue for what they believe is a breach of confidentiality. Although they are not likely to win the suit if the analyst has taken sufficient care to disguise the material, the experience for both parties is likely to be painful, or even traumatic.

Not all patients who discover they have been written about express this sense of violation; some seem to take it for granted that publishing clinical illustrations is an accepted part of the work.

The likelihood that patients may read what is written about them has greatly increased (Gabbard 2000). A number of the analysts interviewed pointed out how the Internet has made psychoanalytic articles easily accessible. Curious patients, looking up an analyst on the Internet, might well stumble on an article that includes material about them. If they are still in treatment, it is likely they will talk about it. If they are not still in treatment, hopefully they will contact their former analyst and discuss it. If they don't, however, there will be no opportunity to explore, understand, and, if necessary, repair what may have felt injurious.

Another negative consequence of disguise that has often been cited is the introduction of misleading information into the literature; the danger is that others may take a piece of disguised information as a fact and make extrapolations from it that are erroneous. An example cited by Klumpner and Frank (1991) illustrated this point. In that instance, a patient described as having a gastric ulcer in fact suffered from juvenile diabetes. Were another analyst to use this case in support of a theory about the psychodynamics of people having gastric ulcers, the disguise would have seriously misled this author and resulted in false information entering the literature. Klumpner and Frank regarded the psychoanalytic literature as archives. From the reports of analysts in this study, it is clear that there is a risk in this assumption; analysts acknowledge that they change many details in order to preserve confidentiality.

This objection to the use of disguise seems based on a misunderstanding of the nature and purpose of psychoanalytic case examples. The data they provide are not, and cannot be, comparable to the data of basic science, or often even social science, since they are most often taken from a single case. Analysts can only illustrate the points they want to make; they cannot prove them. As is nowadays so commonly pointed out, what analysts report is colored by their subjectivity. No measure of reliability can apply. If the analyst makes points clearly and provides relevant clinical material in support of an argument, then the reader may be persuaded to take the author's position seriously. It may stimulate the clinician-reader to compare her own experience and look for examples from her own practice that may be rethought in the light of what she has read. But what has won the reader's serious attention is the author's ability to convey a new understanding and the reasoning behind it.

Clinical observations may be the stimulus for theoretical discoveries, but they can never be the proof of them. Human complexity is too great to be reduced in this fashion. The multiplicity of meanings and functions in any behavior, symptom, or interaction needs to be respected. This is a uniquely psychoanalytic perspective. It must be stressed, then, that *unless* the author's intention is to illustrate something about this *particular topic,* any detail that might be disguised— profession, geographic location, number of siblings, place in sibling order, religion, disease, accident, particular trauma, or even gender— should not be used to support another writer's thesis about that *topic.* To use the data in such a fashion is to miss the point.

Reed (1993) suggests that there should be an unspoken clinical convention among analysts. The reader should recognize the author's specific purpose in selecting the example and not try to draw any other conclusions from the identifying details or use them for other purposes. No details given should be assumed to be factually accurate.

Analysts need to trust that the gist of the narrative, rather than specific details, is related to the theoretical point the author is making and represents the way the analyst believes they in fact operated. Since it is necessary to acknowledge that the analyst cannot be an objective scientist, then readers are simply being asked to judge how well the analyst has made a point. However, unless this convention is accepted, many analysts and non-analysts reading the psychoanalytic literature are likely to assume that factual details are being represented accurately and so may use them erroneously. To prevent this, some analysts suggest that when disguise is achieved by misinformation, a footnote or endnote be provided alerting the reader not to take all the details of the description as fact. The problem with this suggestion is that it tends to undo the disguise. In this regard, it may be better to omit information than to alter it.

Composites

Composites, as a vehicle for disguise, were used by only a few of the analysts in the sample. Perhaps this is because most of these analysts were not writing about syndromes where such a method can be useful. Gabbard (2000) emphasizes quite correctly that when an analyst uses this method, it should be made explicit. An example of the method is Gabbard and Lester's (1995) illustration of the kinds of analysts who might commit sexual boundary violations. In such instances, it is possible to describe personality types and then provide brief fragmentary examples omitting all identifying data.

Writing Up a Colleague's Clinical Material

Having other analysts provide case examples for published work is one way to get clinical material into the literature while ensuring confidentiality. An analyst who contributed clinical material to the study reported in *The Patient's Impact on the Analyst* (Kantrowitz 1996) used the example he provided for teaching purposes. In this way, the analyst used my voice as narrator but his own material, to convey ideas. Obviously, this solution will work for only certain themes and for certain analysts. For the analyst who wants to write, it is no solution at all.

FURTHER THOUGHTS ABOUT CONSENT

Regarding the hazards of asking consent, the analyst-authors in this sample concur with other reports in the psychoanalytic literature on this topic. Aron (2000), Gabbard (2000), and Goldberg (1997) have all pointed to the various ways in which requesting permission may interfere with an ongoing treatment and may be an intrusion in the life of someone who has terminated. A major problem, already noted, is that truly informed consent can never be given since it is always granted under the sway of the transference, even when treatment is over.

At the Beginning of Analysis

Granting that consent can never be truly informed does not inevitably lead to the conclusion that patients will be adversely affected by giving permission. Although patients whose characters are organized around pleasing are unlikely to say no, their transference issues around the wish to please will certainly be stimulated and become manifest around other topics. Once understood, their granting of permission can be reevaluated in this light. In a subsequent chapter, I shall describe analysts who have transacted these reconsiderations with their patients.

While a number of analysts in the sample found no difficulty in making the request for permission in the initial hours, Aron (2000) has reported doing this only for a short period of time, after which he concluded that neither he nor his patients knew each other well enough to feel comfortable with requesting permission early in treatment. He stated that trust and knowledge of the other and their intents and capacity were needed first.

Since most analysts report having some patients of whom they would never ask permission because of particular conflicts or character structures, it is hard to see how one could routinely ask at the outset, when conflicts and character structure are not yet adequately known. Nonetheless, this study has revealed that some analysts do just that, and seemingly with no ill-effects, at least none of which they were aware. It is not clear whether this conclusion was a matter of the analysts' comfort or was "blindness" to the effects of their behavior.

Goldberg (personal communication) has proposed that all analysts should make this request at the beginning of treatment. His argument is that if blanket requests were universal then everyone in the field would share the burden of this problem, and by extension requests would become the norm. He archly states that those who object to the practices analysts employ around confidentiality should not read articles containing clinical material.[1] His point is that the burden that comes with trying to advance psychoanalytic knowledge should not be the responsibility solely of those who choose to write. If his suggestion were followed, asking blanket permission would become a routine part of analyses. Still, most analysts prefer to wait until they feel comfortable that a given patient will not be burdened by the request, though they can still find they have been mistaken once the request has been made. Tucket (2000b) suggests that we should perhaps educate the public to expect the publication of clinical material as an important part of psychoanalytic discipline.

Requests during Treatment or in the Termination Phase

Making the request to use a patient's material during the course of treatment poses other risks. The meaning that the analyst's writing has for the patient may become interwoven with the meaning of the time that the request is made. For example, during the termination phase, patients may experience the request as a way of preserving a connection with the analyst after treatment ends. Depending on the patient's particular conflicts and the nature of the relationship with the analyst, the patient may react to the idea of a continuing connection as pleasurable, burdensome, or something between these possibilities. The

---

1. According to Goldberg, this idea originated with Jeffrey Sterns.

reverberations ensuing from stimulation or inhibition in reaction to the request may then be played out in the analytic process before they were well enough understood to be recognized. Potentially the meaning can then remain unanalyzed. However, analysts today are on the whole sufficiently aware of the impact of their contributions to the process that they would most often be able to note changes in a patient that follow a request. Connecting these matters in the analyst's mind and then bringing them to the patient's attention would likely make this part of the analytic work.

Asking patients for permission to write about them during the termination phase has the advantage that most of the patient's issues have by then been explored and are understood. A disadvantage is that the request itself may interfere with the process of facing and analyzing the issue of separation. In writing about the patient, the analyst links the two of them together on the printed page; the connection is preserved in perpetuity. Although a request for consent may be flattering to the patient, it has the potential for creating a specialness that potentially can interfere with other relationships in the future as one analyst in this sample suggested. It might also inhibit patients from bringing up negative feelings in the termination phase, out of a wish to maintain this positive, special connection. But positive feelings toward the analyst or the analysis are interferences only if they restrict the expression and exploration of negative ones, and this is not invariably the case.

Analyst need to consider the effect on the patient when they extensively search for derivatives related to requests in patients' material and then intensively pursue analyzing this material. Concern, or even guilt, about having made a request may cause the analyst to intrude further into the analysis. On the positive side, when the request stimulates aspects of the patient's character or conflicts that are either already known or newly discovered, a focus on the meaning of the request can be usefully folded into these broader issues. Under these circumstances, the request may serve to highlight or unearth areas that require analytic attention. Finally, once an analyst has made a request, whenever this occurs and however much it stirs in the patient, something has been enacted by the analyst that may place a limit on exploration by the patient. While in most cases the primary motive in the analyst's request for use of clinical material is to make intellectual advances in psychoanalysis as a field, unconscious motives stemming from unconscious conflicts that overlap with the patients are likely to contribute. If the analyst's action concretizes a meaning for the patient, whether he or she feels special, exhibited, or in some other way gratified, then this meaning may never be fully analyzable. There always remains a meaning beyond the meaning to the patient.

Requests after Termination

During treatment, a request for consent may be disruptive but can at least be processed; after treatment, the process is not interfered with, but the feelings stirred may disrupt what has been consolidated and may require further treatment lest they remain unmetabolized or worse. If the former patient does not return to discuss his or her reactions to the request, its meaning and its effects on the patient will not likely be pursued. As a result, whatever negative sequelae occur may remain unanalyzed. Some patients may consciously accept a post-termination request as reasonable for the sake of the profession or may feel narcissistically gratified by being chosen. The latter reaction might suggest that certain narcissistic issues were not sufficiently explored in the analysis. But neither reaction would likely prove disruptive to the former patient's experience of the analyst or the analysis. As such, neither response would seem a particularly detrimental reaction after the conclusion of treatment. But other patients might feel narcissistically injured by the analyst's interest in the profession, or perceive it as revealing the analyst's self-interest and interest in colleagues, rather than the patient alone, and in either case feel used.

If issues of shame, fear of exposure (real or imagined), trust, or revival of childhood experiences of betrayal were stimulated by the request, the analyst may have selected a former patient unwisely or may have failed to have appreciated the degree to which these issues had not been resolved. Patients may react to what they perceive (correctly or incorrectly) as the analyst's view of them or the treatment (positive or negative). As noted earlier, several analysts expressed concern that reading the analyst's account of the treatment might usurp the patient's view of the process. Failure to explore any of these potential reactions might disturb the patient's previous satisfaction about the remembered analysis.

An analyst can remain totally unaware of this disruption unless the former patient chooses to return and explore it. When written material is given to patients after termination, an invitation to come in and discuss their reactions may lessen the hazards of this approach, but the relative brevity of this contact does not ensure that reactions of distress that were not expressed immediately to the analyst will not occur later. Patients may, of course, go back into analysis or psychotherapy with someone else and explore these reactions. Indeed, the impact of the discovery that their former analyst wrote about them may lead some patients to seek further treatment.

Sometimes when former patients are aware of something untoward having been stirred, they do return to explore it. In such instances, the analyst's request may have unsettled a previously "good-enough" resolution, but it may also have provided an opportunity to more satisfactorily rework residual issues. Nonetheless, this work will have come about because of the analyst's initiative and not that of the patient.

Conflicts over Writing about Patients

It should be emphasized again that all of the analysts interviewed were concerned about their patients' welfare. These interviews show that many of them were often consciously conflicted about making requests for permission to write. Nonetheless, once the decision to ask permission was made, analysts at times minimized or avoided struggling with their conflicts about using patient material. Similarly, some analysts who chose always to only disguise patients rationalized these decisions when patients discovered these papers. While this was certainly not true of the majority of analysts who were interviewed, the tendency to rationalize decisions was notable in the sample.

This disinclination to be more self-reflective raises the question of whether analysts unconsciously fear that a request for consent might be more harmful than other less obvious impositions that may not necessarily be so directly recognized or acknowledged. Certainly there are personal artifacts that each analyst introduces into treatments of which they remain unaware, unless it is brought to their attention or comes to be considered for some other reason. But the request to use a patient's material occurs because, however ambivalently, a conscious decision has been taken by the analyst to undertake this action. It is also a conscious decision to opt for disguise alone and risk discovery by the patient.

The likelihood is that when analysts avoid struggling with their conflicts over using patient material, conscious or unconscious guilt over the personal gain they accrue from publishing is implicated. As stated earlier, the financial gain from working with patients is open, acknowledged, and accepted. However, to benefit in some other way from working with patients undoubtedly occurs. One unequivocal example is professional advancement from supervised cases in psychoanalytic training. Benefit also accrues in various psychological ways for all analysts—though it may at times feel suspect and unacceptable. While most often analytic writing brings neither monetary gain nor academic advancement, it is likely to provide some prestige and opportunity for advancement in professional associations. This personal gain comes because these analysts have made contributions that have earned respect from colleagues; the papers or books they have published have informed and stimulated other analysts. In most instances, personal ambition is not the primary reason analysts write, but it may create a secondary gain that many analysts would prefer not to think about. Self-interest is always a motive that is likely to be stronger than altruism. All self-interest is not about ambition. Narcissistic needs may be satisfied by writing, such as exhibitionism or other forms of self-enhancement. Such motives are certainly not restricted to analysts. Published materials in all fields might be minimal if they were restricted for this reason.

Of course, not all publications use patient material, but when they do, analysts may be indebted to their patients in ways that may make them uncomfortable when carefully considered. While guilt about using patient material in ways that serve personal ambition is likely to be at least preconscious, other potential sources of guilt may be less consciously accessible and experienced as more shameful when recognized. Gratifications that are narcissistic or exhibitionistic might be in this category. On a deeper level, analysts may feel guilty about appropriating something that belongs to the patient—the history, the problems—and using it for the analyst's own purposes. In this respect, analysts may feel guilty that they want the patient to give them something, to feed them so to speak, or that they have enacted a wish to be united with the patient forever by the very act of writing about him or her.

The writing analyst has to be willing to tolerate the intrapsychic conflicts stirred up by using patient material. But there are interpersonal as well as intrapsychic consequences. The benefit from publishing papers may be experienced as especially suspect because not all analysts avail themselves of this opportunity. Not every analyst wishes to write, though some who may wish to may not do so because of personal constraints. As Stein (1988a) noted, many analysts cannot afford the time for this financially unremunerative activity, or they may have other priorities for the hours they do not see patients. Other analysts, who wish to write but do not, may be limited by more personal inhibitions. The writing analyst has to be willing to tolerate the envy and competitive feelings—at times manifested in behavior—stirred in some colleagues whose ambitions have not been actualized. Perhaps the combination of conscious and unconscious guilt related to both professional competition and to the use of patient material in the service of their own ambition and other needs makes some analyst-writers avoid exploring their conflicts over this aspect of their motivation.

Patients' rights are emphasized more today than in previous times and this is as it should be. But the importance of communicating clinical material, as well as ideas, for the benefit of the field may concomitantly have become undervalued. Papers that include clinical material are vehicles for the transmission of new ideas that stimulate the growth of psychoanalysis as a discipline. Writing about patients is like walking in a minefield. There are no good solutions. It is natural to want to avoid the discomfort of conflict that thinking about the use of patient material stirs, but analysts are committed professionally and personally to facing internal struggles. The solution is not to stop writing about patients but to face and struggle with the conflict it creates as directly and honestly as possible.

The discussion of difficulties, conflicts, and motives for writing elaborated in this chapter applies to all analysts who write, not the *JAPA* authors alone. Aspects of this discussion will recur in subsequent chapters, but it will not be as fully elaborated as it has been here.

Knowing the contemporary views of United States analysts trained in traditional psychoanalytic institutes, I will next compare them with analyst-authors residing outside the United States most of whom have been trained in institutes sponsored by the International Psychoanalytic Association.

3
International Journal of Psychoanalysis (IJP) Authors[1]

It is often assumed that analysts from different theoretical schools of thought or who reside in different parts of the world are likely both to think and to work differently. Whether these differences are actually as great in the consulting room as on paper is a subject of debate. Whether there are differences in attitudes and practices in relation to writing about patients based on where one resides in the world is the topic of this chapter. The attitudes and practices of thirty-six analysts residing outside of the United States, who published articles with clinical material in psychoanalytic journals between 1995 and 2001, are reported.[2] Their attitudes and practices will be compared with those of the thirty author-analysts residing within the United States, who were described in the last chapter.

---

1. Material in this chapter has previously appeared in slightly different form in the *International Journal of Psychoanalysis* (2004) 85:691–712, © Institute of Psycho-analysis, London, UK. I am grateful to the editors for granting permission for the material to be reprinted in this book.

2. Twenty-one of these analysts are male and fifteen are female. Twenty analysts were trained in psychiatry, six in psychology, five have Ph.D.s in other fields, and five are lay analysts. Neither gender nor discipline distinguished analysts' approaches to confidentiality.

These non-American analysts were published in the *International Journal of Psychoanalysis* (*IJP*), the *Canadian Journal of Psychoanalysis*, *Revista Argentina de Psicoanalisis*, and *Revista Brasiliera de Psicanalise*. Unlike the prior sample from *JAPA* where I chose a random, systematically selected sample because I had a large database, in the current survey I contacted all non-United States analysts who published clinical material in these journals since 1995. I also included articles published from all of 2000 and 2001. My intention was to get as large a sample as possible.[3]

Reasons for Case Selection

Most of the international analysts stated that they wrote about patients in order to illustrate an idea. Six analysts stated that specific transference/countertransference dynamics had been the impetus for writing papers. As indicated in the previous chapter, most of the analysts from the United States also stated their conscious reason for writing was to illustrate ideas. While three United States analysts described writing as a method for understanding and managing countertransference reactions—viewing writing as a kind of self-supervision—none of the international analysts were as explicit about this self-supervisory function of writing.

Writing about Mental Health Professionals

Almost all analysts around the world stated that they would be much more cautious about writing about patients who were in the mental health field or related to mental health professionals. A number of international analysts elaborated that if they had decided

---

3. One hundred and seven analysts were contacted and thirty-six agreed to participate. The material presented in this chapter was gathered mostly through e-mail. A questionnaire was initially sent to the authors (see Appendix) and e-mail exchanges followed with many of the respondents.

to write about patients in the mental health profession, they would never have presented or published this material in their own country. Eight analysts stated that they would never write about mental health professionals, believing it was impossible to preserve their anonymity. Six analysts wrote about the special problem of being a training analyst; under these circumstances, many of their patients would be recognizable to the analytic community and so could not be written about. Two analysts used writing as part of the analytic process; they believed that patient and analyst could work collaboratively both on the published communication about the analysis and on construction of an adequate disguise. The attitudes and practices of analysts from the United States were similar; however, none of these analysts addressed the specific complications of being a training analyst.

METHOD OF CONFIDENTIALITY

Twenty-one of the thirty-six analysts (58%) used disguise exclusively when writing about patients. Eight analysts (22%) always asked permission and seven analysts (20%) varied between these two approaches depending on the particular patient. Analysts using only disguise came from England (4), Italy (4), Argentina (3), Brazil (3), Canada (2), France (2), Germany (1), Peru (1), and Spain (1). Analysts who consistently asked permission came from England (3), Canada (3), Brazil (1), and Peru (1). Analysts who varied their approach came from England (4), Mexico (1), Spain (1), and Italy (1). In the sample of 30 United States analysts, almost twice as many analysts (15 analysts, 50%) chose to use disguise alone as regularly requested permission (8 analysts, 27%) for use of patients' material. The other United States analysts (7 analysts, 23%) varied their approach depending on the circumstances. In both the international and United States samples, three analysts asked permission on only one occasion based on the concern that patients would see the material and recognize themselves due to their connection with the mental health field. In the aggregate, the two groups are similar.

Table 3–1 shows a breakdown of results by country.

Table 3–1. Geographic Location and Methods for Maintaining Confidentiality

	Disguise Only	Ask Permission	Varied Approach
England	4	3	4
Canada	2	3	0
Italy	4	0	1
Brazil	3	1	0
Argentina	3	0	0
Spain	1	1	1
Peru	1	1	0
France	2	0	0
Germany	1	0	0
Mexico	0	0	1
United States	15	8	7

Reasons for Only Disguising

Most international analysts who use only disguise believe that asking permission is an imposition of the analyst's agenda and will disrupt the analytic process.

One analyst wrote:

I am concerned that asking permission will seriously disrupt and distort the analytic process and may be harmful to the patient. Some patients may get excited and others persecuted, but the fact of asking their permission introduces a nonanalytic parameter whose consequences are difficult to judge. Certainly I would find it difficult to claim that I was attending to the patient's needs in doing so. I am sometimes tempted to ask the patient and then I try to work out privately why the temptation. For whose benefit would it be? Mostly I reason that it is to clear my good name, and the result is to put me in the right and to lay the burden on the patient.

Another analyst stated:

My reasons for not asking permission are: (a) Uneasiness on my part, not having incorporated in my practice discussing with a patient and working through all the implications and ramifications of this situation; (b) No benefit for the patient and the treatment and my confidence that the patient will not know about the publication;

(c) In the remote event that the patient would happen upon the publication, I trust that the patient would not feel hurt about the way I speak about him; (d) paranoid traits of the patient that could make the whole treatment very difficult to handle if I asked permission to write. Experience has made me more humble about the capacity of my understanding of the unconscious.

A third analyst's view was:

I would never publish data about someone who would have a great probability of reading it. I have my own synthesis of our shared experiences, and my patient has his/hers. Perhaps the effort to put them together could be too overwhelming for the patient. Furthermore, if we are always trying to provide interpretations to the patient piece by piece according to what we think is his/her ability to digest them, we run the risk of giving out more information than the patient is able to profit from, and has not even asked to receive . . . I believe that bringing up such issues during the treatment is a form of invasion of your own wishes or concerns, foreign to the patient's needs or to the analysis itself. I would rather deal with problems or misunderstandings that could potentially arise afterwards than to create an issue between myself and my patient, just to avoid any future problem for me. I would not say that I am concealing from the patient when I write about our experience together, just as I would not say that I am concealing the fact that I am married, that I have one son, etc. This information is not part of our contract. My writing is about my work with someone, and if I do not reveal his/her identity, and if I do not take an unethical approach, I really do not think it is useful or constructive for them to be informed of my decision.

Another analyst's reason for not asking the patient for permission was a concern about revealing countertransference material:

I used the clinical material of a second patient with accentuated perverse aspects to illustrate how the elucidation of my negative countertransference feelings activated in the analytic process guided my technical handling of the perverse transference. Through this I came to understand some of the patient's perverse intentions and my own unconscious link to them. In so doing, I revealed some very personal and intimate aspects of my private life, thus making the reader a "voyeur" of my intimacy. When I wrote the article I did not ask the patient's permission for publication, as I did not feel she should know of my personal private "links" to her perverse attitudes. It was published in English. I felt safe, as my patient did not have knowledge of that language.

Analysts from the United States had similar reasons for not asking permission. Because their responses were given spontaneously and were oral rather than written, they were often not as fully developed or articulated.

Many analysts throughout the world also stated that when only small examples were used or the material came from a long time ago, they did not feel they needed to ask permission if the patient were adequately disguised and unlikely to read it.

Asking Permission

Most analysts in the current sample who always asked permission believed that this was the only ethical way to proceed. These analysts also offered to show their patients what they had written. These experiences will be illustrated later. Only one analyst routinely asked written permission. Most analysts from the United States who routinely asked permission also believed it was the only ethical practice.

One analyst in the current sample was insistent about asking permission based on her disturbed feelings about the way her analyst had dealt with writing about her.

> I ask permission before I write. Only one time did I do it without asking and that didn't sit well. I feel very strongly about this because when my analyst wrote about me it was such a bad experience. Many friends recognized me. It was humiliating. He never asked me. He just told me. There was this idea of implied consent if you were in analysis. I love to write and I hate it if a patient says no, but I have to live with it.

The impact of the analyst's writing about an analyst when he or she was a patient will be described in the third section of the book.

Individualizing

One respondent's comments epitomize the ideas most frequently reported by international analysts in defense of individualizing their approach with each patient:

It depends. I (asked permission) when a more detailed story and description of the analytic process increased the risk of recognition by the patient or others. If I was sure that the patient would not be recognizable, that alterations in the description would not alter the core issues and/or that there were no chances at all that the patient or anybody in his entourage would read the paper, I might not have asked permission or informed the patient. This is also true if I publish in a foreign journal that I believe the patient will not have access to. In one particular case in which I felt that the amount of recognizable material was not indifferent for the patient himself (though I had informed him that I would avoid or change as much as possible so as to protect confidentiality), I asked the patient whether he would allow me to publish material from his analysis. He responded that he felt proud to be considered an interesting case.

REFUSAL OF PERMISSION

Four analysts each had one patient who refused to give permission. Two analysts who had asked consent, but not yet written up the case, described their experiences.

I felt I had miscalculated the vulnerability of the patient and I regretted not having better evaluated the patient's feelings. The patient did not react with aggressivity against me—but said that she did not want that which was our private relationship to come to the open air. She also added that she thought that if I published the paper with information about her treatment, she would always have this in her mind and this would restrain her from feeling free. I explicitly agreed with her. Her reaction helped me to feel less guilty and at fault. It appeared several times in later material in relation to her feelings that I perhaps was more devoted to my own interests than to her. I was careful in not interpreting the patient's reaction in terms of "you want to have me in exclusivity" or "you are jealous that I have a life outside." Instead, I told her that I felt it was a legitimate reaction on her part that expressed her desire to preserve the treatment. This issue appeared from time to time in relation to certain aspects of her past and of our actual relationship. I discovered myself struggling to overcome my more spontaneous reaction of trying to evade the memory of my request. In the end, I felt that the episode strengthened our therapeutic relationship and made it possible to disentangle transferential issues from more mature forms of relationships.

> I made a mistake with a patient because I asked her based on my wish to use the material for a presentation. My timing was bad. This patient had been in treatment for six years but it was after she had revealed childhood sexual abuse. So everything felt like exploitation. She said, "No, not now." My countertransference feelings were hard. I was irritated, and I'm sure that had some spillover. I did feel she wanted to say yes. Maybe at some other point I would have been able to write about her. At that point in the treatment, she had been wondering how I would rape her and this was the way. I found I could live with [her refusal].

The third analyst did not describe the process. The fourth analyst's patient read the paper after termination and refused to grant permission. The analyst's description of this experience appears in the second section of the book.

In the survey of analysts from the United States, three patients had refused permission. In only one instance did an analyst elaborate his reflections and what he learned from the process. However, several other analysts from the United States gave examples of not publishing despite the patients' permission. The decision not to publish illustrations occurred when subsequent material alerted them that the patient was having a detrimental reaction to the request. Like the second example presented above, many of these patients felt exploited though they did not say so directly, and the analyst chose to bear the countertransference disappointment of not writing or publishing for the sake of the patient's treatment.

TIME OF WRITING OR REQUEST

Beginning

Only one international analyst routinely requested permission at the beginning of treatment, compared with four analysts from the

United States. This analyst, from England, believed that asking at the outset was the only ethical way to proceed.

During

Seven of the international analysts wrote only while the treatment was ongoing, but never at the outset, compared with five analysts from the United States. Three analysts were from England and one each from Argentina, Brazil, Canada, and Peru.

> When I write about a patient still in analysis, this experience has helped me to understand the patient.

> I regret the times I waited until after analysis [was over] . . . there was no chance to explore it. So far, I have found it easier near the end. Because you've been working together a long time and both the patient and you know more about how he or she reacts to things, what it might mean, how and how long it needs to be thoroughly worked through, etc. But perhaps it should be mentioned to all patients as a matter of course early on? I intend to experiment throughout my career [with the timing].

Another reason for asking permission prior to termination was a concern that a request after treatment would revive feelings that might revisit the already concluded analytic experience. The analyst whose patient ultimately refused to give permission reported such a negative reaction. Several United States analysts also chose to request permission prior to termination for this reason.

After Termination

Eight analysts wrote only after the termination of analysis, compared with one analyst from the United States sample. Two analysts were from Brazil and one each from Argentina, Canada, England, France, Italy, and Peru. The Latin American analysts used only disguise, whereas the European and North American analysts made post-termination requests for permission. As stated in the last chapter, the one United States analyst who wrote only afterward said he did so because writing during analysis might lead him to prematurely foreclose ideas about what was occurring in the analysis.

Individualizing Timing of Requests Case by Case

Twenty international analysts wrote either during analysis (never at the beginning) or after termination; their approaches depended on the issues of the patient or the analyst's particular interest at the time.

None of the international analysts expressed very strong feelings about the timing of writing. Those analysts who believed that writing about the patient would be an intrusion or would interfere with the analytic work used only disguise and never asked permission. One analyst, who did not view it as a matter of the particular time in this treatment, thought it depended on the nature of the relationship:

> Provided I feel confident that the patient does not experience unconscious or conscious feelings of being exploited the decision could take place at any time.

CHANGE IN VIEWS

Twelve international analysts (33%) had changed their ideas about how to preserve confidentiality compared with nine analysts (30%) in the United States.

More Concern about Using Patient Material

Eight analysts are now more concerned about the issue of confidentiality and either have restricted where they present and write, or have decided to stop writing about patients unless they ask permission. Five of these analysts are from England, one each from Canada, Mexico, and Spain.

One analyst wrote:

> I no longer write about current patients, actually except for snippets, my main illustrations are twenty-plus years ago. I have seen far

too many patients in consultations who were deeply hurt over the countertransference remarks made by their analysts in papers. The analysts felt that they were just being "honest" about their feelings and mistakes while patients often felt responsible. As time passes these issues are usually less recognizable to patients and have less impact on them even when they do recognize themselves.

A second analyst stated:

I am now doubtful that there is any way to publish case material without it being recognizable because no disguise can disguise it from the patients and there is no way for the patient to know about it that would not distort treatment.

Another analyst, who had used the disguise of changing the patient's sex because she was concerned the patient's relatives might recognize her, stated that she would not use change of sex as a disguise now.

I have moved from a position of thinking that it is satisfactory to take all steps to ensure patient anonymity in order to publish to a position of publication being based on informed consent after termination. I now wonder about the ethics of publishing detailed case material at all because of the risk to the patient's well being of putting highly personal information in the public domain, even when anonymous. I think the appropriate forum for discussing clinical material are individual clinical supervision, clinical seminars, and papers presented at psychoanalytic society meetings and conferences that are closed to the public. I don't think that consent to use clinical material need be sought for these occasions so long as every step is taken to preserve confidentiality and the purpose is learning.

A fourth analyst worried about lawsuits:

I am increasingly more cautious in writing about patients as I have heard about difficulties other analysts have had and as I have participated in discussions at my institute. Two close analyst friends of mine were threatened with court cases in the last ten years; this has certainly affected my attitude. But it still doesn't make me want to discuss the issue with patients or former patients when I want to use their material.

A fifth analyst emphasized the accessibility of publications because of the Internet:

I would not ask patients because I think even when they are ex-patients I still hold a responsibility not to intrude my wishes onto them and that I have a responsibility to preserve myself as someone they could consult again if they needed to do so. I messed that responsibility up to a degree with a patient I wrote about who then read the paper. My failure was not to disguise her sufficiently *and* to have written about a mental health professional. However I am very aware of the illogicality of my thinking and also its increasing untenability, since with the advent of the World Wide Web almost anyone can be a reader of one's published material.

A sixth analyst has stopped writing:

The situation for me is that I have come to the stage where I have stopped writing because of my concern with confidentiality and not knowing how to resolve it. I find asking permission extremely intrusive when the treatment is on going but even more so if it has ended; yet not asking doesn't feel right. It is also clearly very painful for patients to see themselves "objectified" however sympathetically the paper is written, and, therefore, does not resolve the problem at all. If I do publish again, the case material will be very reduced but even then I am unsure how I would proceed.

Another analyst who is a prolific writer stopped publishing clinical material for ten years to give "true privacy " to his patients:

I have also been anxious to protect my ongoing clinical work from the intrusion that can flow from knowing that some of this could, even at a later date, be used for publication. So, for ten years after my last book, I remained determined not to publish any further clinical papers. This gave me and my patients the true privacy that was clinically necessary. It has only been as I approach my retirement, and am now taking on no new patients, that I have eventually decided to publish some examples of my work from that time.

A seventh analyst expressed the hope that the people he wrote about would—if they recognized themselves—preserve their own privacy by not informing others:

I trust that those patients and students, whose work with me I have drawn upon, will appreciate the care with which I have sought to protect their anonymity, so that others too may benefit from those occasions when I have had the chance to learn so much from each of them.

As before, I trust that anyone who recognizes themselves or their supervised work, amongst the vignettes presented here, will still feel able to choose not to have themselves identified by anyone else.

An eighth analyst hoped that guidelines to preserve confidentiality and the analytic process could be found:

> The new technology and easy access via search engines on the Internet and fear of being sued had made me much more cautious and I am still trying to find a way that I feel okay with. In the last five years I have given ten papers at conferences using heavy disguise of clinical material but have not submitted any paper for publication because of this anxiety. . . . To be honest I have always felt it to be something of a betrayal of trust but contained that feeling in the belief that psychoanalysis needs to have clinical papers (a belief I still hold). I do not think there is a way I will be comfortable with it. I hope that as a profession we may be able to specify agreed rules describing what we feel are ethical procedures which respect both personal confidentiality and safeguard analyses from intrusion from our need to publish clinical material.

Eight of the nine analysts in the United States who changed their view now believe they need to ask consent; four of these analysts worried that patients can more easily come upon their material and feel betrayed. As previously stated, only one of the American analysts changed his view in the direction of concern about negative effects of asking permission because he believed it complicated the treatment by intruding the analyst's interest. However, two other analysts from the United States, who declined to be interviewed and therefore are not counted in this sample, indicated that they had been sued and did not want to discuss it. One of these analysts has chosen to no longer write.

Less Concern about Using Patient Material

Two English analysts, one Canadian, and one Italian believe that over time they have felt less concern about using patients' material in their published papers. The other four American analysts who changed their views now believe asking consent posed no problem for the treatment and had seen no derivatives that suggested interference with the analytic process. One English analyst succinctly expressed the sentiments of this group.

> I have become less anxious over the years about writing about patients as I feel that the quality of the analytic relationship is the principle factor involved.

Recognition of Increased Complexity

Several analysts stated that over the years they had come to realize the issue of confidentiality was much more subtle and complicated than they had appreciated earlier in their careers.

One analyst wrote:

> Trying to answer your questions I realized that I had not thought enough about the whole issue before and that I had come to some ideas more out of habits and defense than from sound arguments.

Another analyst's response summarized many of these views.

> Writing about patients and the analytic process appears indispensable for the progress of knowledge. I have changed in the sense that when I started writing (in the 1970s) I did not even ask myself about getting permission. Afterwards I began to think that I should ask, and now I think that it depends on pondering many factors: the characterology of the patient, the possibility that the patient gets in touch with the publication (or) that people who know the patient get in touch with the publication, the effects on the course of treatment—not everything can be worked through—and the effects on the patient after the treatment has ended. I am feeling, more and more, that in many cases the reason for not asking permission of the patient, and not disclosing that I am using his/her treatment as an illustration, is more a defensive one on my part.

Parochial Legalistic Concern of United States

But other international analysts believe the concern with confidentiality is a more parochial issue.

One analyst stated:

> I feel that confidentiality as a theme is more relevant in the North American area of influence. It is not discussed much here.

Another analyst wrote:

> I think it is lamentable that fears of the practices of the courts of the United States make confidentiality so much an issue. A certain jurisdiction of societies . . . can become the source of excessive adjudication. Perhaps more normative and clear laws that protect the patient's right to confidentiality are necessary, but also the possibility under certain conditions—respect for anonymity of the patient, given sufficient disguise in order not to be recognizable, respect for secrets, etc.—are also necessary in order to publish clinical examples in order to permit better transmission of the knowledge to young professionals.

A third analyst claimed his right to publish but averred that he would feel more cautious if he lived in the United States:

> I consider it my right to use, under appropriate circumstances, clinical material in scientific communications. Moreover, I believe that we cannot progress as a science without assiduously resorting to the sharing of lots of clinical material. However, I must admit that I would exert more (self-serving and defensive) caution if I practiced in the U.S., given the climate of legal suits there.

DISCUSSION

Limits in the Comparability of the Samples

Although the sample size (36 compared to 30) of the two groups is relatively close, there are many differences in the data. First, almost all the United States analysts that I contacted (30 of 36) agreed to participate in the study. In contrast, a much smaller proportion of international analysts (36 of 107) agreed. It is likely that the United States analysts were willing to tell me their views and practices because they were familiar with my work and me. They trusted that I would maintain their confidentiality. Approximately half of the analysts residing outside the United States who participated either knew me personally or were familiar with my work; they expressed enthusiasm about the project being undertaken. I assume many of the others did not have this personal basis to support their participation in the survey. There are, of course, many other reasons why analysts might choose not to respond to an invitation to participate. Some reasons include not being interested in the topic, not having available time, not believing they could communicate well enough in English (three analysts responded in their native languages; in one instance I was able to translate myself, in the others I found a native speaker to do so), not believing that the findings would be of any value, or not valuing research itself for personal or professional reasons.

A second difference was that the United States sample was drawn from only one source (articles in *JAPA*) while the international sample had a much wider database (articles from *IJP*, Canadian, and Latin American psychoanalytic journals). I had hoped I would have a large enough response from several countries to be able to consider differences in outlook based on culture and training. The sample turned out to be much too small for any consideration of this topic.

Thirdly, the method of collecting the data itself was not comparable. All thirty United States analysts were interviewed on the telephone for 30–60 minutes. During that time, I could ask the analysts to elaborate their ideas and clarify what I did not understand. In contrast, over half of the international analysts did not provide as full or as detailed material since their responses were confined to answering the questionnaire. However, ten of these analysts elaborated their responses in subsequent e-mail exchanges. In these instances, the analysts' openness and apparent comfort with this medium made it seem as rich and detailed as the telephone interviews. On the other hand, the written replies allowed the analysts more time to consider and elaborate their responses. In the international sample, there were also three telephone interviews and one in-person interview.

Limitations of this Sampling

Given the relatively small number of responses from the community of analysts residing outside of the United States, one cannot assume that their views and practices are representative of this group. Nor can one assume that the sample of analysts from the United States is representative of the views and practices of all United States analysts. However, since the United States sample was drawn from only one journal, mostly, though not exclusively, contributed to by analysts trained in institutes sponsored by the American Psychoanalytic Association, more uniformity might be expected since analysts trained in institutes with different theoretical orientations were not numerous. On the other hand, in the United States, analytic viewpoints and practices have become increasingly diverse and multi-theoretical in almost all psychoanalytic training. There is also increasingly a view, and some supporting data, that adherence to theory is less directly related to issues of practice than had been assumed (Kantrowitz 2003, Spezzano 1998).

Another limitation in representability exists because many authors who published, and who are intellectual leaders in psychoanalysis, may not have published in these particular journals at the particular time period I selected.

Conclusions

Granting all the above limitations, what can be learned from this data? First, the representation of similar views and practices does not appear to be related to geographical location. Analysts the world over seem to be divided about the method for preserving patients' confidentiality. Somewhat less than half the sample of analysts (42%) around the world asks permission of their patients to write about them at least some of the time. This finding represents a change in attitude or practice in the direction of seeking permission or not publishing for approximately a third of the sample (33%).

Analysts have fantasies about analysts who do not live in their region of the world. United States analysts anecdotally stated their beliefs that only they and analysts from Great Britain would be concerned about the ethics and effects of writing without obtaining patients' permission. Some analysts residing outside the United States reported their beliefs that lawsuits would be of concern only to North American analysts. These assumptions were not supported by this project. Overall, the analysts responding to this study showed great diversity in their views, but it was not based on where they trained or the geographical region of the world in which they lived.

In summary, based on surveys of international analysts, analysts' geographical location does not seem to be a major determinant in relation to their ideas and practices about preserving patient confidentiality in written material. While more than twice as many analysts still use only disguise than regularly ask patients' permission to write about them, analysts around the world are increasingly concerned about the accessibility of published material. Many analysts are restricting where they present or publish, and some are choosing not to write if they do not believe it acceptable to ask patient permission for use of their material.

Fortunately, some analysts are finding that even when patients whose permission has not been asked discover they have been written about, they are still able to salvage the situation and sometimes they both learn from it. Some analysts also believe that asking permission to write about patients can become a useful part of the analysis. This material will be presented in a later section of this book. Current trends are to individualize one's approach in terms of the particular patient, the time of the request for permission, and the manner of dealing with untoward consequences.

Having compared the contemporary attitudes of traditionally trained psychoanalysts around the world, I will next present a generational comparison to show their views twenty-five years earlier.

4

Comparison of *JAPA* and *IJP* Authors between 1977–1981 and 1995–2000

Informal conversations with my colleagues about this study revealed that most of them assumed analysts had not been asking patients' consent prior to the last two decades. This chapter presents data about a generational comparison of attitudes and practices of analysts when they published in the *Journal of the American Psychoanalytic Association* (*JAPA*) and the *International Journal of Psychoanalysis* (*IJP*) between 1977 and 1981 and their views in 2003 at the time of their interviews. The current attitudes and practices of this group who published two and a half decades ago will also be contrasted with the attitudes and practices of analysts who published in these same journals and in the *Canadian Journal of Psychoanalysis*, *Revista Argentina de Psicoanalisis*, and *Revista Brasiliera de Psicanalise* between 1995 and 2000.

Many of the analysts who published papers in *JAPA* and *IJP* 1977–1981 are no longer alive. Therefore, in order to have a large enough sample, every analyst with a published clinical example in these volumes who was still alive was included. Fifty-one authors were located. They were first contacted by e-mail, or by letter or telephone when no e-mail was listed. Forty-four analysts provided material for this study. Thirty-four were men and ten were women. Thirty of the participating analysts were from the United States. Analysts residing outside of the United States who participated in this project are from England (5), South America (3), Canada (1), France (1), Greece (1), Holland (1), Israel (1), and Italy (1). Thirty-six of these analysts had backgrounds in psychiatry; two of these analysts also had Ph.D.s in psychology. Six others had Ph.D.s in psychology; two were British lay analysts.[1]

All but two of the thirty United States analysts were interviewed on the telephone for 30 to 60 minutes. Two United States analysts and nine of the fourteen international analysts responded by e-mail; sometimes this communication involved several exchanges to obtain more detailed information.[2]

Changes in Attitudes and Practices

The majority of analysts (33 of 44) who published over twenty-five years ago still practice confidentiality as they did in the past. Even when they indicate a greater awareness of potential problems from patients discovering their own material, the analysts who believe in using only disguise (19 analysts, 43%) still think there is a greater risk of interference with the analysis (or after termination, with the patient's life) from asking permission than from the impact of patients' inadvertently finding they have been written about. However, a quarter of the sample (11 analysts) previously using only disguise now either varies their approach or always asks permission. No analyst in this sample changed a view in the direction of using only disguise. Seven of the eight analysts who now vary their method, more often ask for permission unless it is a matter of short vignettes or they believe it is a certainty that the patient will not read the literature.[3] Their ideas are similar to the

---

1. Of the seven non-participating analysts, three analysts were too ill to respond. One analyst was too busy to participate. Three analysts did not respond.

2. Three analysts from England and one from Italy were interviewed on the telephone. One analyst from Greece responded by letter. Each analyst responded to a semistructured interview or written questionnaire about his or her attitudes and practices in relation to confidentiality of published material (see Appendix).

3. One analyst has not yet decided what to do about this problem but is affected by the current climate where an expectation of consideration of patients' rights prevails. Currently, this analyst feels inhibited from writing but believes that her decisions will be individualized for each patient when she does return to writing.

other eleven analysts who had always varied their approaches. Three analysts who changed from always using disguise alone to now always asking for consent joined the view of the three analysts who always believed this method was the only ethical practice. Neither gender nor professional background nor age discriminated among the attitudes, practices, or changes of approach of respondents (see Table 4–1 below).

Reasons for Maintaining Original Attitudes and Practices

Those analysts who continued to employ only disguise believe, as they did previously, that asking permission will disrupt the treatment. Most of these analysts offered the now familiar reason that transference made truly informed consent not possible. The three analysts who always asked patient permission at the earlier time continue to believe that no other way is ethical. They will not write about a patient if they believe that asking will create a disturbance in analysis. Eleven analysts who have always varied their approaches believed then and now that it is necessary to consider the treatment context. If they believed they could sufficiently disguise the material, so that even the patient will not recognize it, they did. Otherwise they asked the patient's permission or did not write when they thought it would be disruptive to the treatment.

REFUSALS OF CONSENT

Six analysts reported that patients have refused permission for them to publish clinical material; two of these analysts routinely ask patients' permission and have been refused by more than one patient, though many other patients gave their consent.

Table 4–1. Generational Comparison of Analysts' Attitudes and Practices in Publishing Clinical Material, 1977–1981 and 2003 (N=44)

	Disguise Only	Vary Approach	Always Ask Permission
1977–1981	30 (68%)	11 (25%)	3 (7%)
2003	19 (43%)	19 (43%)	6 (14%)

Comparisons of Attitudes and Practices with Analysts Publishing in 1995–2001

In the earlier era, sixty-eight percent of the sample, compared with the current forty-three percent, would have employed disguise alone. Compared to analysts' publishing in *JAPA* and the international journals of psychoanalysis between 1995 and 2000, the current views and practices of the sample publishing two decades before indicate that fewer chose disguise alone, while approximately twice as many vary their approach depending upon the patient and/or the analytic situation. The ideas of both these groups were similar to analysts who published in *JAPA* and international journals from 1995 to 2002. As indicated in the previous chapter, a slightly larger percentage of analysts residing outside the United States (58%) who published in the international journals chose only disguise as their preferred method for maintaining confidentiality than the United States analysts (50%) currently publishing in *JAPA* (see Table 4–2 below).

The majority of analysts who published between 1977 and 1981 now choose to vary their approach depending on the patient and circumstances. Since many analysts who published in these journals over

Table 4–2. Comparisons of Analysts' Current Attitudes and Practices in Publishing Clinical Material Between Analysts Who Published in JAPA and in IJP,[4] 1977–1981 and 1995–2001

	Disguise Only	Vary Approach	Always Ask Permission
JAPA & *IJP*: 1977–1981 (n=44)	19 (43%)	19 (43%)	6 (14%)
JAPA: 1995–2000 (n=30)	15 (50%)	7 (23%)	8 (27%)
Internat[5]: 1995–2001 (n=36)	21 (58%)	7 (19%)	8 (22%)
Combined *JAPA* & *IJP*: 1995–2001 (n=66)	36 (55%)	14 (21%)	16 (24%)

4. The 1995–2001 international sample also includes analysts publishing in the *Canadian Journal of Psychoanalysis, Revista Argentina de Psicoanalisis,* and *Revista Brasilia de Psicanalise.*

5. *International Journal of Psychoanalysis, Canadian Journal of Psychoanalysis, Revista Argentina de Psicoanalisis,* and *Revista Brasilia de Psicanalise.*

two decades ago are no longer alive, obviously we cannot determine if their views would have changed. This means we cannot determine how representative the surviving responding analysts' views are of this earlier generation of analysts nor how changing cultural attitudes might have affected their perspectives.

The previous chapters have focused on analysts' reasons for selecting their chosen approach to preserving confidentiality. This chapter concentrates attention primarily on the reasons some analysts have changed their attitudes or practices.

REASONS FOR CHANGES OF ATTITUDE AND PRACTICE

Conformance with Cultural Norm

Two analysts who have changed their practice from only disguising to asking for permission have done so because, as one put it: "It is currently the custom." They both were unsure if it was the wise thing to do but believed that analysts should be responsive to the present-day thinking of colleagues. One of these analysts has been surprised that there have not been difficult clinical repercussions from asking permission to publish clinical material.

> Now I ask and some say no; some agree; and some don't like it. I think it always has an effect but never a long-lasting one. I look for its effect very carefully. I explain that I share my experience with the analytic community. We have to share our experience to learn from one another.

The other of these two analysts explained his current thinking and practice:

> Before the last six–eight years I never thought about this issue, then reading papers about confidentiality and talking to my colleagues, I began to consider its implications differently. I didn't think about confidentiality previously as I do now. Then I just avoided identifying information. I wouldn't be so cavalier today, but I still don't think it's so great to ask. I ask if I don't think it would injure the alliance or effect the treatment. But I worry that I don't think enough about how special the patient may feel. If I think a patient would be hurt or humiliated, I won't ask or write about them, or if I

decide to write, I write in a general way so they wouldn't be sure it was them. If I wrote in a more detailed way, I wouldn't do it until the treatment was over. I've had only one patient ask to read it and he said it would be fine long before I ever actually wrote about him. Later, after the analysis was over, he came back and asked to read what I wrote and was fine about that.

Increased Awareness of Patients' Rights and Autonomy

Five analysts changed their views because they came to think differently about patient rights and autonomy. One analyst stated:

Although in the past I didn't ask permission, I did my best to disguise material. If a patient asked me not to write about him, I didn't and I never wrote about analyst-patients. But I've come to appreciate the concerns of privacy rights—it's less a concern that a patient would catch me in the act [than this newer appreciation of the patient's right to privacy]. I don't think I'd take a categorical position. It would depend on the stage of analysis and the stage of the transference. It's introducing something that isn't coming from the patient but is my own interest. In that respect it's an intrusion on the process and the analyst's neutrality. If I did it, it wouldn't be until a late stage of analysis and I probably wouldn't do it with someone suspicious. If I had any real concern that my patient would see it, like a patient in the mental health field, I would certainly ask permission.

Another analyst wrote:

I certainly have changed my mind over the forty years of my practice, becoming more and more cautious about confidentiality. I presented oral reports of analyses in sessions of work in my society and institute. I never have published the report of a whole psychoanalysis, but have used short fragments to illustrate a topic. It was easy to disguise the identity of the patient. Nevertheless, it has happened that patients have read the publication and have recognized themselves, without noticeable effects. In those instances, I had not asked permission from those patients. But I have become more and more reluctant to publish even small fragments.

I was deeply impressed by the position of Robert Stoller, who not only asked permission but also gave the text to read to the patients, and would not publish without their corrections and agreement. See in particular Mrs. G. in "Splitting." We have a colleague in France who does the same: Joyce McDougall.

Of course, this practice raised problems. Usually it concerned ended treatments so it did not influence the course of the analysis. It showed the patient that his material was "his" and that he or she was being treated as a person as much as the analyst who does not have more rights than the patient.

A third analyst said:

> I never used to ask permission, but rather disguised as thoroughly as I could. Now this no longer seems respectful of the patients' rights for autonomy. I am going to try something different. I am going to ask patients' permission about using clinical material before starting the analysis.

A fourth analyst put it briefly:

> The times have changed and so has my thinking. Patients have a right to decide whether or not their material is published.

A fifth analyst explained that a personal experience led to his reconsidering his practice:

> Around 1980 I would not have asked permission, though I would always have disguised and only written when I thought there was no chance of the patient reading it . . . people who weren't reading the literature but just interested in getting better. But later a patient like this went into the field. I was very upset about that, thinking he might read my article and be upset by it. I worried that it might not be as innocuous to him as it was to me and that he might think he could be identified. It didn't feel right. Earlier I hadn't been treating many people in the mental health field and had just avoided writing about them, but this example made me think about it more. I always ask people in the field for permission and show them what I've written, because how can they know what they are giving permission for if I don't? I would only ask someone who felt comfortable with display. We'd talk about exhibitionistic and voyeuristic experiences that were important to them. The asking permission then brings in more material that can be worked on in the analysis. One person I asked refused permission because she didn't like the way I described her mother. Though that brought more material too. I did not publish it.
>
> Today I would question writing about anyone without asking permission. A certain amount of selfishness comes in about wanting to

write. In the old days I felt I wanted to move ahead in the field and writing was a way of doing that . . . something crass like that. Now I'd only write if it really added to the field. I'd be much more conscious of how the patient would feel about being written about and would feel it essential to get permission before publishing.

A sixth analyst discussed "not having solved the problem" of writing about clinical material in the changed cultural climate. Previously this analyst did not ask permission, but now she appreciates a different view that "patients have a right to be asked" for use of their material in published papers.

> I haven't yet found my place in this dilemma. I am much more aware of patients' rights and concerned about patients' reactions, but I am still hesitant about the effect of asking. It is possible to write in less immediacy [with more distance] and detail by using a supervisee's material. But I think we need detailed material to be published so that we know the differences in how we work. It is very important for the future and development of our field to be exposed to and to appreciate the differences among us.

Negative Effects of Patients' Discovering Papers and Reading about Themselves

Two analysts changed their views due to disquieting experiences when patients discovered material about themselves.

> In the 1970s and early '80s, I disguised material as best I could. One person in the field recognized himself. I apologized and it was okay. But I began to worry about it. I had written about a child and I worried that when he grew up if he might find it and recognize himself, but he does not appear to have done this. But then I had patients whom other analysts had written about. These patients had found the articles about them and had been upset because of unflattering things that were said. I decided I would no longer write about people in the mental health field. Later I wrote a book and had the people I wrote about read the sections about themselves. These patients, who were not in the mental health field, were in ongoing treatment. I don't think it was detrimental. For one patient in particular, it enhanced her sense of being important in my life; she had been disappointed that our relationship was so limited. I think it helped

her sense of worth. But I worried because it was for my benefit and not the patients' primarily. I wouldn't write if I had something derogatory to say about a patient. That could be very detrimental if they read it. I just wouldn't do it.

The second of these two analysts described the combined effect on his views of his patient's reaction and changed attitudes about patients' rights.

> Around 1980, I didn't ask patients' permission if I could adequately disguise their material. . . . One time a patient found a piece about him several years after the analysis. I had disguised it but not sufficiently. I gave a dream that my patient recognized. He was very upset and contacted me. We met and discussed it. The analysis had been a good one. He felt I described it beautifully. He was impressed by my care and gentleness but felt that the dream was recognizable and that he had been a guinea pig for me as I shifted my theory. He did recognize my emotional commitment to him. I was able to repair his hurt and then it was all right. This patient had a major impact on my awareness of the effect of writing about patients. But also the climate had changed and that influenced me too. But mainly I realized that I had never been comfortable writing about patients without their permission. It was not so much about the safety for the analyst of not being sued as concern for the safety of the patient's right to privacy. Whatever you do creates a reaction. It's better to be ethical in your approach and deal with the consequences. I never ask anyone during analysis, only afterwards. I haven't written up full cases. I am much more aware of the effect of writing about patients now.

Changes Based on Self-Reflection

One analyst's change of view and practice was based "not on bad experiences or changes in ideas about writing—all of which came later —but from a more internal experience" in relation to himself and his patients.

> Before 1990 there was only one time I asked a patient for permission; it was a long case write-up and I thought because of the detail I should do that. In other earlier instances I had never gotten permission. I wasn't thinking in those terms. The examples were not from people in the mental health field; they were heavily disguised and I

didn't think they would ever see it. I kept the true sense of what went on but I changed the details. But the book I wrote used so much clinical material and many people were in the mental health field that I didn't think I could do it without getting permission.

Going through this process was an enormous strain. I wrote 150 pages without knowing if it would see the light of publication. Then there was the concern about screwing up ongoing analyses. I had four people in ongoing analyses and six people coming back after terminated analyses to talk about the write-ups. I worked really hard to give them freedom to say no against my wishes for them to say yes. It was intense and wonderful and I'm glad I did it, but I wouldn't do it again. It took too much out of me. It was a terrible strain.

Another analyst, who has always varied his approach to writing depending on the circumstances, expressed similar sentiments.

Throughout my career, I have been very hesitant about using material from analyses in my writing. I acknowledge the value of such examples, but feel very worried about the impact of publication on analysands, for many reasons. In the first IPA congress I attended as a candidate, I went to a talk by a senior analyst from my country, and within minutes realized the patient being discussed was a high school friend of mine, also a mental health professional. I was upset. Since then I have heard of many such situations, and know many people who have been hurt. Disguising thoroughly and "thickly" creates serious problems of distortion, and is used at times as a pretext to fit the case more to the writer's theory or self-image. Asking permission may imply making "an offer you can't refuse" to a patient who feels dependent upon the analyst. Consent may be transferentially motivated and may be regretted later on. Even if not regretted, consent may express narcissistic or exhibitionistic needs that the analyst should not have encouraged.

The issue for me is not only confidentiality, but also the fact that an extensive case report, using diagnostic terms and confident interpretations about personality structure, is in my view counter-therapeutic for the analysand, fixating the analysand's image rigidly, in a way that the analytic interaction itself hopefully does not do. In my clinical work, I value very much the fluid and open-ended quality of the discourse, its capacity to create a transitional space, and I feel that for the analysand to read definitive interpretations in writing sabotages this.

My solution so far has been to only use brief vignettes, which do not disclose anything the patient would consider confidential, instead of describing minute issues in the analytic encounter itself. When they were very brief, disclosing utterly nothing of a personal nature, I asked no permission. When they were a bit longer, I asked permission, letting the analysand read the whole paper, and trying to explore patiently any indication of ambivalence. In addition, I have disguised details and wrote the example with the assumption that someone sometime might guess who the patient was, and tried to think if anything in the material might embarrass my patient if his or her identity became known. If there was anything like that in it, I gave up the example altogether, and searched for other material. The one longer case I wrote up, I wrote with almost no biographical detail (no age, no profession, no marital or parental status), focusing only on the analytic interaction in the consulting room; and I only presented it in faraway locations outside my country, avoiding its publication in any journal that is likely to reach my countrymen.

My personal solution to the frustration of not writing up my cases is writing about historical figures or fictive literary figures, where I can enjoy discussing and interpreting life stories (which fascinate me) without damaging confidentiality and without risking my therapeutic contribution. I have also come to accord more respect for the controversial case studies (by Anna Freud, Kohut, and others) where we have come to realize that the patient was really the analyst. Giving up one's own confidentiality may be more fair than giving up someone else's secrets.

Another analyst, who still believed that disguise is the wisest practice had been greatly troubled by the experience of one of his patients who discovered she was written about without permission. The patient was disturbed, not only by the tone of what the analyst had written, but also by the fact that it had been done without her permission. This analyst had become increasingly concerned about patients' discovering their material and their reactions to it. Like many other analysts interviewed for this book, he has found himself disinclined to include clinical material in publications. Instead he restricted its use to teaching. Five other analysts, who continued to believe that disguise without asking permission was the best method to preserve confidentiality, have decided to stop writing clinical material for publication. They now present in different cities, publish in foreign journals, write about non-clinical issues, or use no illustrative material. Some other analysts write about supervisees' cases rather than their own.

Not all analysts who publish believed that it is necessary to be so concerned about patients' reactions provided the patient who is written about and the manner in which the analyst writes are carefully considered. Many of these analysts felt they would deal with the consequences of a patient finding the material and thought this was preferable to intruding on the analysis or on the patient's life afterward. One analyst described it this way:

> It works out positively if the patient feels that the analyst is really trying to help and has a good intention for sharing the material, that it is not just gossip. We still read what Freud wrote. I tell my patients I am following in Freud's tradition and only write what I believe will be helpful. One time a patient discovered I had written about him and came to see me very upset. I explained that I tried to disguise as well as I could and was very sorry that this had happened. But I said that unless we write, how would others learn. He understood and then it was all right.

DISCUSSION

Over the past decade and a half, there has been a shift in judgments in the world about what is permissible and what is a violation when publishing clinical material. As previously noted, while some psychoanalysts have reported being sued, most analysts who have been subject to litigation report having won these suits. The result, however, is that some of these analysts have decided to no longer write. In the last few years, confidentiality has become a subject of books and papers (Goldberg 2004b, Levin 2003). Although guidelines (Gabbard 2000, Tuckett 2000b) have been published for use of clinical material and recently papers (Aron 2000, Furlong 1998, Gabbard 1997, 2000, Goldberg 1997, Lipton 1991, Reiser 2000, Renik 1994, Stoller 1988, Tuckett 1993, 1998, 2000a,b) have discussed the merits and problems in various approaches, no single approach has been found to be satisfactory. It is increasingly clear that every choice has its hazards. The topic of ethics itself has rarely become an explicit subject in psychoanalytic journals, as of 2003. However, it has been an arena of debate in journals treating ethics in relation to psychiatry practices (Brendel 2002, 2003, "Carter" 2003). Ethics will be discussed in the fourth section of this book.

Historical Reasons for Adherence to a Disguise-Only Approach

Adherence to a medical model, a hierarchical view of analyst and patient, and a belief in the patient as the only subject of inquiry, undoubtedly contributed to many analysts continuing for so long to believe that only disguise was needed when publishing clinical material. Under certain circumstances—such as very brief vignettes—most analysts still believe only disguise is necessary. What is noteworthy is that eleven analysts who only disguised clinical examples twenty-five years ago have changed their view; eight have concluded that there are many circumstances—such as longer clinical presentation and material from patients in the mental health professions or recognizable by mental health professionals—where patients' consent for publication of clinical material is required. Three others have decided that they now will ask consent in all circumstances.

A SEARCH FOR FACTORS THAT DISCRIMINATE BETWEEN ANALYSTS WHO SEEK CONSENT AND THOSE WHO EMPLOY ONLY DISGUISE

Even two and a half decades ago, a few analysts (3 in this sample) believed all patients, under all circumstances, should be asked permission; when this approach was not appropriate, they maintained that the patient should not be written about. Eleven others had also frequently requested permission. What distinguished the group of analysts who asked permission from patients several decades ago from others?

Age, Gender, and Professional Training

They were not younger; only two of the fourteen analysts who asked permission are under seventy—and one of these two only by a year.[6] Of the eleven analysts who changed their attitudes or practices, only one is under seventy. Therefore, age is not an explanative variable. Nor do gender or professional training discriminate among the groups.

Time of Training

Whereas the late 1970s and early 1980s was an era when authority was being questioned and individual rights asserted, most of the analysts in this study who published in the organization's psychoanalytic journals were trained at an earlier time when these ideas were not so prevalent. Therefore, the time of training was not a significant factor.

Training in Child Analysis

The groups who always varied their approach or always asked permission do have a higher percentage of child analysts; six of the thirteen analysts (46%) in this category work as child analysts compared with three of the nineteen analysts (16%) who still believe in using only disguise; four of the eleven who have changed their views are also child analysts. These numbers are not enough to be significant but may suggest a factor for further reflection. Perhaps training in and working with children made these analysts more sensitive to this issue. Many of the child analysts discussed their concerns about the effect on their child patients of reading about themselves as adults. They did not believe it was appropriate to rely solely on a child's consent and always asked for the parents' permission as well. They thought children might feel differently over time. They also tried to imagine how a child might feel if he or she happened to read about himself or her-

---

6. Thirty-seven of the forty-four analysts in the sample reported in this chapter are over seventy years old.

self at a later time and tried to write with sensitivity to this possibility. Two of the three child analysts who still believe in only using disguise were among the analysts who gave the most detailed attention to, and expressed the most concern about, patients' reactions if, or when, they found articles about themselves. Perhaps this added concern about the impact of later discovery led some child analysts to think that permission was necessary when writing about children and then led them to consider other instances where it also seemed desirable.

Writing about Patient–Analyst Interactions

Another distinguishing characteristic of this group is that they have among them three analysts who have innovatively written on patient–analyst interactions. These analysts, therefore, have been among those who have contributed to changing ideas in the field. Their work likely influenced analysts' views about the importance of including the patient's perspective about the publication of their clinical material. Three other analysts in the group that changed their views about seeking patient permission could also be characterized as innovative in introducing a focus on process.

Personal Experiences, Values, and Beliefs

I have not found a satisfactory explanation that allows characterization of any group. I tend instead to think the choice of method for preserving confidentiality is based on individual factors. Values, beliefs, sensitivity to cultural changes, and personal experiences—for better or worse—all contribute to both constancy and change in approach. I am inclined to think the particular choice an analyst makes to protect confidentiality requires understanding a multiplicity of other individual factors. Some analysts were always more conscious of patients' rights and autonomy whereas others developed this awareness as the professional climate changed. Some analysts have changed their practices out of fear of lawsuits, regardless of whether or not the suit is likely to be successful; other analysts have changed their practices and views because they have become more sensitive to the fact that patients may be hurt and feel betrayed by the discovery that their material has been used without their permission. However, other analysts still believe that if what one presents is sufficiently disguised and sensitively presented, and if no material that would shame or humiliate the patient is included, then even the patient discovering they have been written about will not be ultimately detrimental. Most analysts who continue to maintain that disguise alone is preferable have either not had patients find articles written about them, or believe that when this material has been discovered they have been able to discuss the experience in a manner that alleviated the patient's distress.

Whether they are asking consent or only disguising the clinical material, analysts want to believe the decision they make will be the one that least adversely affects the patient and the analytic process. As such they may at times remain "blind" to information that contradicts their beliefs. In Sections 2 and 3 of this book, analysts' perceptions of patients' reactions and first-person accounts of patients' reading about themselves will be presented. The reader can then make a judgment about these decisions and their effect.

CHANGE IN REASONS FOR WRITING

Analysts who write are people who want to write. Certainly in this desire there is personal self-interest as well as the wish to contribute something of value to the field. A few analysts were very specific in stating that in their earlier years they believed publishing advanced their careers; now that they were older they wrote only when they thought it was a really new idea.

HAZARDS OF WRITING

The exposure that published material affords is, however, janus-faced. It gives recognition and sometimes admiration, but it also leaves the author open to criticism and sometimes envy. Analyst-authors take a risk in relation to their colleagues by putting their ideas forward. When they write about patients, they also risk something in relation to their patients. As previously stated, when analysts write about patients, there are no solutions without problems. Not writing would be a problem for the field. Therefore, non-writing readers need to appreciate the risks as well as benefits involved in writing for analysts-authors.

REFUSAL OF CONSENT

It is not true, as some have assumed, that patients cannot and do not refuse to give permission. Numerous analysts in these studies report that they have had patients who have not consented. Six analysts in this group of forty-four had patients refuse. Some analysts who make it a policy to ask all patients before writing have been denied consent by several patients. But then there is a countertransference reaction to deal with. Some analysts have reported struggling to keep their patients' interest foremost; these reports are less troublesome than those claiming no reaction to the refusal. As one analyst in this group described it: it is an exhausting experience to try to make it possible for one's patients to say no, while at the same time one is very much wanting them to grant permission. There are some ways of asking and writing that are likely to be upsetting to most patients. However, when analysts choose patients carefully, write and ask with tact and sensitivity to the individual patient, we need to wonder why some patients are distressed and others are not. No doubt each individual case requires separate reflection.

USING WRITTEN MATERIAL FOR ANALYTIC WORK

Two analysts who published in *JAPA* and two analysts who published in *IJP* between 1995 and 2002 raised the idea that the written material could be used in the treatment to benefit the patient. These analysts were much less conflicted about involving patients by asking their permission. None of the authors in this current sample who had published two decades earlier brought up the possibility that getting permission and using the material that emerged could be employed in this fashion. However, it was clear from interviews that many of these analysts did pursue this material in that manner.

Analysts subscribing to a relational theoretical perspective have expanded the technique of actively working with reactions stimulated by patients reading clinical material. Many of these analysts now use the written example as a stimulus for clinical work. The ideas and practices of analysts who identify themselves as relational theorists is the topic of the next chapter. Relational analysts' use of writing as a stimulus for clinical work will be discussed in the second section of the book.

5
Psychoanalytic Dialogues Authors

The previous three chapters have provided data about the attitudes and practices of analysts who have been trained in institutes approved by the International Psychoanalytic Association. The assumption, possibly not warranted but formally accepted, is that they have been trained in a similar manner and, therefore, share a similar set of theoretical beliefs and practices with similar clinical interventions. In fact, there may be considerable variation among these analysts in their theories and techniques (Kantrowitz 2003, Spezzano1998).

This chapter provides data about the attitudes and practices of a group of United States analysts who have separated themselves from this historically mainstream training. They founded institutes where their own theories and techniques are taught and a journal where their ideas are published and debated. They designated themselves relational analysts. I will provide a brief summary of their theoretical perspective and their journal's background before describing their views and methods in relation to preserving confidentiality.

The central assumption of relational analysts' thinking is that a person's character and relationships will be manifest in the relationship with the analyst. The residue and core of unconscious phenomena show themselves in the current interaction with the analyst. It puts relationships, both external interpersonal relationships as well as internal object relations, at the center of the theory in the place of dual drive theory.[1] A second assumption is that any interaction between two people is jointly created, rather than the creation of one person's mind. A patient's relationship with analyst A is different from what might have formed with analyst B; each analyst will bring out different aspects in the patient. It is a source of variance in the analysis; therefore, the analyst's countertransference needs to be analyzed and understood as well as the patient's transference. The transference/countertransference intertwining is the starting point of interpretation and analysis.[2] How and to what extent this interaction becomes the central focus of analysis varies among relational analysts. What they share is a different lens for viewing the material. They look for the role they play in what emerges with the patient. This central idea shapes their technique. Many relational analysts have become particularly interested in enactment, multiple self-states and self-disclosure. The extent to which they explicate their contribution to the patient or to the reader also has considerable variation.[3]

Psychoanalytic Dialogues, first published in 1991, was the inspiration of Stephen Mitchell who was the founder and first editor. His idea was to establish a journal that would allow debate about current ideas in analytic thinking. There would be a lead article and discussion about

---

1. Modern conflict theorists would agree that unconscious phenomena manifest themselves in interactions with the analyst. Both external interpersonal relationships and internal object relations are given much greater focus than in previous times. However, intrapsychic conflicts and interpretation of drive and defense remain central to the theory and technique of most analysts who identify themselves in this fashion.

2. While classically trained Freudian analysts had viewed analysts as a "blank screen" for patients to project their conflicts upon, by the 1980s these ideas had begun to change. The real characteristics of the analyst were increasingly acknowledged as playing a role in what transpired between the patient and the analyst. Countertransference was no longer exclusively seen as interference to the process to be analyzed away. It became viewed as a potential source of valuable information that was part of the process. The transference/countertransference encounter became a central focus of analysis, but never as exclusively as with relational theorists.

3. Modern conflict theorists would also maintain that an appreciation of countertransference and other sources of characterological contribution by the analyst need to be owned and analyzed, but they would be far less likely to share these insights about themselves with the patient.

it that introduced divergent perspectives.[4] *Psychoanalytic Dialogues* quickly became the main forum for dissemination of theoretical ideas and clinical techniques introduced by relational analysts. These ideas were debated by both other relational analysts and analysts with different theoretical orientations.

Thirty-one analysts[5] who published articles with clinical illustrations in *Psychoanalytic Dialogues* between 1995 and 2002 were interviewed. With one exception, all interviews were conducted on the telephone for thirty minutes to an hour as had been done with analysts publishing in the *Journal of the American Psychoanalytic Association*. One response was obtained by e-mail in a manner similar to my contact with most of the international analysts. Nineteen of these analysts were male and twelve were female. Twenty-nine of these analysts had PhDs in psychology; one was a psychiatrist and one had a doctoral degree in mental health. Gender did not discriminate among the attitudes and practices. The fact that all but two analysts came from the professional discipline of psychology makes it impossible to comment on the effect of the background discipline.

Slightly more than half the analysts interviewed (16 of the 31 analysts, 52%) who had published in *Psychoanalytic Dialogues* varied their method of preserving confidentiality. For the majority of these authors asking for permission was the default position. However, when the material presented was only a short vignette, most of these analysts did not believe they needed to request permission. The other half of this

---

4. Over the years other journals, like *JAPA*, have also included this kind of format.

5. Fifty United States analysts published clinical examples in *Psychoanalytic Dialogues* between 1995 and 2002. I was able to contact forty-five of these analysts. Nine did not respond. Three analysts stated they were too busy and two, who initially gave tentative agreement to being interviewed, did not follow through. Four of the analysts interviewed did not identify themselves as relational analysts. One considered himself a modern Freudian, similar to the majority of analysts publishing in the *Journal of the American Psychoanalytic Association*; another identified with object relations theory and intersubjective views; a third saw himself as a self-psychologist; and a fourth as eclectic in the clinical sphere and intersubjective theoretically. Many of these analysts indicated that multiple theories influenced them but that relational theory permitted an integration of their views. I chose to ask all of these analysts, rather than a randomly selected group, because I realized fewer of them would know me and therefore, understandably, fewer would be likely to agree to an interview.

group was almost equally divided between a commitment to only disguising clinical material (7 of the 31 analysts, 23%)—though five of the seven analysts had on at least one occasion asked permission—and always asking for permission (8 of the 31 analysts, 25%). Most, but not all, of these analysts will not write about a patient in a mental health field unless they have asked permission. In other words, unless the illustration is very brief, twenty-four analysts (77%) in this sample prefer to ask permission. If the five analysts who at least on one occasion requested consent are added, then twenty-nine analysts in this sample (94%) have asked consent of patients.

CONFIDENTIALITY

Always Only Disguise

Two analysts always only employed disguise when writing about their patients. The first[6] of these analysts had strong negative feelings about asking permission and used clinical material very sparingly.

> I write only small vignettes and use only disguise. I'm dismayed about the trend of introducing asking permission in treatment. I see it as an intrusion; it would be better afterward, but I've never done that either. I never write about people in the mental health field. When I write about someone, I disguise heavily and my examples are very brief. I write so even the patient won't recognize it. To ask permission would be to introduce how I think about a patient. It puts jargon and theory into how I think about the patient. That isn't how I talk with patients. It puts things in their mind that wouldn't be there.

This analyst raised the idea that asking permission may be intruding the analyst's agenda not only into the work, but intruding the analyst's thoughts into the patient's mind.

The second analyst was concerned not only that asking permission might create an interference with the patient's process but that it might also place a constriction on the analyst.

---

6. The first analyst's self-described theoretical position was as "an object relations theorist with intersubjective views," not as a relational theorist.

The way I think and the way I communicate are somewhat different. I just disguise. I believe asking distorts the process. If I were thoroughly honest I'd say I'm also protecting my privacy to think in a certain way that I don't always share with the patient. I'm also concerned about patients feeling used. I suppose there are occasions when I'm also concerned a patient might not agree to the material being published.

This analyst added the issue of the privacy of his thoughts that would be revealed to the patient by reading what has been written. He was concerned as to how his wishes would affect the patient but then also questioned the effect on him if the patient's wishes clashed with his own wish to publish. Asking permission, then, could be an intrusion on both the agenda of the patient and that of the analyst.

Disguise Preferred

Five other analysts use only disguise as their method of preserving confidentiality; however, on one or more occasions they had asked permission. The first of these analysts had asked only one time. His motivation for asking was based on clinical factors rather than related to a modification of his way of thinking about dealing with confidentiality.

My decision to ask this patient's permission was not so much about my clinical writing as trying to assert myself into her treatment. I made it an issue between us to try to engage her passivity. I don't write about people in the mental health field who are my patients, though I have about supervisees' patients, but they and the supervisee are heavily disguised. When I write about my own patients I do it with circumspection. My clinical examples tend not to involve too much demographic information. They are about things in the session, things no one could connect to the patient. I haven't done too much writing that tells about lives outside of treatment. Usually I disguise so fully that I feel comfortable it won't be recognized. Usually my writing is about people I've finished treatment with. I've always been tormented by this issue though and that hasn't changed. What's changed more is recognizing the need to protect my own confidentiality when I work—mine and my patients. I'm more aware how subject to interpretation everything is. People who read bring their own sets of assumptions to it. So I have to be concerned how it will be taken and used.

This analyst mentioned the concern about the readers' view of the analyst and his intentions. He said that, by making his thoughts transparent, the analyst might paradoxically be leaving himself open to being misinterpreted by his colleagues.

The second analyst in this group viewed disguise as the preferred default position but recognized special circumstances when he would ask permission.

> Most of the time I disguise. I don't put in the giveaway facts. The patients have been in treatment for a long time. I never write about people in the mental health field. If I feel like the disguise is sufficient, then I think it's overkill to ask. But if something about the patient is so central to what I'm writing about, then I ask because the person might identify himself if for any reason he read it. I still write it in a general way so no one else would recognize the patient. I've had former patients say no, turn me down and I don't know the lasting ramifications of that. My preference is definitely to disguise and not to ask.

This analyst introduced concern that the ramification of asking permission of former patients and of its being refused may remain unknown.

The third analyst in this group of three asked permission only once and he did so because the patient was in the mental health field. Otherwise he disguised age, ethnicity, profession, location, and frequently wrote aggregate cases. No patients had ever found a published case he had written about them. But this analyst, unlike all the others who advocated disguise as the preferred method, believed his choice was suspect.

> When I write, I write my take on patients, feelings they evoke in me, and usually these are things I never say. If someone I was supervising told me this, I'd ask why. I think I should want my patients to know [I think this analyst means that his commitment to a theory of the co-construction of meaning should make him think it was advantageous for his patients to know what he thinks and feels, but he does not actually feel this]. Maybe this is cowardice. I think I don't do it the right way. No one has ever found what I've written, but I worry someone will find it. I wouldn't take that chance with someone in the mental health field. So in that one instance I asked. I don't think I do it the right way but it's a convenience.

This analyst believed that he should want his thoughts and feelings about his patients to be transparent to them, but he sensed that he was resisting doing so. He was self-critical about what he viewed as a personal inhibition. He theorized it would be preferable to be open and self-revealing in ways other relational analysts describe, but he was stopped by feelings that he did not describe further.

The fourth analyst always employed disguise only unless the patient was in the mental health field. She had done this only on one occasion. In other instances, she preferred to use a composite.

> I remain true to the treatment process but everything else is changed, even the symptoms. I've never let a patient read the material, but I've only asked permission once and that was because the patient was in the mental health field. I never write about anyone in the public domain. I try to preserve not only the patient's privacy but my own. I publish in journals that don't have a wide circulation.

The fifth analyst had asked patients' permission at the end of analysis or afterward, but her strong preference was to disguise.

> My preference is to disguise so thoroughly that the patient can't recognize it. I write vignettes without identifying data or create composites. It's coercive to ask. The pull to comply is enormous . . . to please you. Or you end up feeling beholden to them. It's a mutual back scratching. Are they really free to say no? I don't think so. But once you create composite how veridical is it? How much does it distort? I try to keep the feeling quality consonant with the actual material, but still. . . . It makes me angry when analysts say there's no problem. Any time anyone says no problem, there's a problem. If disguise is a problem for the reader, I'd rather take that chance than mess something up with the patient. I'd like things to be less hierarchical, but this is bad in a different way. I never assume that a patient won't read nowadays, though I did ten years ago. I try to alter key elements that are irrelevant to the case, like creating a costume that draws your eyes away from something. I also try to put in as little background information as possible. I worry if patients do recognize themselves whether they will feel objectified, humiliated, even though I don't pathologize or put in anything that hasn't been talked about. I've asked permission of only two people. I struggled for a year because I couldn't find a way to disguise them. I wanted to write a case about someone who couldn't express his wants. It's paradoxical because I wanted something. So maybe I was reenacting something with

him. The goal for him might have been for him to say no. But he didn't. But I was more comfortable because my asking was in our work.

This analyst's conflict between her values and preferences and her personal desire and ambition to write vividly convey the struggle many analysts feel now that they no longer are confident that patients will not read what they write. This view is very similar to those expressed by the more classically oriented analysts.

With the exception of the first analyst, who was not identified with relational theory, and the last analyst, who was focused on how troubled she was when she had asked permission, all these analysts brought up the issue of their own loss of privacy in addition to the privacy concerns of their patients.

Change in View from Using Disguise Alone to Asking Consent

Three analysts described a change in their views and how their approaches evolved over time to asking for permission.

One analyst stated:

> I have written and heavily disguised the material and not asked permission. I don't do that anymore. I used to see it as an intrusion, and it can be, but it also can be enriching. Now I ask permission and offer patients the opportunity to read it.

A second analyst reported:

> I've changed my way of thinking about this and what I do over the years. In the 1960s I wrote up patients' data, never told them, and just disguised it. I think everyone did then. It was the old medical model; analysts just wrote and published. But I had a misadventure. Other people couldn't recognize the patient, but the patient could. I had no idea my patient would see it. He was in a different, unrelated field. But his wife was angry about the way he was changing. She searched out everything I had published, found a paper she thought might be him, gave it to him, and he was justifiably upset. It was after termination. He came and talked about it. He came several times and he left not angry. But I thought it was a bad thing to have happened and I felt I had to do something different from then on. After this experience I felt that no matter what I did, it was possible

to be found. I still didn't tell patients. I chopped up data, disguised it heavily. But I was concerned. I felt caught between doing something that intrudes and being found out.

Then about fifteen years ago, I began asking permission, showing it to patients if they wanted to see it. At times it brings up something that gets analytic attention, but is it really analyzable? I don't know; it's hard to generalize. It has something to do with the degree of trust two people have in each other. Some people I wouldn't write about; you have to have a lot of mutual trust to do it. If my patients want the disguise changed or something left out, I do that. I feel better doing it this way, reassured by the patient that it's okay. But I'm not at all certain that the patient benefits by it. You intrude and useful things can come of it. But I'm not sure if it's better than if you never did it.

A larger proportion of my patients are now in the field. One advantage of this approach is sometimes my patients don't feel what I've written is an accurate picture. Then we try to understand it and find a more accurate picture or get clearer versions that each of us has. It gets used like any other material that I introduce, like if I'm sick or have made a mistake based on a countertransference. Once you see it, it's an everyday experience that the patient may know something, but if the analyst says it or if the patient sees it through reading what the analyst has written, it takes on another caste.[7]

This analyst's observation that while patients often "know something" about the analyst's views it takes on "another caste" once the analyst actually says or writes it, is central to the understanding of the impact of the move from employing only disguise where patients can have fantasies about their analyst's view about them but lack confirmatory evidence, to the contemporary practice where many analysts ask permission and show patients what they have written thereby revealing more of their reactions to the patient. The transformation from ambiguous fantasy/perception to concrete, actual data that confirms or disconfirms fantasy constructions has broader implications for analytic theory and technique than debates about methods of preserving confidentiality. I will return to this in the next section when I discuss relational analysts' use of written material in analytic work.

Another analyst's former rule of always asking permission has evolved and changed to a more complex approach.

---

7. This analyst identifies as a modern Freudian, not a relational theorist.

I had a rule at one point that I had to ask permission when patients came to treatment. I gave them a paper to sign. But after a while I realized they didn't really know what they were signing. Then for a while I wrote very short things that were disguised and I didn't ask permission. Then about five years ago I realized that I needed to write things to be clear for myself. So I did. But it wasn't for publication. Then I needed to write something for a presentation. The patient was in a termination phase. I thought that asking then might interfere with the process, so I didn't do anything with the paper. A few years later I submitted it to a journal and they accepted it. This was about three years after the patient's termination. It so happened that the patient returned shortly before the acceptance. So I asked him what he thought about my publishing something about our termination. He said fine and was happy for me that I was doing it. He saw it as something I was doing in my world, and not really about him. I was really glad that I hadn't intruded on his termination. I wouldn't have published it without his okay though.

Always Ask Permission and Show Material

Eight analysts always asked permission and showed the patients what they wrote either at the time of the request or before publication. Three of these analysts emphasized that what they wrote had to be "real"; otherwise it would seem hollow. They all disguised by omitting rather than changing biographical data. They never made composites. Two analysts did not write before asking their patients' permission. One of these analysts stated that no patient had ever refused to give consent.

My patients are curious about what I'll write. It hypes up the transference, which gets analyzed later. There seems a universal response of genuine interest in what I'm writing. Patients are usually eager to read what I've written, but after they read their interest gets diluted because it usually feels like a responsible representation of what went on and they are satisfied with the degree of anonymity. Later they get curious about the meaning to me that I'm writing about them. If I didn't ask for permission, I'd feel covert in relation to the patient. I'd feel it and know it all the time as a secret and it would affect the treatment.

The second analyst believed all her experiences of asking patients' consent to have been positive.

> Asking permission stirs up things to work with. In the beginning I wrote first and then asked permission. One patient refused. I had already put in so much work. So now I ask before I write. The only patients who have refused were ones who were abused. They don't want me to say how bad it was. It meant a lot to them that I was respectful and asked. The process of asking and sharing what I write can sometimes create intense bonding.
>
> I'm very concerned about confidentiality. I had one patient running around saying that's me. I worry that later the patient might regret it. I had another patient who didn't care what I wrote but she didn't want to read it. Ultimately, I didn't feel right about that and I had her read it. She found it amazing, like seeing a photograph from another time.

The third analyst introduced the idea that asking permission may bring complications but believed that the outcome is positive. What is stirred up becomes part of the work.

> I can't imagine writing about a patient without asking permission. It feels like a betrayal. Asking brings complications in terms of the patient feeling special. The very personal way I write introduces things I wouldn't naturally be introducing, but it acts as an opportunity to explore things.

The fourth analyst had only written about two patients and had asked permission of both. In these instances, he had advised them that he would show them what he had written to be sure the disguise was good enough before it was published. He was explicit about not according them veto power over what he wrote.

> One person was in the field and was concerned about being recognized because she had told people she was in analysis with me. Reading what I wrote brought back something from earlier in the treatment that had a new impact on her. It allowed us to rework something I had done that had been very upsetting to her. This was a positive experience. The other patient had been excited that I was writing about her but infuriated by what I wrote because of the way she understood my countertransference. From an ethical point of view, if there's any chance that someone could be recognized I can't write about them. I also believe it's wrong not to ask permission.

This analyst made clear that the outcome of asking permission may not always be positive, but he maintained that ethically he believed there was no other choice.

The fifth analyst also acknowledged that asking permission introduces complications so that he had focused on being sensitive in terms of the timing of the request. This analyst also believed that it was wrong not to ask for consent.

> Some patients I ask and show what I've written and we talk about it. Sometimes patients don't want much involvement in relation to my writing; others do. If they think I'm getting the picture wrong, we talk about it and clarify and then I'll alter or expand the perspective if I come to understand it differently. For other patients reading what I write gives a clearer form and organization to understanding themselves. But some people feel used. I always disguise very heavily and think there's very little chance of anyone recognizing my patients. So if I think it might be disruptive at the time I'm writing, I might not ask then, but I would eventually before it was published. I've never had a patient I told I was writing about them who didn't want to see it, so I think about what's going on between us at the time I ask, but I always ask eventually. I believe it is wrong not to ask permission.

The sixth analyst told patients early in the treatment that he often writes and asked for a general permission. He said that he would share with them what he intended to publish if they wanted to see it; most patients did want to read it. Usually, he did not write until the later part of treatment. He waited until he was somewhere near a final stage of a paper but had not yet submitted it before showing it to patients. If patients thought their material was identifiable, he took it out. If something was misremembered, he corrected it. On one occasion, he decided not to publish the material because the patient wanted so much changed.

A seventh analyst always asked permission except when writing very brief vignettes. She viewed treatment and writing as a joint venture.

> I do a lot of internal work before I ask a patient. I think about the meaning to the patient. When I give what I write to a patient I have them read it, edit if they want. I correct that and then give it back to the patient to check again. It's a collaborative process.

This analyst highlighted mutuality in the process. Her position contrasted with that of the fourth analyst, who was equally committed to asking consent, but who made it clear that patients had no veto power over his writing.

The eighth analyst also stressed the reciprocal nature of the process of negotiating about how to use patients' material. His belief was that asking permission was the only ethical way to publish. However, on one occasion he "violated" his own belief system.

> I only write about process and never a full case. I always ask consent. I believe the patient owns the story and it's exploitative not to ask permission. Asking consent reflects the respect and reciprocal nature of relational ethics. I give patients editorial and veto power about the way they are represented and disguised. One time I violated these principles and wrote without getting permission about a treatment that fell apart. The patient had subverted the treatment and I disliked him. He had a consultation and then he left. I felt there was no way to ask his permission. So I massively fabricated his life and gave almost verbatim process. If he did read it, he might think it was familiar but he wouldn't think that it was his material for sure.

This analyst saw his one-time disguise-only publication as a violation of his own ethical beliefs. His description of the situation suggested that his countertransference dislike and anger with this patient may have played a role in his departure from what he believed to be ethically correct procedures.

The first three analysts who were committed to asking patients' permission agreed on the need to write authentically and to be open and collaborative with their patients about what they had written. They also agreed that patients' reading what they had written stimulated the transference in ways they believed were beneficial. However, they conveyed different senses about how they thought about their impact on their patients in relation to writing about them. The first analyst seemed to consider his patients' responses to the actual written material as almost bland. He thought most of his patients' reactions to being asked permission stirred interest in what the analyst would write about them, but he did not refer to any sense of conflict. The second analyst was similar on these counts; only abused patients said that they minded. Both these analysts conveyed a sense that there was a positive relationship of respect in which transference issues are stirred up but that the writing itself never stimulated negative, disruptive reactions. The second analyst's belief in the importance of feeling honest caused her to disregard her patient's conscious wishes. She claimed that it worked out with the patient gaining a positive feeling. But what does it mean to overrule your patient with your own agenda even if the result is "not upsetting"? The third and fourth analysts acknowledged possible complications. The fifth analyst offered concrete instances of both positive and negative reactions by patients. The sixth analyst expressed a more textured and complex sense of his patient's reaction. What occurred seemed to have been therapeutically beneficial, but this analyst lets us realize that there was more conflict in it for both him and his patients.

The seventh and eighth analysts focused on asking permission as reflective of analytic collaboration, a precept of relational theorists. The eighth analyst was emphatic about his commitment to seeking permission as a respectful and a reciprocal way of working; however, despite his strong convictions on one occasion he overrode these principles and wrote without asking consent about a negative experience with a patient. It is certainly beneficial to the field to have these negative outcomes in the literature. Nevertheless, like the one analyst who was so strongly committed to disguise and on two occasions overrode was because of her wish to publish, this analyst does not seem to have considered the possibility of not publishing given that it went counter to her values.

Preference for Asking Permission and for Showing Material

Sixteen analysts varied their approach to preserving confidentiality depending on their view of the patient's character and conflicts and the nature of the transference at the time they were writing. Some of these analysts had previously used disguise alone but no longer thought of this as a preferred practice. They now chose to ask permission when they believed it would not be detrimental to the analytic work. When they did ask permission, they also showed patients the written material.

TIMING OF REQUESTS

Requests Early in Treatment

Three analysts preferred to ask permission early in treatment. One analyst described his thinking:

> I talk with most patients early on before it's an issue of something I am actually planning to write. Not right at the beginning because then I don't have a relationship, but early on. I tell them if I publish or present a full case, I will get their permission, but if it's only about my reactions, or a theoretical point or a question of technique, rather than a detailed look at their lives and dynamics, then I'll just disguise and not seek permission. By and large, that's agreeable. The exceptions are primarily people in the field or those who ask me not to write at all. When I write I disguise heavily. I take something in a session that felt powerful and change it radically. I try to stay honest to the experience. I can only do that if what I'm writing is a moment in a session. So that's what I write about. But if a patient should come upon this and recognize himself, it's not totally out of the blue. One patient in the field came upon an example about him. It was fine.

Requests in the Middle of Treatment

The majority of the relational analysts asked for permission during analysis because they made the writing an active part of the work with the patient.

One analyst stated:

> I almost always ask during treatment, though some patients I ask in advance and have them sign a consent for permission. With others if I think about writing at a place in the relationship where I feel it's meaningful to talk about it, I do it before I write; with others, having asked in a general way earlier, I start to write and then ask later on. I don't ask if what I write are only brief vignettes.

A second analyst said:

> I've only asked during treatment. It seems intrusive to ask and reopen it afterwards. Also it's most alive for me then and I use it in

the work. I always ask before or simultaneously as I write and almost always show it to the patient.

A third analyst reported:

> If the patient is in treatment, I tell him I only write when a patient has finished analysis. I write it up and disguise it, but I do not ask permission. I never write anything surprising, hurtful, or offensive, but I don't recontact the patient because I feel it's an intrusion.

Another analyst provided reasons for his decision to ask permission only late in analysis.

> I've asked late in treatment. My freedom to ask had to do with a confidence that the patients would experience it as collaborative.

Requests and Reasons Not to Request after Termination

Two analysts in this sample had written only when the treatment was terminated, but neither analyst was committed to a belief that this timing was the only time to write.

> I have never asked permission in an ongoing analysis. I can tell a narrative better when the treatment has ended. It's not a rule that I don't, but I think if I wrote while it was going on, it would affect the treatment. I've never thought about this consciously before; it's just what I've done. Perhaps it could affect it positively. When I write I pay more attention. I think when I do that the work becomes more rich and varied.

Another analyst, with one exception, only asked for permission after termination.

In contrast, one analyst stated that it was specifically when a patient was no longer in treatment and that he had no further contact with the patient that he would not ask permission. He envisaged it as an intrusion and not useful to the patient since it could no longer be made part of the work. Under these circumstances, he made a composite or disguises, but did not go into great detail.

Another analyst stated that he also tried to avoid asking after termination because it felt like it would have been more of an imposition than it would have been during the treatment itself. His asking afterward would most often occur with someone who was in the mental health field.

> If I ask afterwards, I've chosen very carefully and I'm relatively certain how they will respond. Sometimes they come in and discuss it. I go along with whatever comes up as we talk. I wouldn't want to ask someone and then not produce something. I say I'm thinking of writing something and if they say okay, I say I'll send it to them when I've written it. If they don't want to see it, but are in analysis at the time, it always comes up again as part of the analytic work.

Requests Based on State of the Transference

Still other analysts (2) made their decision about when to ask according to the patient's state or the nature of the transference rather than thinking about it in relation to a particular phase of the treatment. One analyst stated:

> I don't have rules about when to ask. The unfolding transference/countertransference process influences my decision, but you never know when something is done. I never ask permission when someone is in distress or intensely in some aspect of the work, or at other times of vulnerability.

Another analyst reflected on the difficulties:

> It's a struggle to sort out how and when to ask patients, to have them involved in a more collaborative process. Asking adds complications to the work; when it's already very intense, it doesn't seem like a good idea. Patients can feel exploited. When patients see that I've written something, it sometimes raises anxieties, negative feelings. They wonder if I'm thinking about writing about them, what I would write, if I would show it to them. That can be analyzed. I think it affects my writing more than the treatment itself.

Patients' Reactions to Being Asked Permission

Many of the relational analysts reported that their patients were pleased, felt special to have been the subject of their analysts' writing. A frequent description was that they were "interested," "curious."

Many patients were reported to have accepted the request, talked about it briefly, and then it disappeared as a topic. But not all analysts reported this experience. One analyst elaborated a more complex, complicated process.

> I never had anyone say fine and that's it. They ask why I want to write about them. I give the reason and I weave it into the material we've been working on. The fact that I'm writing can make them feel special and that we're a team. For some, it feels it's taking away from our intimacy if it's put out for others to see. I say what I put out there is only a piece of the relationship. Some patients talk about it more, others less. Sometimes people feel exploited. I wonder if they or I don't question the whole process enough. I also wonder do I pick people to ask who won't ask anything too complicated or resist too much. I've never had anyone say no, but there are lots of people I don't and wouldn't ask, so maybe that's why.

Most of the relational analysts described their patients' reaction to being asked permission to publish an article as reflective of issues that were alive in the analytic work.

One analyst reported:

> My patient is pretty cynical. He said he knew I did things for self-serving reasons so this was just another example of it. He thought people didn't help other people. He mocked that I wrote or taught. Anything I wrote would be ridiculous and would not help him or others in the field. His reaction fit in with the focus current in the work.

Five patients gave permission for use of their material but did not want to read what had been written. One analyst explained that his patient feared that reading his account would confirm her negative perception of him and solidify her negative transference.

> It's a dynamic in the treatment. Am I open to her? Am I getting the full complexity about her rather than my theoretical perspective? She worries I'll be like a train going down a track and I'll ride over her like she's a blade of grass, crushing her out. She worries if she reads what I write that she would see this transference fear was a reality. She loved that I was writing about her, but there was this issue: Was the treatment for her or me? So I was anxious when I asked her and she sensed this. She didn't like my imposing my anxiety on her.

She saw that as my issue and she didn't want the responsibility to absolve me of it or not.

Some analysts described patients' capacities to view writing as something related to the analysts' professional lives and focused less on how it was about them. These patients seemed able to compartmentalize the analyst's need to make professional contributions from the clinical work. Patients who were themselves mental health professionals often had an appreciation for why writing was needed for the field. But other patients may also have separated the personal from the professional. One analyst conveyed the way she thought patients were able to maintain this stance.

> There are patients who have a sense of privacy and a comfortable separation from my writing role. They give me permission to use their material, but they feel a distance between their personal lives, which is our work in analysis, and the analytic world. They have a comfortable relationship to what I'm doing professionally. They are focused in their internal world and not interested in what I'm communicating to my colleagues. In these cases, I ask permission but don't offer to show what I've written; however, if they say they want to see it, of course I say they could.

Showing the Written Material

Two analysts described their thinking about the procedure of showing patients the material.

One analyst stated:

> I always have the patient read it in the session. I don't want them to take it home, put it aside, or to read it and be pissed off and not process it with me right away. Sometimes patients say, "On my time?" I accept that but I explain. Usually they say okay and do it then. I've never had anyone really pissed off, but then on some level I think they always are. If I can sense that, I bring it in. There are momentary direct reactions. Like, "So I'm just fodder for your writing." That's pretty open and direct and we can explore it. It's the secondary and tertiary negative transference reactions that I dig for. Usually what is specific about the writing itself resolves pretty quickly.

The second analyst reported:

> When I've written something, I give it to the patient in the wait-
> ing room before a session so we can discuss it right away. I make what-
> ever changes they want as long as it doesn't distort what occurred. I
> make clear that the purpose of the writing is to show me not them;
> for that reason, some poetic license may be taken about their material
> in terms of how I disguise it. I don't write about patients in the field.
> Generally, the writing is not a major event in the treatment.

PATIENTS' REACTIONS TO READING
THEIR OWN CLINICAL MATERIAL

The experiences of relational analysts when their patients read
about themselves will be presented in the next section.

Patient Refusals

Five analysts reported that they had patients who had declined to
have their material published when their analysts had requested permission. Some of these analysts had more than one patient refuse permission. All five analysts accepted and respected their patients' wishes.
All were disappointed not to be able to write those particular papers.
None of them believed it had posed an interference with the work.
While five analysts in a sample of thirty-one is not a large number, it
supports the data from classically oriented analysts that some patients
are able to resist the power of transference idealization, fear, or wish
to please, and make decisions based on evaluating how they feel. Unfortunately, the analysts did not reflect on the factors that may have
enabled these patients to say no. They also did not address why they
had misassessed them and had expected them to agree. Only one of these
analysts elaborated his reaction to being refused. Most of the analysts
made it clear that they ask many patients. So, perhaps, they are not as
upset by a refusal as their more traditionally trained colleagues who
ask less frequently and, therefore, may have more invested when they
do. I regret that I did not inquire about this at the time.

DECISIONS ABOUT WRITING

Deciding Not to Publish

On some occasions, analysts decided against publishing material even though they had been granted permission. Three analysts interviewed in this sample made that decision. One analyst described what occurred.

> The patient wanted so much changed that I ended up not using it. He was upset with things I said. He was very angry, that got worked out in treatment. I wasn't aware that what I wrote was so different from what he thought I was thinking. It was very useful in the treatment, but I felt I had to give up publishing the article.

The written example in this instance clarified that the analyst had not understood how the patient had perceived the analyst's communications. The clarification was beneficial for the analytic work but the article was never published.

Writing as a Stimulus in Analytic Work

The topic of writing used as part of the analytic work will be explored in a chapter in the third section of the book.

Thoughts about Ways Papers Are Written

Many of these analysts carefully reflected on the manner in which they wrote about patients.

One analyst stated:

> The way I write vignettes now is to leave it ambiguous about what will happen next. I think it's misleading to write here's what happened and this is what was going through my mind and this is what happened, as if it's cause and effect. I'm leery of that kind of writing. I don't want to say I did a weird thing and the patient got better or I made an interpretation and the patient had her first orgasm in years. I'm suspicious of that kind of linearity. I'm interested in using clinical

material to show my state of mind at the moment and my choices with no implication for the future.

In part, it's about my reactions to other people's writing that makes me sensitive to my own. People often use two sessions to present a point. I wonder about the 1500 other sessions. Naturally, they've said lots of other things that have led to this moment, but they don't show it because they are pushing a point of view. But maybe that other stuff is just as interesting or important. I'm concerned about being misleading. So I just try to capture a moment. Even without the patient reading the material, the patient and the relationship with the patient powerfully influence the writing. That's necessary for the writing to become compelling. Clinical writing is quite impassioned; it's not conceptual in the way I think of it.

A second analyst reported:

I think of writing as a kind of affirmation of the relationship I have with the patient; writing honors it. Yet I do write things that are negative. I've written about things I've done that I'm not proud of. I've written about negative countertransference; the patient was aware of it, it was part of our dialogue.

A third analyst focused on what he had learned:

I think it's important to write about all sorts of issues with patients and have patients read it. There are surprises for me too. One treatment I felt was not going anywhere. I brought it up in the treatment and the patient told me he thought I saved his life. My surprise when he said this became an impetus to write about it.

A fourth analyst said:

I think in writing I'm more self-revealing than I am in sessions. So when a patient reads it, it may feel like this communication is suddenly sprung on the patient, and the communication isn't primarily intended for the patient, yet it's focused on what goes on between you and the patient. So it's almost like overhearing a conversation about you.

A fifth analyst conveyed his feeling constrained:

I think when I ask in advance it puts limits on my thinking and writing. I don't do it as freely. But if it's too disguised or fabricated that detracts from it being meaningful. I can analyze patients' concerns about what I'll write, but I think thinking about their concerns constrains what I would write. If someone doesn't want me to write about them, of course I don't.

A sixth analyst reflected on the meaning of his tone:

I try to write in a charitable, diplomatic fashion. I see writing as part of self-analysis. If I'm writing about a patient with a negative tone, it informs me of something inside myself that I need to think about. It's part of a process of self-reflection.

A seventh analyst noted how writing increased self-scrutiny:

When I write I bring discriminating factors [I think the analyst means conceptualizations are made when he writes that did not consciously inform what occurred in the clinical situation] that I don't necessarily have actively in the work with the patient. It brings a different gloss to how I think than what I say in treatment. It creates a pressure on me about how I write knowing the patient will read it. I have to cross that divide. It exerts a conscious and unconscious pressure on what I write. I would not focus on pathological elements as much as I otherwise might, but what I write isn't so much about that anyway so that's not so much a problem. But if I had a place in my article where I might want to emphasize that, then I would tone it down. But if I were in a bind, it would provoke self-scrutiny. It would make me ask myself why I would want to do that. I'd question the arousal of an unconscious negative countertransference or become alert to a hypersensitivity in the patient that I hadn't previously thought of. The goal of clinical writing is to expose clinical process including errors so we can communicate with everyone. When you write you should lay it out clearly and scholarly.

These analysts' reflections about writing make it clear that the view of and motivation for writing differs among analysts. For most it clarifies their thoughts. Many of these analysts believe patients' reading what the analyst has written can become part of the communication with the patient; they believe in the importance of negative reactions to patients being public both to their patients and to readers of the psychoanalytic literature. Some analysts believe that these negative reactions have to be processed first in the work with the patient, but other analysts think this processing can be done if and when the patient discovers the clinical writing.

For some analysts the thought of patients' reading what they have written is inhibiting; it limits what they write. For others, the effect was to make them sensitive to tone, use of language. It increased their attentiveness to being respectful of patients. But many analysts fear that the fact of patients' reading what is written limits the topics that can be written about.

Patients and Issues Not to Write About

Some analysts wrote to illuminate their own thinking and understanding. They had no intention of publishing what they were writing. One analyst described this process:

> Sometimes I can only get through an obstacle I'm experiencing with a patient by writing about it. When I immerse myself in writing about a patient, it enhances my sense of understanding. The crystallization for me is different from talking about a patient in supervision. Writing puts me in contact with my patient and myself, who and what I am in treatment. But this kind of writing I have no intention of publishing; it's just to help me with the work.

All analysts made explicit that they would never write about a patient who had asked them not to do so.

One analyst stated:

> I have a profound sense of privacy. Patients I write about have to have enough comfort with themselves that they won't be narcissistically knocked off balance by my making use of them this way. I don't want the writing to make them feel too special, intruded on, betrayed, or exhibited. Someone who could weather that: those are the people I write about. There's a synchrony in our work and in what I write; they don't have shame about it. But of course, there's always a possibility I can be wrong in how I think it will be and that it could traumatize the patient. Then we would have to work with that. I wouldn't write about countertransference elements that would be painful and hard to work through. Even if you work it through in a hundred different ways, I think it still is wounding so I'd soften it or omit it.

A second analyst also emphasized his feelings about privacy:

> I won't write about something that feels very private between us, even if it's not identifiable and the patient won't see it. I feel

when a patient is entrusting me with something that personal I don't want to use something that personal between us in that way. It feels unfair, like a betrayal. Imagining that a patient would read what I write affects the writing. It leads me to curb my irony. I wouldn't want patients to see this side of me—sardonic or ironic —a detached place. I'd keep that out of the account, though if I actually was sardonic or ironic *with* the patient I would write about it.

A third analyst expressed a worry about both patients' vengefulness and embarrassment:

> There are some people I wouldn't write about: some who are litigious or vengeful. I don't like to publish about people's pathology. I look for how strongly something is worded; I wouldn't want something that would be disturbing to a patient in print. One time I did that. I put in a patient's hallucination in a session and the patient said it was too embarrassing. So I took it out. I wouldn't put in things that would embarrass someone, but sometimes people work it through and feel differently about the same content. Then it's all right. One patient who felt humiliated [I think he means by a former therapist] wants revenge by having me write about it, but I also wouldn't write about something while it was as actively gratifying either.

A fourth analyst stressed a gut feeling of constraint:

> I have a gut feeling about what not to write about. I was asked to write a case of a lesbian patient in analysis of whom I have a couple. I didn't because I felt that the delicate tension in the work would be broken. Then there's the countertransference issue of feeling the patient is too special to me to share and I take that seriously: the patient's need for a self-object, for example.

A fifth analyst emphasized that material written needed to be understood first in the work with the patient:

> I would only write about negative countertransference in the context of understanding what that said about me and as part of the process of working it out with the patient. I would only do it if it were part of the ongoing work. It's not a big departure from what's going on normally because I use a fair amount of countertransference self-disclosure in analysis.

A sixth analyst considered issues of confidentiality and shame:

> I wouldn't write about things like weird perversions; it's too con-
> crete, too identifiable. I wouldn't write anything that would make
> patients uncomfortable, that was too acutely shameful to see in cold
> print.

A seventh analyst was concerned about patients' vulnerabilities:

> I wouldn't write about patients' vulnerabilities that felt too pain-
> ful or difficult for them; you want to offer safety and enclosure in
> the treatment. If a patient were paranoid, I wouldn't write about the
> patient.

An eighth analyst had particular concerns about patients with histories of trauma:

> I struggle with whether it's okay to write about patients who have
> experienced traumas. I don't think I'd ever ask a patient who had been
> traumatized. I think they'd feel shamed.

A ninth analyst focused on the relationship of the topic written
about and the issues in the current work:

> I never ask anyone when I think they'll feel it as an intrusion. Many
> patients would find it narcissistically wounding. I think that erotic
> transference/countertransference is insufficiently written about but it's
> difficult to do. When I write about negative transference or counter-
> transference, I'd only do it if it were worked through so nothing new
> or not previously understood in treatment, would be written. I can't
> ask someone if experiencing me as separate pains them. So I wouldn't
> bring up writing with them. With patients who can acknowledge and
> enjoy separateness, it can be enhancing. But I'd also never bring it
> up while a patient was working on competitive or oedipal issues.

This analyst posed subtle questions about transferential issues. He
wondered whether the patient's knowing that the analyst is writing
about him is disruptive. The effect of asking permission when patients
are in the midst of competitive or oedipal issues raises interesting clinical
speculations. One can wonder whether the analyst imagined that asking permission would defuse or intensify the feelings and conflict. It
might conceivably go in either direction depending on the patient's
psychological organization and defensive structure. But this analyst was

emphasizing that focus on the analytic work takes precedence over writing about it.

One analyst specifically questioned the effect on the field if writing is restricted for all the clinically sensitive reasons cited by many of these relational analysts.

> I'd think two or three times before writing about sexual transference or countertransference because of the potential of feeling exposed and shamed. It's easier to write things about aggression. I've become more scrupulous over time. But it is an insoluble problem. If you are really scrupulous then certain things won't get written about, things that feel humiliating or exposing to a patient or anything not comfortable in the countertransference. Some of the most important things to write about are these very matters, like disastrous treatments or ones that languish and don't have breakthroughs. It's necessary to learn from bad experiences and from sensitive and shame-inducing moments. These examples are hard to let patients see, but if we don't . . . well, that's a big problem for the field. When I'm comfortable with my countertransference, I'm comfortable asking. But when I'm not comfortable or not sure of it or what I'll expose, in these instances I mainly don't write.

DISCUSSION

While the material provided by all the analysts interviewed for this book indicates a trend toward seeking patients' permission when publishing their clinical material, many more analysts who publish in *Psychoanalytic Dialogues* asked permission and showed their patients what they had written about them than those who published in *JAPA, IJP*, or other international journals. Understanding the theoretical underpinning for the analysts' self-revelations makes it easier to see why relational analysts are more apt to ask patients' permission and to show them what has been written than are analysts whose training has traditionally been to maintain both neutrality and more personal opaqueness. It explains why relational analysts experienced less conscious concern about their patients learning what they think and feel about them. For many of them, the transparency of their reactions to the patient is an essential part of analytic work.

Given the relational analysts' philosophic commitment to analysis as a co-constructed process, it logically follows that they would perceive less interference in the work by the introduction both of their professional agenda and of information revealed about themselves in the written piece. In this respect, the issue about asking permission has implications for both theory and technique that go far beyond the matter of political and ethical correctness.

DISGUISE ALONE

When relational analysts did choose disguise alone as their preferred method for preserving confidentiality, their reasons were similar to the more traditionally trained analysts. But they also added worries about the loss of their own privacy. Although it is increasingly common for all analysts to include descriptions of their countertransference reactions in published material, relational analysts more consistently include such material and often do so in more detail. A tension between a theoretical commitment to self-revelation and a personal discomfort with such openness exists for some members in this group.

ASKING PERMISSION

Relational analysts, because they believe in the co-creation and mutuality of the analysis, view asking permission and showing patients their clinical material as enriching to the analytic process. Only a few of the more traditionally trained analysts shared these views; as a result, many more of them had far more conflict and anxiety about asking their patients for permission. However, many of the relational analysts also expressed considerable conflict about how, when, and what to write—and if they should write at all.

STRUGGLES WITH CONFLICTS OVER PUBLICATION

It should be noted that some relational clinicians tended to minimize their sense of conflict about asking permission and its ramifications in a way that was similar to some of the ways more traditionally trained analysts minimized their struggles about using disguise alone. Neither group wishes to believe that they are doing something that may adversely affect a patient's analysis. Therefore, they may minimize the potential problems and as a result may have reduced the complexity of their reflections about it to evade internal struggle. Nevertheless, it should be noted that the majority of analysts interviewed for this book, regardless of theoretical orientation, were self-reflective and acknowledged that every choice poses potential problems and did not reduce the level of complexity and conflict when describing the process of their thinking and the effect on their patients.

The analysts in this chapter were similar to others in this book in that sometimes their wish to publish overrode their conflicted feelings about how this might impact the patient. When patients were mental health professionals, most analysts remained restrained about publishing material. While most of these decisions seemed to reflect concerns that these patients might be more easily identifiable, a greater degree of personal identification may also have increased their sensitivity.

CONSIDERATIONS OF CONTENT AND STYLE

Relational analysts devoted more thought to the affect of content and style of writing than most, but certainly not all, traditionally trained analysts. I cannot be sure that this was not an artifact of their being the group that I interviewed last—two years after the analysts who published in *JAPA* and a year after those publishing in international journals. I may have asked more about this aspect of their thinking as my own questions and concerns deepened about it based on the earlier interviews.

OVERALL COMPARISON

Overall, relational analysts do believe that as co-creators of the analytic process, they can introduce their ideas and writing without as much concern because they presume that patients gain something from this interaction. Provided the patient's privacy can be maintained, they do not see involving the patient in clinical writing as much of an intrusion of their own agenda.

In the next section, I will illustrate and discuss how this perspective extends to their use of writing as a stimulus for clinical work. I will also recount the perceptions of all analysts in this study of their patients' reaction when they read about themselves.

II

ANALYSTS' PERCEPTIONS OF THE EFFECT ON PATIENTS

6
Background Literature

A small literature on patients' reactions to reading about themselves has developed only in the last fifteen years. Initially, when analysts gave their patients written material about themselves to read, it was done because these analysts believed it was the only meaningful way for patients to be really informed about their consent. Analysts' accounts then began to weave together their patient's reactions to the consent process and to reading the material, as well as the elaboration of these reactions in the ongoing analytic work. Some analysts, primarily but not exclusively those with a relational theoretical orientation, then considered whether they showed patients material about themselves for ethical purposes only or also for therapeutic benefit. A literature in which the analyst employs written material intentionally as a vehicle for clinical work began.

PATIENTS' REACTIONS TO READING

In the first article in the psychoanalytic literature on patient's reactions, Stoller (1988) stressed the importance not only of asking patients to read what their analysts write about them but also of including the patients' reactions in the report. His focus was both on the ethical aspect of such requests and on the question of clinical ramifications. He emphasized that when patients read their analysts' papers, they try to find clues about how the analyst has experienced them. Pine (1990), in the acknowledgments that preface his book *Drive, Ego, and Self*, described the process of requesting permission and his inclusion of his patients' responses. Patients' reactions to his request and to reading his write-ups became part of analytic work for those who were currently in analysis; for patients who had terminated, it was a process of reworking and reevaluating their analytic experience and their relationship with him. His view was that this process was productive rather than destructive. However, he recognized that he had introduced a parameter with unknown consequences.

Other analysts have also shown their patients what they have written and asked them to contribute their observations to the final publications (Karme 1988, Lafarge 2000, Stein 2000, Stern 2002). After termination, Stein (2000) asked a patient for permission to use his material. She was apprehensive because it described "unsettling and potentially shocking extra-analytic material" (p. 187). She included the written response of the patient who stated that he was able to read the article "without excessive ecstasy or pain" (p. 187). It confirmed what he believed the analysis had been about; he recognized himself. It was "not fun" (p. 187) to realize he had evoked revulsion in his analyst but he believed her capacity to be with him and contain this experience had held him in his working through and understanding of himself. While the patient could still recognize these unsavory aspects of himself, he believed that he had changed substantially and that others had confirmed this.

During the termination phase of a treatment, Karme (1988) invited a patient to provide her view of their work for a paper. Although pleased to be asked, her patient worried that the audience of readers might misunderstand their work and that its presentation might change things in "an irreversible way and I'd lose all my gains" (p. 277). Karme interpreted that the patient felt that her needs were going to have to be sacrificed in favor of the analyst's and related this fear to the patient's loss of her trust in her mother when her mother had become ill and died. The experience of loss of trust in the analyst was thereby woven into loss of trust in relation to the analyst's use of the patient material as well as the imminent loss of the analyst in the termination.

The question that needs to be raised is how can anyone be sure of neutrality under these circumstances. Of course, we are always faced with similar situations in which we have to ask whether we are defending ourselves and our self-interests or interpreting the patient's projections.

Reading their analysts' accounts apparently often stimulates and recreates patients' central transference paradigms. Lipton (1991) described a patient's masochistic submission to his request to write about him as a parallel to his submission to parental authority. The patient then felt this submission entitled him to special consideration as he previously had enjoyed with his parents. When recreations such as these are recognized, analysts believe they are beneficial to analytic work. Presumably this benefit is due to the affects becoming alive in the present situation with the analyst and making what has been intellectually understood a current emotional reality.

Patients' awareness of analysts' papers may also provide a representation of the analyst's other interests (Crastnopol 1999, Friedlander 1995, Gerson 2000, Pizer 2000). Some analysts view awareness of analysts' writings as an intrusion of the analyst's agenda, stimulating unwieldy transference complications (Furlong 1998), while others assert that it can have a beneficial aspect. A variety of functions and meanings have been attributed to the role and meaning of the "other" for the particular patient. Friedlander (1995) and Gerson (2000) believe the introduction of the analyst's writing as a "third" facilitates both an analytic and a developmental process. Friedlander, a Lacanian analyst, believes this introduction makes the patient's unconscious wish to maintain the gratification of a private dyad conscious. For example, when he told a patient of his plan to write about her, she accused him of introducing a third party into their relationship. The loss of freedom to maintain "secret opposition to the mores of civilized life reflects a change in psychic structure that coincides with the passage from a mother–daughter matrix . . . to a framework that is significantly more complex" (p. 19).

Gerson makes a similar point about a developmental advance being stimulated by an increased awareness of the presence of a third. He defines the function of the third in oedipal terms, namely, as making clear that the patient cannot be part of the primal scene. Writing helps the analyst hold the patient's experience in mind and makes it an object of reflection for both patient and analyst. He believes there is a need to be in a relationship with an "other" that extends beyond the intimacy of the patient–analyst dyad. The knowledge of the analyst's writing for a professional community introduces this "other." This triadic structure benefits the patient because it "disrupts and contains the intensity and insularity of dyadic relating" (p. 263). For Pizer (2000), the patient's awareness of the analyst's commitment to the professional community provides a sense of containment and safety. It assures the patient that the therapist is not afraid to have others become aware of the details of what is occurring between patient and analyst.

Furlong (personal communication) believes it is a logical error to equate professional writing with a "third party." The writing itself, though addressed in the imagination to outsiders, does not create a triadic structure. It is a mental product that begins with only one person, the analyst-author, and a discussion takes place with a second person, the patient, who is under the influence of transference. In order to be structurally a "third," the third must actually stand outside the dyad with an independent point of view. A real third party looks critically at the narrative constructed by the dyad and asks if it is missing something. In this respect, it is similar to the role of a consultant, or what I am doing in reflecting on the interviews presented in this book. The imaginary addressee cannot act as a third because it fails the test of independence.

Her point is well taken; nevertheless, something new may still be productively introduced into the relationship provided the effect of its impingement is given analytic attention. Discussion with the patient of the analyst's wish to communicate dyadic interactions to an audience may expose or stimulate fantasies about the patient–analyst relationship in the patient, the analyst, or both. For some patients (and possibly analysts) the writing stimulates an experience of being "special." Many analysts have concerns about this potentially gratifying effect of informed consent, but if the reaction is acknowledged and analyzed, it could serve as a stimulus for deeper exploration. For other patients (and possibly analysts) a publication may disrupt a sense of specialness and privacy for better or for worse. Again, the possible benefit from this disruption requires that patients be able to reveal and analyze their reactions. Analyst too may benefit from private self-scrutiny. I am not suggesting that therapeutic benefit comes only from insight and interpretations, but in the context of analysts' introducing their own agenda, the meaning of it to their patients needs to be understood and not inferred. It is too easy to become self-serving and to believe the effect is the way one wishes it to be.

Crastnopol (1999) also believes that patients' awareness of their analysts' writing about them provides an experience of containment, but she views containment in a broader way. She believes that partaking in the professional side of the therapist's life, insofar as he or she is the subject of an article, provides a wider community for the patient as both a source of mirroring and kind of holding environment.

The number of articles written about the benefits that can be derived from reactions to patients' reading about themselves have increased (Beebe 2004, Brenner in press, Feiner 1996, Ringstrom 1998, Scharff 2000, Schwaber 1997). Papers can serve as a catalyst for reviewing work together (Beebe 2004). They can also provide an opportunity to understand and redo previously painful experiences. When Feiner (1996) asked to write about his patient, the patient thought that his analyst had been bewitched by and had submitted to the dictates of his profession. By then submitting to his analyst's request, the patient thereby became in turn his victim as he previously felt he had been conned and victimized by his mother. Feiner concluded that his request, although honest, was an exploitation. Fortunately, the open exploration of the patient's reaction allowed an undoing and negation of the experience of being conned.

Similarly, Ringstrom's (1998) request for permission to publish clinical material recreated an old predicament for his patient. The thought of refusing filled the patient with terror and fear of the therapist's retaliation; yet agreeing was an act of submission and self-betrayal. The feeling of a life-and-death struggle from the patient's childhood was activated. Recognition of the similarity of the present conflict to the patient's past, previously encountered in their work, enabled the patient and analyst to see that the therapist was caught in this trap as well—to not ask felt like a submission, to ask felt like an aggressive act—and for the patient to experience the dilemma differently.

Brenner (in press) also believes that his patient's reading his paper aided in resolving a pathological grief reaction to his mother's traumatic death and difficulty in terminating analysis. Reading the paper provided the patient with a documentation of both the fact of her death and the history of his treatment and life. This documentation may have enabled him to symbolize and differentiate himself from his mother in a manner that solidified and internalized the fact of her death. The paper also provided a tangible connection between the patient and analyst, a bond that may have paradoxically enabled the patient to leave.

USE OF THE WRITTEN MATERIAL AS A VEHICLE FOR THE CLINICAL WORK

Several analyst-authors have written about introducing the experience of patients reading the analyst's writing about them as a stimulus for analytic work. Lafarge (2000) views this process as a useful step in de-idealization of the analyst. She was apprehensive that her patients would experience her request that they write their own accounts of treatment and subsequently read hers as an imposition of her interests. Her perception is that the experience helped her patients to see her as not viewing either herself or the work as perfect in the way they had imagined. In one instance, it also stimulated competitive issues that led to one patient's taking more responsibility for her own ambitions.

Crastnopol (1999) believes patients' reactions to reading her accounts may clarify misunderstandings and make her as the analyst aware of previously unrecognized countertransference responses. Her belief is that many patients accept being written about because they have a wish to be part of their therapists' lives in a fuller way. She provides an example of a patient who was first pleased to be asked permission but then revealed ambivalence in a dream. Like Karme's patient, she expressed the concern that the outside world might not accurately understand what went on in her treatment. When the analyst wrote about this experience, the patient believed that the therapist had not conveyed clearly enough that the patient had "felt less accepting and more ambivalent about the dream therapist's distractedness" (p. 454). The therapist acknowledged that she may have unconsciously wished to avoid the thought of having been careless and hurtful to the patient. The patient also expressed her wish to view her therapist's writing about her between sessions as signifying an involvement with her, but considered this idea preposterous. Crastnopol describes a process in which she and the patient share their formulations and readjust their understanding in the process. She gets more in touch with the patient and the patient gets a greater trust in her. She thinks it is wishful thinking or denial to believe that the impact of writing about patients will not be part of the dyad's intersubjective experience.

Pizer (2000) believes writing metaphorically contains and integrates the patient's experience in the treatment. His writing interest "bring[s] patterns into awareness and enhance[s its] clinical use" (p. 250). In addition, he believes that the analyst's gratitude to the patient for permitting use of the material may deepen "a loving bond that opens further potential space in the treatment relationship" (p. 250). He offers an example in which a patient's reading his paper, and their negotiations around the details of the written material, enabled his patient to see how the analyst held his patient and his patient's subjective experience in mind and how he worked to provide for the patient's needs. He believes there is a safety for patients in knowing the way he thinks about his work and in his sharing what he does with a professional community. With a second patient, reading about a treatment she had broken off with Pizer led the patient to wish to return to him. This patient believed that what Pizer wrote was more about himself than about her, but this was precisely what reassured her and made her feel a wish to return to treatment. She saw the way he thought about his work as showing he was of "sound mind" and "high seriousness" (p. 257), in contrast to her family.

Bridges (unpublished paper) argues that the function of patients' reading accounts of themselves depended on their individual dynamics. She offered to share a draft of a chapter for a book with eleven ongoing and five terminated patients in which she describes a clinical interaction with each one of them. All patients were in psychotherapy. The fourteen patients who gave permission had reactions varying from pleasure in feeling validated to anger in feeling betrayed. Some patients had different reactions over time.

One patient had hoped to find written documentation of the therapist's warm feelings toward her in order "to diminish her shame at the depth of her longing" (p. 14) for the therapist. She was hurt and shamed not to have found this. The patient highlighted in red the passages that hurt her feelings and stimulated shame. Then later, reviewing the chapter again, she highlighted in blue passages in which the therapist expressed feelings and thoughts about her. She saw that even though the therapist had not written as much as she had hoped for about her own feelings and thoughts about the patient, they were, nevertheless, present in the manuscript. When she realized the discrepancy between her initial reaction and what she later came to recognize in the chapter, she was able to see the extent to which her affective state shaped her perceptions.

Another patient who at first found the therapist's formulations distancing came to realize that it was also a relief to see the therapist as an observer who stepped back to view the process. This patient had previously had a therapist who had been unable to maintain sufficient therapeutic distance. Other patients, who at first used the material to self-sooth themselves in the therapist's absence, later experienced new anxieties when recognizing that a level of separateness between themselves and the therapist was implicit in the written material.

While many analysts currently believe that it is beneficial if reading their own clinical material unearths some part of the patients' perception of the countertransference (Bridges unpublished paper, Crastnopol 1999, Lafarge 2000, Pizer 2000, Scharff 2000, Stern 2002), others believe it may interfere with the analytic process (Furlong 1998, 2004, in press, Stein 1988b). These analysts offer voices of dissent. Furlong (1997) believes that patients' knowing that their analysts write about them reconfigures their perception of their analysts' internal lives, activating their curiosity and sometimes upset. Questions about the nature of the analyst's desire for the patient arise, such as: Why does the analyst need or wish to communicate about the patient to outsiders? It reveals to the patient the particular area of the analyst's interest, perspective, or overlapping conflicts. She is skeptical of Pizer's conclusion that his papers have provided a holding environment for his patients. Rather, Furlong (2004, in press) believes he is reassuring his patients that he is "a nice guy," someone whom they can trust. Furlong worries that such reassurances may obscure and block access to some transference anxieties.

Viewing the introduction of the third from a Lacanian perspective, Furlong argues that asserting that writing can act as an imaginary third for the therapeutic dyad misrepresents that fact that until it is peer reviewed the draft is "still under the power of the analyst's or the patient's fantasy and therefore incapable of performing in itself a triangulating function" (2004, p. 6). She explains that the symbolic third introduced by Lacan is explicitly related to the recognition of differences, such as sexual or generational, and thus symbolic of "castration," in the sense of incompleteness, the impossibility of completely satisfying desire, and the limits of ever really knowing another. Thus, both the meaning and function of "the other" is the opposite from Pizer, and probably Crastnopol, but may be closer to the anxiety-provoking implication dawning on Bridges's patients about the separateness between their therapist and themselves. Furlong cautions that for therapists to present themselves as good and reassuring, as completely trustworthy, is to recaptivate the patient's ego in a narcissistically mirroring relationship with an omnipotent other. But analysts with different theoretical orientations might argue that some patients need precisely this experience for a period of time.

Stein (1988b) voiced his cautions about the effect on patients when they read their analyst's writings. He neither asked permission nor showed his patients what he wrote. He specifically warned against analysts encouraging patients to read their analyst's writing. At best he assumed this practice creates "a difficult intellectual resistance and at worst lead(s) to an irresolvable transference mess" (p. 402). Like Furlong, he stressed the downside in the use patients make of what they believe they learn about their analyst. Patients' awareness that their analyst is writing about them touches off an inner disturbance, most often in the form of "hidden competitive, voyeuristic and exhibitionistic impulses" (p. 395). While he did not estimate that this disturbance would be great enough to prove disruptive to analysis, and was *not* advocating that analysts should stop clinical reporting, he alerted colleagues to be watchful for clues in dreams, slips, or symptoms that might reveal repercussions for patients. Stein believed that patients in the mental health profession would sooner or later imagine that they were the subject of their analyst's papers. While sometimes their assumption might be correct, often it was not. He thought that patients wished to be written about because they wished to believe that they had taught their analyst something and wished to see themselves as collaborators.

While Stein concurred that analysts learn from patients, he did not recommend directly acknowledging this contribution. On some level, there is likely an unconscious fantasy that this "intimate collaboration is equivalent to sharing in the conception of a child." Analysts may also share this unconscious fantasy; when they do, it can lead to inhibitions about writing about patients.

Stein believed complications in analysis of the transference may arise from patients' reading even their analyst's theoretical papers. Several patients who read his paper "The Unobjectionable Part of the Transference" (1981), began to present themselves as "objectionable" so as to show him that they could discard this resistance. It was necessary to recognize that this rebellion was itself a kind of conformity; he acknowledged that this expression of hostility was the first to appear in the transference and enabled him to usefully approach deeper levels of hostility. He quickly added, however, that he was not suggesting that patients should acquire their ideas by reading what their analysts write and emphasized that it is best for the transference to emerge in the ordinary course of analysis. Nonetheless, Stein was acknowledging what some contemporary analysts, whose papers are cited in this section, have found, that is, that writing can be put to therapeutic use.

The issue of whether it is best to let affects and transference emerge "in the ordinary course of analysis" has been closely debated. At present, there is no evidence to answer this question. There is, however, heated feeling on both sides about the choice made. There are those who find reviewing clinical descriptions useful in stirring transference and those who believe as Stein and Furlong do. An argument made by the first group is that interrupting the analysis to respond to the writing stimulus can be made consistent with analysis. Some analysts see it as no different from a request to see a consultant, sit up for some sessions, or to take medication. In other words, it is an adjunct to the treatment that may be of benefit to the patient. This argument ignores the crucial difference that these latter requests, though departing from standard practice, are made for the patient's benefit only, whereas the request regarding publication entails potential gain for the analyst.

Furlong and Stein present concerns related to a loss of the natural asymmetry when patients come to view themselves as collaborators in analytic publications. Not only is there a concern that defensive aspects and unconscious meanings may be obscured, but also there is the danger of merger with an omnipotent other. Their views provide a caution and counterbalance to the contemporary trend toward equality central to the co-constructionists' view of analysis.

In the section of the book that follows, I will provide accounts that may help readers draw their own conclusions about this debate. I will present analysts' perceptions of the patients' point of view. Their reactions to discovering material about themselves, being asked permission, and being shown the material reveal a wide range of response from benefit to disruption of treatment. I will also examine examples of analysts using their papers as vehicles for therapeutic work.

7
Effect on Patients—
JAPA Authors[1]

In the first section of this book I described the views on preserving patients' confidentiality of thirty analysts who published clinical material in *JAPA* between 1995 and 2000. These analysts debated the advantages and limitations of employing disguise alone versus disguise coupled with patients' consent. In this chapter, I am reporting the experiences of these same thirty analysts when their patients read clinical material taken from their analyses. Some of these patients had been asked for permission to use their material and were shown what was written. Other patients had been written about in disguise without having been asked for consent and then discovered and read the material.

As I indicated at the beginning of this section, the literature on the ramifications of patients' reading material about themselves is small, but has increased in recent years (Bridges 2003, Casement 1985, Crastnopol 1999, Friedlander 1995, Gabbard 2000, Gerson 2000, Lafarge 2000, Lipton

1. Material in this chapter has previously appeared in slightly different form in the *Journal of the American Psychoanalytic Association* (2004) 52:101–123, © 2004 American Psychoanalytic Association. All rights reserved. I am grateful to the editor for granting permission for the material to be reprinted in this book. The permission was conveyed through the Copyright Clearance Center, Inc.

1991, Person 1983, Pine 1990, Pizer 2000, Ringstrom 1998, Scharff 2000, Stoller 1988). It is important that knowledge of the clinical consequences of patients' reading about themselves become part of the psychoanalytic literature. The current project is a continuation of these enterprises.

As stated earlier in the book, thirty psychoanalysts were selected in a random systematized fashion and were interviewed on the telephone for thirty minutes to an hour. They reported the ways in which they worked to ensure patient confidentiality. They were asked to recount their experiences when patients' consent was granted and about the ramifications of patients' reading material about themselves. Patients' reactions to two different situations were described: when they had not known their analysts had written about them and when patients had given permission for their material to be used.

PATIENTS WHOSE PERMISSION WAS NOT ASKED

Eight patients read articles about themselves or heard themselves presented when their analysts had not asked for permission. All these analysts were upset that such a mishap had occurred. Their views on the effects on their patients were less uniform.

Patients Perceived by Their Analysts to Be Untroubled

Three of these analysts did not believe that their patients' discovering a paper written about themselves had been detrimental. Each accepted the patient's unperturbed reaction to this discovery at face value. One analyst had "agonized" over the decision not to ask for permission. He thought his patient would grant it but worried she might not. He thought she would be excited about his writing about her, but also worried that she might devalue him if the article were not accepted since this was typical of her. Eventually, a friend of the patient read the article and showed it to her.

> The patient recognized herself and was excited by it. It was a nar-
> cissistic gratification. She knew it was unlikely that anyone would
> identify her. She thought that I was special because I had had an ar-
> ticle published and that she was special because I had written about

her. At the present time (six years later), the patient is still in treatment. I don't see that this incident has played any particularly important part in our analytic work.

A second analyst, who had not asked for permission, described being "shocked and horrified" when this former patient, who was not in the mental health field, appeared in the audience as he was about to present. He was sure she would recognize herself in the material.

> I called her aside and told her that what she was about to hear was about her. She said it was fine. [My policy is not to] ask permission because I wonder why introduce the fact of writing when it may be protecting against a non-event? Mostly I write to illustrate an idea, e.g., projective identification. Patients wouldn't care if they were used for an example of that; it's not something that has meaning to them. I disguise the examples; the historical data are transformed as well as the particulars of the exchange that I imagine could be recognized by the patient. To have asked permission would have caused trouble for me, for the patient, for that analysis. I don't want trouble.

The third analyst was giving a paper in another geographic area over five years after the termination of the patient's analysis. The patient's sister, who had entered the mental health field but had not been in it at the time of the treatment, was in the audience. After the presentation, she came up to the analyst and said that she knew her sister had been in analysis with her, and that from the history she thought the analyst was describing her sister. The analyst told her she could share this with her sister and that if her sister wanted to, she could be in touch with her. Her former patient then contacted her. This analyst described exploring the patient's reaction.

> I told her she could read the paper or not and since it had not yet been published, that I would delete her material if that would be her preference. I explained that I hadn't asked her for permission because I thought it was hard for patients to say no and that it was a burden to put a patient in that position. She found that interesting and credible. She expressed surprise that I thought her worth writing about. We talked about her reactions to her sister's hearing the material. She wanted to read it. She thought it was fine to publish it. She was someone who I thought would be open to criticizing the paper and me. Given that the cat was out of the bag, that it had already been presented, and that I had thoroughly gone over it with her, it would have

been bending over backwards not to have published it then. My preference remains that I wished that she had not known about it. I told her that with her giving me the go-ahead, I was going to publish it. I told her she might over time feel differently about my writing this and publishing it. [If that happened,] then she could contact me to talk about it. Some years later, she returned about a different issue and she talked about it some more. She felt complimented by it, interested in me and how I focused on my countertransference issues, and that my work with her had helped me. It was a messy situation. I still would not have spontaneously asked this patient because of her trouble with aggression and a difficulty in saying no. My ideas about using disguise, even with this mishap, haven't changed.

Patients Perceived by Their Analysts to Be Upset

Two analysts reported that their patients were very upset after reading about themselves.

One time a patient read something I had written. I changed her to a male, added from another case, and made it a composite. Nevertheless, she recognized it and was upset and felt exposed. I asked if she thought anyone could recognize her. She said no, but she had told others that it was in the paper. Thus, she'd exposed herself. It was traumatic.

One time a patient read something I'd written about her. She was furious when she found it. It took a very long time to work that out. She thought I was evil, corrupt, that I had used her. Some perception that she took what I said as negative about her, though it was actually very admiring of something about her. But mainly she used it as a pretext to express her sadomasochism.

An Analyst Upset by a Patient's Coming to a Paper about the Patient

One analyst reported an upsetting surprise encounter in the course of an ongoing treatment.

I had an experience giving a paper and the patient, who was in a different field, showed up in the front row. It was spooky. How do you respond in the moment? Recognition? Friendliness? I felt she was spying on me. The next day in analysis we talked about her not telling me she was coming, the impressions of hearing me, etc. So what goes on when the subject of a paper unexpectedly appears or someone hears your talk or reads your writing about another patient? This is all current material and being explored between us in treatment.

Analysts Sued by Patients

As reported in the first section of the book, two analysts stated that they were sued by former patients for having used their material without asking consent. Neither patient won the suit; in both instances it was judged that the material was sufficiently disguised and that the patient had suffered no harm. One of these analysts was too upset by the experience to discuss it further. This analyst has been hesitant to write ever since. The other analyst described the experience:

> One time I wrote a case and the patient read it and wrote to the ethics board and wanted to press charges that I had done this without his permission. He could recognize himself but no one else could. The incident I wrote about was very specific to him. The ethics board said I'd done nothing wrong. He was someone in the mental health field. One reason I hadn't asked him was that he had moved to (a distant place), but actually I don't know if I would have asked him even if he had been here. I thought his complaint was a reflection of the transference. The situation put me through the wringer, but it didn't change my view that we need to write.

PATIENTS WHO CONSENTED WITHOUT BEING SHOWN THE MATERIAL AND WHO READ IT LATER

A few analysts who requested their patient's permission but did not show them the written material described their patients' reactions as unremarkable, when they later read about themselves. One analyst, however, was concerned when he learned that a patient, no longer in treatment, had read a paper written about himself. The analyst was uneasy because he could not explore the patient's reactions.

I heard that one patient (seen in a clinic setting), who had come back to treatment there later, had read a paper of mine and recognized his material. I did not know what his reaction was and that made me uncomfortable. Did he feel I understood him? Did he think that he was special to me? A reaction like that could spoil a later treatment. It could be like idealizing a first love so that nothing later could measure up and that could ruin later relationships with others if not analyzed.

Some patients may become trapped in unresolved idealizations, and potentially a patient could respond in this fashion. Nonetheless, a question can be raised about whether the analyst may also be overestimating the continued power of their particular relationship in his concern that things could be worked out only with him. The analyst did not seem to consider the possibility that the former patient could work out his reactions in his present treatment.

THE IMPACT ON PATIENTS WHEN ANALYSTS SHARE THEIR CLINICAL WRITING

Twelve analysts had shown patients the material they had written about them. Seven of the twelve analysts had always asked permission. The majority of analysts who gave their patients papers to read had used verbatim material. When verbatim accounts are reported, it is almost impossible to disguise the material so that patients will not recognize themselves.

Written Material Shown at the Time of the Initial Request

All analysts in this sample believed that once permission was requested, they needed to accede if a patient asked to read the paper, or be willing to forgo use of the material if they believed it undesirable for the patient to read it. Several analysts made the point that the things they were writing about had always already been shared with their patients; consequently, there were no surprises. One analyst emphasized that as he was drafting the paper, he was consciously "keeping in mind" how the patient might react to reading it. Another analyst remarked that material, illustrating hate in the countertransference, could not be shown to the patient; some analysts who have shared such countertransference reactions with patients perhaps would dispute this point. There are, however, other difficult and potentially untoward consequences of showing patients material written about them. One analyst illustrated with two examples:

> Sometimes patients feel proud, feel special and important to be written about. One time a patient wanted to show others, to boast, and I worried it would lead to exposure but it stopped. We looked at the tug [of the exhibitionist wish]. Another patient read and thought about the paper scientifically.
>
> Another patient refers back to a piece of countertransference I wrote about in a paper and he uses it to get at me. He does it angrily. In some way, it points to something which may be helpful to me but there's a lot of anger behind it.

Three analysts considered showing the patient what they had written a highly unusual occurrence, even though one of these analysts always asked for consent. Another analyst stated that if a patient were uncomfortable about not seeing the clinical report, he would suggest that the patient consider not giving consent. However, he granted that there were special circumstances, such as writing about someone connected with the mental health field, when he might feel obliged to show the patient the paper in order to assure him or her that the disguise was adequate.

> One time during a termination phase I gave a patient a copy of a paper about him because while he was not in our profession, members of his family were and knew he was in analysis with me. I was concerned that he would be recognized, though he was not. I wanted to make sure that he knew exactly what he was consenting to. The patient returned it, edited with red marks. I don't really know if there was any detrimental effect to his reading it. Issues of narcissism and masochism came to the fore. Was it a masochistic submission to my request? These issues of masochism and sadism would likely have come up in termination anyway but the publication focused it. Did he really want to do it? Or was he submitting to me? It brought back sadomasochistic fantasies from adolescence. This patient had previously been in analysis with someone else who had been wild and crazy and the patient went along with it without questioning it. I wanted

to be sure he felt he had a right to say no without my being angry with him. The patient was a thoughtful and caring person. He added to the disguise but tried to be careful to do it in a way that didn't distort the material. I didn't write about my countertransference in this paper because I thought it would disrupt the termination for him to read it. On the surface the patient responded well, but it stirred up a lot of competition. Whose insights were these? Were the ideas mine or did he give them to me? These competitive feelings and thoughts had been hidden behind masochism. So this reaction was a sign of his growth that he could be openly competitive and not just eat it.

Perhaps it is easier to be more explorative when patients have knowledge of the specific material that is being used. Aware of the details, patients may not as easily avoid thinking about the request or their reactions to it. Analysts may then in turn feel impelled to more thoroughly pursue their patients' reactions.

Only one of the twelve analysts who showed his patients written material routinely offered to do so. Apart from the patients' granting permission, however, he did not allow any input from them about what he had written.

> Many people I now see come knowing that I write. I discuss the possibility that I may write about them in the initial interview. When I decide to write I describe to the patient what I intend to write and offer an opportunity for the patient to read it but not to negotiate about the history, material about the process or the disguise though certainly they have the opportunity to have it withdrawn and not published. I've never had anyone ask me not to publish what I wrote. If a patient has a disagreement or correction about a fact I have gotten wrong, such as the age of a sibling or the time some event occurred, I do correct that. But I use patients' materials in very limited ways.

Requests Perceived to Be without Complications When Patients Read about Themselves

Half of this sample had not found that showing patients written examples led to any notable complications in the treatment.

> These patients have read the vignettes and it hasn't become a topic for conversation. They have not pursued the issues, though I was open

to talking about it if they did. I assume my asking has an influence on the work. But I don't really have evidence of what it is. The patients are under the influence of transference and might not feel free to say no so I try to be cautious about whom I ask.

I never write about a patient until treatment is over and then I wait at least a year. I used to tell all my patients at the start of treatment that I did at times write about patients after the treatment. I would send them a copy and ask for their permission. I'd disguise it. The patient would then write back giving me permission. I've never had a patient refuse. One patient wrote that reading it felt just like being back in analysis.

The patient read it, we met, and he liked it, agreed with it. Even though he thought I'd done a good job of disguise and had left out all identifying data, he thought there was a remote chance that someone might sort it out and given that risk, he was uncomfortable with a few lines. We went over them and none of them seemed necessary to the flow or to the arguments. I offered alternative ways of putting the material that he agreed to—there were only a few such changes and that was the end of it. I said I didn't know if it would be accepted or whether there would be revisions, but I promised I would show him what I'd revised if it happened and get his permission.

After termination, I contacted one patient and told him I wanted to write about him and wanted him to read it. He gave a written consent and gave some suggestions about what I'd written. He thought I had underplayed certain things about him that he had found hard to face about himself in the analysis. I thought this was a testament to the work. I offered for him to come in and discuss it, but he didn't feel that was necessary. In this instance, I was particularly careful because I was describing something which had legal ramifications.

When patients read what I write, their main reactions are narcissistic injury. They feel I've not paid sufficient attention to them. They feel insufficiently important. They think what I've written is accurate but they thought I would tell their full life story and instead it's about ways of looking at theory or just a paragraph about them. It takes me a long time to write so usually the material is from several years before. I prefer it be from long enough ago so that I understand its meaning since I find it takes time and understanding changes and develops over time.

> One patient had been talking about the topic I had written about. I asked permission and I wondered if we could talk about it. I told her that if she wished to read it that was okay or if not that was okay, but I also told her that I wouldn't publish it without her permission. She was very thankful. She took it home, read it, cried about the things I'd written. The only thing she wanted to change was the disguise. So I changed that. We explored what that had meant to her. The repercussions were minor and mostly positive. She didn't feel used. The patient was several years into her treatment at the time and is still in treatment. I don't see any notable ramifications. She is the only patient from whom I have ever asked for permission and to whom I have shown an example.

The last analyst quoted wrote about the same patient on a second occasion. In the latter instance, the patient had said something "brilliant and witty" that had hurt him. He was reluctant, though unclear about why this was so, to address this with her directly. Instead he wrote a poem about it that he felt he needed to show her, since it both came directly from his experience with her and included a phrase she had used.

> The patient was flattered but also guilty that I had kept from her that she hurt me. She was grateful that I wove her phrase into my poem. She did not think it was a big deal and wondered why I felt I had to hide it. I expressed in my writing my admiration for her skill, my envy of her ability to express herself so beautifully, and my shame about what she had seen and revealed about me. How did this effect the treatment? Despite the fact that this patient has had considerable suffering, she has an amazing sense of humor and a mobility of cathexis, a real flexibility. I haven't found more in the work [suggestive] of any interference.

In this instance, the analyst was very forthright about his reactions to the patient, as well as self-revealing in the work. The impact on the patient of reading what her analyst had written, as well as his self-disclosure, may not have interfered with the analytic work, but it would be unlikely that it did not have some influence on its direction.

Analysts' Withdrawal of Patient Material

Two analysts reported withdrawing patients' material because of what followed the request for consent. It is notable that neither of these analysts had at first thought of the request as something that would stir conflict in these patients. Their accounts show how each of them expanded their understanding of the dynamic complexity that was stimulated.

Both of these analysts spontaneously reflected on the effect their patients' reactions had on them and what they learned from the process.

> During treatment, a patient, not in the field, read something I'd written—not about this patient—and gave me another example that confirmed the point I was making and said I could write about that. I thanked her. But then over the next sessions, I noticed there was difficulty in our working. This was a patient who had been exploited by her family. I realized that she felt exploited by this even though she offered it. It was a really compelling example and the temptation was there to use it. So it was really an issue of whether this treatment was going to be for her or for me. I told her that I was revoking her permission and promised I would never use the example.

> The first paper I ever wrote, I asked the patient's permission. It was a lengthy analysis and this was about a year or two from the end. The paper had been accepted with a need for revisions at the time I asked her permission and gave it to her to read. The patient gave me permission, but I ended up feeling she was not free to say no and that it would harm the treatment if I published it. I felt she had reservations she couldn't directly express. For example, she was resentful that I would advance myself at her expense. She had a younger, very successful brother whom she would have liked to have cut down, toward whom she felt really vengeful. She said it was fine to publish it and suggested some minor changes, but I realized that for the health of her treatment I could not publish the paper.

> So I withdrew her permission. The treatment prospered, but I was very unhappy. It was my first analytic paper; I had put a tremendous amount of work into it, hundreds of hours, and to feel I couldn't publish it! I was surprised what a huge role this had in the analysis. I was very naive. I just assumed analysts wrote about patients. I thought it was just accepted that it was done to advance the science. I didn't give a thought about how it would be a transference/countertransference issue. What a hot potato! I put in a lot of work, and then I realized that this material didn't just belong to me. It cost me a lot, but I learned a lot. I saw that I was putting my fate in her hands, to grant or deny me something important to me.

The last analyst initially conceptualized the use of patients' material in relation to an issue of ownership. But once he involved the patient with his writing agenda, he understood the problem that arose in terms of a transference/countertransference that was stimulated. The meaning of the writing and the request were different for analyst and patient. The reverberations of the request undoubtedly brought certain conflicts of the patient to the fore. Since the analyst recognized them, this occurrence may be viewed like any other for the patient in which some action imposed by the analyst brings forth important material. However, the long-term effect on a patient, an analyst, and on a treatment in which an analyst declares a wish for something from a patient that is other than is usually expected is not known. In this particular instance, the analyst was very clear that he felt he learned something very important from the experience.

Reactions to Patients Who Read Material and Then Refused to Give Consent

Three analysts reported that a patient had refused to give permission. Two of these three analysts elaborated their reactions and the subsequent process.

In the first example, the refusal was accepted matter-of-factly. In the second, the analyst persisted, putting the material aside and then asking again. At one point the patient would give consent and then later rescind it. The analyst was spontaneously reflective about his reactions to his patient's refusal and described gaining insight into its meaning.

> I had only one patient who said absolutely no. Her suspicion of me and my motives was about everything and included the idea that I would be using her. Her fantasy was I would use her material for my self-interest, to get promoted, tenure, etc. I asked her only once again and when she again said no, then I dropped it. Suspiciousness remained as a general topic but the specifics of writing about her didn't. Maybe it will come up again in termination.

> When the patient refused, I had to do a lot of work to stay with the patient's feelings and not get caught up with my own reactions. I was surprised and hurt at the refusal and it took me a while to under-

stand the patient's position. At first the patient was adamant and I pressed it. Then I realized I had to back off and I left it to be understood over time. What I came to understand was that it was like you took a picture; it stole the patient's soul; that's how she felt it. It fit in with so much other stuff of her being fearful of what I'd do to her, but it brought all this to a head prematurely. It touched things she needed to deal with so I didn't think there were any long-term negative consequences. It made the patient angry as if I were stealing something from her. It was like reacting to an analyst getting pleasure from interpreting or any other libidinal investment in the work.

Therapeutic Reworking of Patients' Reactions to Reading about Themselves

Two analysts incorporated their writing about their patients into the therapeutic work.

> I haven't asked permission or shown material in more traditional analyses, but with one patient who had been traumatized, I asked her to read a chapter. I knew this patient would find out. It was six years into treatment, a long treatment that is still going on. This patient had so many fantasies of being special, had been involved in some boundary violations, and had paranoid tendencies. I felt if I was going to write about her, I needed to discuss it with her. She felt it was offering something to others and wanted to do it. Some traumatized patients have felt so useless, worthless that when they get to a place when they feel helped, they want to give something back . . . to feel a participant in helping others. There's a collaborative mirroring, supportive element in showing a patient what is written. At the time of publication, I showed it to her and she didn't have much to say about it. She was surprised I chose this aspect of the work to write about. It didn't seem very central to her. I'm sure there's a lot more to it. The analysis of the meaning of my writing to her has not been fully explored.

The other analyst asked permission from two patients and showed them what she had written. This analyst believed that a major advantage in showing a patient material was that it can allow a useful deidealization of the analyst. However, she thought this approach was contraindicated if the patient was a mental health professional.

> I don't think it would be useful to share written material with some-
> one in the field because it would likely become intellectualized. Hav-
> ing the analyst's perspective for these patients [who are not in the
> mental health field] is useful in part because it de-idealizes the ana-
> lyst. When my patient read the material, she thought I had under-
> stood her but not perfectly, which she would have wished, but then
> she came to feel that it was okay that my understanding was not per-
> fect. With analysts or candidates, it might serve as a resistance. It also
> might result in reifying some point of view or analytic technique.
> Candidates tend to scrutinize my writing. If it were about them, it
> might be hard for them to be critical or hard for them to develop dif-
> ferent, independent ideas. I would worry that it might interfere with
> formation of their own analytic identity.

This analyst thought she was more exposed by the vignettes than
her patients were. She worried about the deleterious effect of writing,
for example, promoting intellectualization or reifying some aspect of
the analysis, and wanted to be sure her patients could say no if they
wanted to. Yet, the issues of exposure for her patients and their feeling that she wanted something for herself, which she had expected to
arise, did not come up with either patient. One patient, who was in the
termination phase, gave her permission.

> When my patient read the vignette, she had a positive reaction. It
> made her feel special. She was also able to bring in what had not felt
> good in the analysis. She was happy with her disguise in general but
> had reactions of wanting to change what I described in some small ways.
> We were in agreement about what had happened, but she had a need
> to correct me in a way that was related to the competitive issue. I agreed
> to the corrections when I agreed with the patient, which I did. A cen-
> tral issue stirred for her by reading what I wrote was her competitive-
> ness. She had the feeling I would achieve fame by writing. This patient
> wanted fame but she didn't want to do anything to get it. The other
> thing was that what I had done wasn't perfect. She had thought of my
> doing analysis as my way of being special. My willingness to come up
> with a description of doing an analysis that wasn't perfect, and her own
> distress that her analysis was not perfect, then led the patient to think
> of our work somewhat differently. She wanted to get the most she could
> out of analysis and began to make more of an effort. The issue that I
> had dreaded coming up of my own self-interest did in a way, but it
> was in a way that was workable and not at all dreadful.

The other patient, who had terminated two years earlier, had come back a number of times for a few sessions. The analyst wrote her a letter requesting her permission and invited her to come in to discuss it. She did not charge the patient for this or any session related to discussion of the written example.

> This patient had felt really helped by her analysis. The patient was excited about having her analysis written about. She wrote a letter describing her understanding of how her analysis had worked. I felt her to be a real collaborator. These sessions and then the patient's reflecting on them seemed to crystallize aspects of this patient and our analytic work. The patient became more aware of me [as a separate person] and my countertransference responses, for better or worse. It made the work feel more intimate to both of us, mostly in a positive way. This patient came two or three times to continue working on what this write-up brought up.

This analyst had approached these patients about writing with "a great deal of anxiety." It seemed to her "a violation of her training." She thought her supervisors and colleagues would disapprove. When she presented this material, she found it was quite controversial. However, she was reassured that everything that came up was "workable" and helpful to the patients in that it stimulated a deeper exploration of problem areas.

PATIENTS' REACTIONS TO READING ABOUT OTHER PATIENTS

Another issue not often addressed is patients' reactions to reading what their analysts have published about other patients. Two analysts recounted these experiences.

> One patient was deeply upset after reading an article I wrote about another patient. It was a patient I liked so much. I wrote that in the early years of the treatment, I found I looked forward to the patient's hours and that he made me feel like a genius with everything I said to him, etc. Later this dynamic fell apart. This other patient reacted that she was certain that I was not this fond of her. It stirred up a special injury from the past for her. This patient was not in the field, but she read everything I wrote and I would never have been able to

write about her. Writing about patients not only affects the patient written about but other patients who read.

Some patients do read my papers on the Internet. Then they argue with me about the ideas in them; they hear ideas from the paper in the interpretations I make to them and say things like I'm pushing those ideas on them. But no one has brought any concern about his or her own material or about what I revealed of another patient. No patient ever asked to read what I have written about him or her.

The first analyst commented on the seldom-noted effect of competitive feelings stirred by reading about the analyst's other patients. In this respect, analysts need to consider how any of their patients who read the psychoanalytic literature may react to descriptions of other patients. Analysts also reported that patients reading about other patients have assumed the papers were about themselves. They sometimes equally erroneously concluded that papers were about people they know. Often reading the analyst's papers stirred a wish that their analysts would write about them.

ANALYSTS WRITTEN ABOUT BY THEIR OWN ANALYSTS

Seven analysts had the experience of their own analysts having written about them and of reading this material. This material will be presented in the third section of the book.

DISCUSSION

The examples given by these analyst-authors reveal a wide range of reactions by patients as perceived by their analysts. It must be kept in mind that except for the reports of the seven analysts with their personal experiences of reading what was written about them, these accounts are all reports of how analysts processed their patients' experiences. We cannot assume that these patients would have given similar accounts of their reactions. In addition, while accounts of patients' distress and the process of exploring its vicissitudes are likely to approximate at least a part of patients' reactions, the long-term ramifications of reading about themselves still remain unknown.

When analysts report that patients seem to have had little reaction to reading material about themselves, this may or may not be entirely accurate. Sometimes patients are forthcoming with their analysts or former analysts about their reactions, but sometimes they are not. Sometimes they do not know themselves what they feel until a much later time. Sometimes what they initially feel changes over time. And sometimes what they say may be just how it is and remains that way. Conscious acceptance does not mean that unconsciously reactions and meanings may not be more complex and contradictory; unless systematically pursued, these reactions may never be revealed. However, the existence of unconscious reactions does not necessarily mean opposition to the analyst's publishing their material. A central question is what impact the request and reading have on the analytic process.

When patients do not continue to talk about their reactions to their analyst's request to use clinical material from their treatment, it may be that they are accepting the need for such illustrations in the field. They may not pursue the issue further because they accept, and wish to accept, this request as something separate from the analytic work. But when patients actually read material about themselves, the separation between the scientific and the personal would seem much harder to maintain.

Analysts themselves would like to maintain this distinction between scientific and clinical work. The wish to maintain this distinction may be why most analysts in the sample stated that their reason for writing was to develop and illustrate ideas. Only a few gave the more personal or more clinical reason that writing provides a supervisory function or, more specifically, helps them deal with countertransference reactions. As I discussed in the first part of the book, minimization or avoidance of struggling with conflicts about analytic clinical reporting may have multiple meanings and unconscious motives.

THE ANALYST'S WISH TO ACCEPT MANIFEST CONSENT

Most analysts are thoughtful about which patients to ask for use of their material, but once they ask, the temptation may be to expeditiously accept patients' consent. They want to believe that there are no untoward ramifications of patients' reading about themselves that play out in analysis or that adversely affect patients' feelings about their analyst or the analysis. If analysts sincerely thought that the effect of patients' reading about themselves or their treatment would be detrimental, they could not in clear conscience make these requests. Analysts who believe asking for consent is detrimental use only disguise or do not write about patients at all.

Some analysts in the sample who have never asked permission and whose patients had read or heard papers about themselves tried to maintain that not asking was still the best policy. Though their patients had recognized themselves, or someone else had identified them, these analysts continued to state that it was not likely that such recognition would occur. These incompatible ideas—that patients would not likely recognize themselves, though at least one of their patients had done so, that they would never ask permission because transference would make true opposition impossible, and then that discovery had not been a problem since patients had been able to openly assert their reactions—were presented simultaneously and without the analyst's recognition of the contradiction. Patients' discovering material written about them is disconcerting to analysts; when thinking about it, the analysts' usual logic and reasoning becomes disrupted. Analysts need to avoid seeing these contradictions. They want neither to hurt their patient nor to give up writing. This kind of denial, which could be thought of as a version of splitting, appeared nowhere else in these interviews. Yet many of these analysts rationalized their ways of dealing with confidentiality.

It needs to be remembered that many patients never discover that they have been written about. It is this fact that allows many analysts to continue to believe that the preservation of confidentiality by employing only disguise is a viable approach. The reports of the analysts in this study illustrate a wide range of behaviors in terms of how extensively and intensively patients' reactions were pursued. Some analysts maintained there were no repercussions. Some accepted whatever manifest reaction the patient reported and pursued it no further; others offered opportunities for exploration and elaboration; still others looked for displaced reactions and continued to follow the ramifications over time.

Once again, since requests for permission derive from an external professional agenda, continued pursuit of their meaning with patients is a janus-faced issue. On one side, the tracing and searching of a patient's reactions reflect the analyst's efforts to ensure that the meaning to the patient is understood and analyzed. On the other side, however, the analyst's continued focus on this question can be experienced by the patient as a further intrusion, a distraction from the patient's agenda. Once the request for consent is made, there has been a concrete disturbance of the "natural" unfolding process of analysis. Ringstrom (1998) and some of the analysts I interviewed illustrated that the request and writing may be enactments by the analyst. Only a few analysts in the sample openly worried that the request for consent and the patient's reading of the paper might submerge issues or inadvertently concretely repeat core conflicts or distract patients from other dynamics.

PATIENTS' REACTIONS

Patients' reactions to reading about themselves varied considerably. Some were much more forthcoming about their reactions than others, though for some this may have been influenced by the extent to which their analysts inquired. When patients openly expressed themselves, and the meaning of being written about was explicated, their analysts often seemed able to productively analyze this material. Analysts who had themselves been written about as patients often stated that issues similar to those stirred up by their own experiences of reading about themselves came up for patients in ways related to the dynamic issues for each person. But only one analyst in this sample openly questioned what added impact the analyst's having concretized a particular meaning central to the patients' primary conflicts through the request for consent or through reading the example might have created. The one analyst who did raise this concern had been written about when a patient. The effect of concretization is not known. And even if there were some data that reflected interference or that indicated no adverse consequences, we could not generalize these findings.

Another unexplored area was the fantasies that may have been stimulated by the analyst's request, and the patient's reaction to discrepancies between fantasy and what the analyst actually wrote about the patient. If fantasies of importance are stimulated by informed consent, and the analyst's account of the patient turns out to be a brief vignette used to illustrate an idea, some analysts have observed patients' disappointment. Though these analysts may then have attempted to analyze this disappointment, they did not describe these interventions in the interviews. Such iatrogenically generated experiences of disappointment are likely to produce echoes in the transference and can create complications for the analytic work.

Have patients sufficiently explored their fantasies and interpretations of their analysts' motivation and countertransference, either in other areas or specifically in relation to the issue of their having been written about? If the analytic work has not included such a focus, will the later discovery of a paper that includes their clinical material stimulate this kind of inquiry? What are the reactions of patients to their analysts, as perceived through the medium of analytic writing? What do patients think they have learned about their analysts' feelings about them? Does the analyst raise these questions with them? Should the analyst? Would raising them be intrusive as these thoughts might never have come up were it not for the article that the patient read? When are analysts conscientiously pursuing the effects of introducing their writing, and when are they simply pursuing their own external agenda? When is such a scrutiny beneficial, and when may it be detrimental?

I am not posing these questions as disguised suggestions since I believe the answers to these questions depend on both the patient's issues and the nature of the relationship and analytic work between each patient–analyst pair. I am suggesting, however, that every analyst must carefully weigh these questions in relation to each individual patient. Clinical writing can never be totally objective, free of the analyst's relationship to the material presented. This relationship is not necessarily the analyst's countertransference.

THE EFFECT ON WRITING OF KNOWING PATIENTS WILL READ

When analysts write about patients with the thought that their patients may read what they are writing, this has some effect on how and what is written. A number of analysts in the sample emphasized that they would never write anything that they and the patient had not already discussed. Analysts who write about diagnostic issues, such as using patient material to describe some syndrome, strongly preferred to use disguise without asking consent; as previously quoted, they were concerned that patients would find some view about them that had not been processed in analysis and might experience it as narcissistically injurious. Particularly when writing about syndromes, analysts had concerns about the impact of their tone.

Consciousness of tone seems a desirable consequence of analysts' awareness that patients may read their papers. Analysts in this sample all seemed respectful and caring about their patients. While this may partly be an artifact of the sample, it may also reflect a sociological trend. Perhaps the shift in ideas about authority and the view of the analyst as a participant in a process has resulted in increased professional humility, and recognition of the commonality of human vulnerability and ensuing difficulties.

In the past, when articles communicated a view of the patient, with the analyst thought of as merely a silent filter for the material, the primary concern was often whether the analyst's words had the "right" tone or whether patients might feel misunderstood or objectified were they to read the analyst's account. Now that the analyst is apt to include countertransference material, there is an additional concern about the meaning this implicit and explicit self-disclosure may have for the patient. Gabbard (2000) has made a similar point.

A number of analysts in the sample stated explicitly that knowing their patients would read their papers meant that there were issues they would not be able to include, such as reporting negative countertransference reactions, unless they had been explored with the patient. But this sacrifice of material might include any area, which they believed might hurt or humiliate the patient. Of course, the analysts have not always been accurate in their assessment of their patients' sensitivities.

It is clear that an awareness that the patient may read what is written influences, and may at times even reshape, what is communicated; at the very least, this means that certain kinds of data will be omitted from the literature. Some analysts who employed disguise alone also stated that their articles were guided by anticipations about how the patient would react to reading it, even though they never expected that to happen. The implication of these restrictions on what analysts feel free to write about patients means that there is likely to be skewing of what is presented in the psychoanalytic literature. Although it seems reasonable that cautions such as these be employed, readers should be aware that in accounts of patients, all might not have been told. This point will be returned to several times later in the book.

SELECTION OF PATIENTS

All of the analysts in the sample stated that they were highly selective both about which patients they would ask for permission and about which patients they would show what they had written. Most analysts cited compliant, masochistic, and paranoid patients as ones they would never ask. Patients who had been used or abused were generally excluded, though there was one notable exception in which just such a patient was thought by the analyst to be someone for whom there would be a therapeutic benefit from the collaborative process. Most analysts would not write about people in the mental health field; even fewer would consider writing about them without asking their consent and showing them what was written. Other reasons for not requesting permission included concerns that the analyst's request might stimulate shame, fear of exposure, exhibitionistic wishes, excitement or inhibition, narcissistic injury or gratification, or a revival of childhood experiences of betrayal. However, since being written about will have a meaning for any patient, it would seem that the particularity of the meaning may not always be the crucial element in an analyst's decision. What seems crucial is the extent to which the analyst believes these meanings can be analyzed in the aftermath with a particular patient.

INFORMED CONSENT

For the most part, these analysts knew their patients quite well before asking permission and so were not likely to ask someone who would not be agreeable to granting it. The care and reasoning underlying the process of selection likely explains why almost all patients who were asked gave their permission. To what extent consent was influenced by the transference cannot be assessed, though analysts are increasingly aware of the role it plays in skewing patients' responses toward giving permission. Many analysts debate whether a therapeutic alliance can meaningfully be distinguished from a positive transference; both are likely to lead patients to agree with their analysts' requests. Again, readers of clinical reports need to remember that cases presented may not be representative of the breath of analytic practice, since consenting patients or those about whom analysts believe they can safely write may differ in various ways from other analysands.

THE IMPACT ON PATIENTS OF BEING WRITTEN ABOUT

Even if there can be no truly meaningful informed consent because of the influence of the transference, does this mean that giving permission must be harmful to the patient? If patients are gratified or feel special is it likely to harm them? If feeling special is central to a patient's character, it seems likely that it would become a subject of analysis in any event. If compliance is an issue, this can be analyzed as it emerges in other areas and, at a timely moment, be related to a "too easy" acceptance of a request for consent. One analyst pointed to the detrimental consequences if a sense of specialness was not analyzed, namely, the continuance of a fantasized, idealized relationship that might spoil future relationships. If the meanings of feeling special or gratified had not previously been explored, then the analyst's request might have stimulated an area that could benefit from elaboration.

Nonetheless, the gratification, sense of specialness, or any other meaning that being a clinical example in one's analyst's paper has for a patient, will to some extent be concretized for patients who know that their analysts have written about them. The long-term consequences of an experience that cannot be fully analyzed are not known. There are, of course, many areas in every analysis that are not fully analyzed. The focus on the limitations placed on elaboration of this particular enacted area is because it has been created by the analyst's request. It is stimulated by an action that the analyst can choose to make or refrain from making. Nor can generalized assumptions be made, in our present state of knowledge, about what the long-term effect of this experience will be. Undoubtedly, reactions depend both on the particular issues for each patient and on the nature of each specific analytic relationship.

Based on the reactions of the patients described in this study, there are many different reactions and they may also differ over time. Patients' seemingly casual acceptance of their analysts' intent to write or to have actually done so, does not necessarily mean that on a deep level it is fine with them; but neither can we assume that these patients are being defensively bland. Patients' initial negative feelings about being written about, when their material is well-disguised and tactfully presented, cannot automatically be equated with "harm" to patients. Patients may work through their initial reactions and no longer feel hurt, and they may gain useful insights about themselves through analyzing their reactions. Of course, this working through may never happen. In the latter instance, patients may experience the disruption of a sense of well-being that came from an appreciation of an analytic experience up to that point in which they had felt known and understood. But what constitutes harm, just as what constitutes therapeutic benefit, is very complex and not easily defined. Only further research into these reactions can provide clarification in this area.

To return to the question raised at the beginning of this discussion: What do patients do to make it acceptable to themselves that their analysts write about them? I wonder if many of the patients selected by their analysts for asking consent not only tend to be "reasonable," manifesting "unobjectionable positive transferences" (Stein 1981), but also tend to use compartmentalization as a defense. Patients who are not disturbed by their analyst's writing about them may be able to separate the writing from the analysis itself. They may also be able to hold in their minds the complexity and "doubleness" of experience. If patients are able to view what their analysts have written about them as being both about them and not about them, just as they have come to understand transference feelings as both about and not about the analyst, then perhaps they have been able to attain a distance that makes it acceptable to them that their analysts use their material. Analysts have to hope that such a solution is possible.

COLLEAGUES WHO READ MATERIAL ABOUT THEMSELVES

Similar concerns exist in relation to the material in this current project. Listening to these analysts, I thought how fortunate I was to be writing papers and a book in which I had permission to use the examples. My choice of disguise to maintain confidentiality was ensured simply by removing all identifying data except the pool from which the sample was drawn. Both the sample and the pool were large enough to ensure anonymity.

Nonetheless, I have the responsibility of thinking about how each of the analyst-authors in the sample might react to the use of the interview material he or she provided. Respect and appreciation for those contributing their thoughts and clinical examples is an essential part of this process. A patient once said, "You can tell me anything you want provided you put it in a proper envelope." Generally, this is true. Most of what one wants to say can be said with tact. But there are limits, and sometimes thoughts must be sacrificed to avoid causing feelings of disrespect or other forms of hurt. Just as analysts agree that some patients should not be written about, there may be some material that is too potentially hurtful, too personal, or too elusive to be put into words. At the same time, I have the same responsibility to readers that each analyst has when writing about a patient, that is, not to sidestep issues that are central to the work presented. In this book, the most salient issue that might upset the analysts who volunteered to be interviewed is my addressing their tendency to want to make it "all right," a temptation to ignore the possible negative reactions, to minimize, and so avoid struggling with, their own conflicts over using patient material.

All the reflections presented in the discussion section of this chapter about analysts' perceptions of, and reactions to, their patients' reading about themselves apply equally to the analysts who published in the other psychoanalytic journals. The fact that they are not repeated in detail in each section is to spare the reader the tedium of repetition. I will next report the perceptions of analysts who reside outside of the United States.

8
Effect on Patients—
IJP Authors[1]

Analysts residing outside the United States (19%), who published in the *International Journal of Psychoanalysis* (*IJP*) and three other international journals between 1995 and 2001, were less inclined to show their patients clinical material than United States analysts (40%) who published clinical illustrations in the *Journal of the American Psychoanalytic Association* (*JAPA*) during the same time period. In this chapter, I will report the perceptions of international analysts of their patients' reactions, when they were shown or discovered material written about them.

PERMISSION ASKED

Eight analysts asked for their patients' permission to write about them and showed them the written material, compared with twelve analysts in the United States. Three of these analysts were from England,

---

1. Material in this chapter has previously appeared in slightly different form as part of a paper in the *International Journal of Psychoanalysis* (2004) 85:3–22, © Institute of Psychoanalysis, London, UK. I am grateful to the editors for granting permission for the material to be reprinted in this book.

two from Canada, and one each from Peru, Italy, and Germany. A variety of patients' reactions were described.

Patients Perceived by Their Analysts to Be Untroubled

Most of these analysts simply stated they were not aware of any problems. One analyst elaborated the experience:

> Both patients in my article were informed about publication. I did not have the feeling that they were disturbed. I felt the first was very interested in my review of his case and in seeing the article. The second apparently did not mind. Perhaps the fact that one was an intellectual, interested in academic subjects, while the second was not particularly interested in psychoanalysis and did not have a good command of English is important. In the first case I certainly felt that he had a narcissistic investment in my view of his problem. I felt that he felt I had a special interest in his case and that this promoted his interest. This was a subject of analysis for some time. In neither case did I feel that publication interfered with the analysis. Both felt sufficiently disguised and confidentiality was not an issue. My impression is that telling the patient that we intend to publish his case, while respecting his confidentiality, is the best recourse. Disguising the case masks too many of the relevant problems. Publishing in a foreign language is always seen as less menacing. The special interest [that the analyst has] in the case must be thoroughly analyzed. The patient always feels that he is "special," either because his case is so unusual or because he feels that he is particularly interesting to us.

Patients Perceived by Their Analysts as Ambivalent Although Consenting

One analyst described patients who agreed in spite of ambivalent reactions to some aspect of the experience in connection with the paper.

> The first time I wrote about a patient, it was after we stopped. I sent the paper without warning. She was a professional person and I thought it would be fine. It was a big mistake. She was quite angry. She said it had come out of the blue, not registered, what if someone else got it? I quite understood and apologized. She said it was fine to

use. There were things in it she did not recognize but she trusted me that they were true. The second patient had also terminated. He felt a little disturbed because it brought back painful things, but he also thought it was fine to publish it. The third patient, also terminated, had a generally positive reaction. This patient wanted details of an affair left out in case her children read it and recognized her. She came back to talk about the paper a few times.

This analyst recognized that her failure to prepare the first patient contributed to the patient's distress. She conveys how each patient's response reflected the particularity of the patient's circumstances.

Patients' Reactions Change over Time

Another analyst who sometimes showed what she had written to patients gave two examples of its effect and contrasting outcomes. The first example was described earlier in Chapter 3 where the patient considered granting permission but ultimately rescinded it. Here is the second example:

> The patient was still in analysis but it was coming to the end. I said that I was giving a paper using some of his material in a distant country, where he could not be recognized, but that I was also thinking of publishing it, and I did not want to do so without his consent. I gave him the whole paper to read. At first he was outraged. His reaction was a painful reliving of the analytic experience described. I think his partner said it wasn't all that bad. After mulling it over, he decided it would be all right. I had changed the sex. He also suggested several other changes because of things he'd told people about, and I agreed. After these experiences with [these two patients], I realized how very upsetting working-through these experiences can be, though they can be productive too. They are pretty grueling for the analyst too.

This analyst's example makes clear that one cannot assume that patients' initial reactions reflect what they may come to feel over time. Another analyst stated that most of her patients had said they didn't want to see the paper, but one read it later and discussed his reactions in a follow-up visit.

> He felt a bit embarrassed to read it, as it reminded him of how disturbed he used to be. However, he expressed pleasure that he had

been of help to psychoanalysts (and to me). I gave him plenty of time to explore how he felt, and asked him if he regretted giving permission at all. I am sure it is complicated, but I did feel with this particular man that the overall reaction was pleasure at having been of help. I didn't think it was hindering postanalytic work for him.

Reactions to Patients Who Read Material and Then Refuse Consent

Four analysts in this sample had patients refuse to give permission. One analyst describes the painful exploration that ensued.

> A long case history of the analysis . . . about, an unconscious collusion between patient and analyst and how I eventually managed to see what I was doing and extricate myself from it, which freed the patient from it too, at least to some extent. Because the material was so revealing, I waited till the patient's analysis was over and then asked his permission. I rang him up and asked him to come to see me, and explained what it was about, outlined the main topic, and said I would not publish it without his consent. I said I thought he would find it upsetting to read, but that I thought the topic had been important for both of us and for psychoanalysis and that I would like to publish it if possible. We had two more meetings about it. He was very upset, partly, he said, because it brought the whole analysis alive to him again, and partly, I added, because he felt that my alliance to my discipline and colleagues felt to him stronger than my loyalty to him. He agreed. He suggested several additional bits of disguise, but he was very uncertain about publication, even in a foreign language. He pointed out, quite rightly, that his foreign friends would read it and would probably realize it was he. He said he'd like to think about it some more. He did, talked it over with his wife and came back saying that he really didn't think he wanted it to be published, and I agreed at once. He has come to see me since then to discuss an important life decision, and it is my impression that although this discussion about publication was very perturbing to him, it led to further and deeper understanding of himself and his analysis.

All analysts are distressed by patients' refusals when the analyst has an investment in writing about them. When analysts and patients continue to explore the patient's reactions, sometimes patients change their minds, either in the direction of consent or refusal. The process of exploration is difficult for both patient and analyst. More often, analysts decide not to persist with their request. The consequences of patient's refusal on the feelings of both parties frequently remain unexplored.

Permission Asked and Material Not Shown but Later Found by the Patient

One analyst asked for her patient's permission, did not show her patient the material, but then made use of the patient's finding it in the analytic work.

> I hadn't shown the patient what I wrote about him in the case I asked for permission. But he bought a book in which his was one of the clinical cases mentioned and he told me he was very proud to be "used." What followed was a severe narcissistic acting out because he showed the book to his ex-wife who was very hurt because it revealed his having a lover. This was dealt with in analysis; it was part of his total lack of recognition of the "Other" in favor of his narcissistic pleasure to be the case of a gifted albeit disturbed person.

Perhaps the analyst's initial decision to not show the patient this material reflected a preconscious awareness that he might use it in a hurtful fashion. The patient's action may also reflect a transference response to having found something that he assumed was meant to be secret. The meaning of having and of discovering secrets was not discussed by the analyst. Nevertheless, the analyst was able to make therapeutic use of the patient's action.

MATERIAL FOUND BY PATIENTS WHOSE PERMISSION HAD NOT BEEN ASKED

Five international analysts had patients who found and read material written about them: three from England and one each from Argentina and France. Only two of these analysts elaborated the consequences that followed.

One analyst reported:

> Only once has a patient recognized himself in one of my books. He bought it in a bookshop. He was first very ambivalent about it, but . . . he admitted that he was the only person who could recognize himself, and he found that the account given by me of his thinking processes and of the ongoing work together was completely true to the image he had of himself and he was thankful to me that I had not taken anything from him for myself. He felt completely respected.

A second analyst elaborated how he worked with his patient around her distress:

> A mental health professional saw the one paper I have published about a professional. This occurred after the analysis had finished. She recognized herself and asked to come in and talk to me. I confirmed that it was her case and that I had not asked her permission having thought my disguise was sufficient to protect her privacy. She thought she was recognizable despite some radical changes and I tended to agree with her. She was angry and disappointed. I told her I understood her reasons for this and that I had not asked her permission because I had not wanted to intrude the matter into her analysis at that time (the last year of a long analysis). I said I understood that it was an intrusion now and that I was sorry about that and that this was an issue I still had not resolved for myself and that I continued to think that (a) it was not right to intrude into an analysis and (b) there was a proper need to publish clinical material. I admitted I did not know how to put these two needs together and said I was sorry she had been a victim of this. She queried whose need it was to publish and we looked at her thought that she had been the victim of a narcissistic analyst who wanted to see his name in lights. (This was not an overriding belief and if I am honest, it has some validity.) I think she (and I) were pleased we had met and I think there was a genuine clearing of the air without any resolution being reached. Near the end of the session we discussed payment and I said that I did not feel it would be right to charge her since it was my action that had caused her to come to see me.

The experiences of both these analysts indicate that a sensitive and respectful dealing with patients who have stumbled upon their material can salvage an unfortunate situation, and also may deepen and solidify positive and appreciative feelings of the patient for the analyst and for the process. It should never be patients' responsibility to assume a role of understanding and acceptance of their analysts' desire to publish their personal material, whether for the analysts' personal or professional motivation. Under circumstances when patients do accept and understand their analysts' wish to publish their material, and especially when they have not been asked before they discovered it and potentially feel betrayed, it is likely that the analyst will also feel positively and appreciatively toward a patient. These patients seem to be able to appreciate the personal work they have engaged in and, at the same time, to accept and understand professional reasons for writing about their material.

The Therapeutic Use of Patients' Having Read Material about Themselves

Similar to the United States analysts, very few of the international analysts actually thought of the use of the writing as furthering analytic work. However, there were two international analysts who deliberately used the consent process and the written material as part of analytic work.

One analyst described his thought process:

> There cannot be any rules about this, because discussing it and showing the writing to the patient has to become part of the analysis itself, and the patient's responses to the idea handled and interpreted analytically within the psychoanalytic framework. If the particular case does not allow for this, then the question cannot be brought up at all, and this might mean the material could not be used. When I got in touch with an ex-patient, he simply confirmed that he had no objection and was satisfied with certain disguising elements, and said it was interesting to be reminded of episodes in the analysis. On the one occasion when I have done this in the course of an analysis, I showed the patient the whole article I had written, which included a lengthy description of herself, so that she could understand the context of my thinking about her. This had powerful results within the analysis. I was anxious about what the effect would be, but the patient felt recognized in a way that meant a lot to her. We were able to discuss her feelings about what I had done and her response to it in a way that helped the analysis to develop in new directions.

The second analyst stated that he saw working with written material as part of the analytic process. In this respect, he is similar to the relational analysts who will be discussed in the next chapter, but he is, nonetheless, different in that he is careful not to be drawn into exploration of his personal motives for writing about the patient.

> Asking patients about writing I see as part of the analysis. I watch if there are narcissistic or paranoid reactions. I try to make timing right to explore narcissistic anxieties, to keep reactions open and quickly move on to the more profound anxiety. The subject then moves to the anxiety itself. I've written about six patients. One said fine and never wanted to read the paper. Two patients had sexual curiosity about how I viewed them and what it meant for the relationship. One patient objected to how I characterized her mother. She thought I was too hard on her. We worked on that. It didn't have to do with what I'd written but something internal. It led to work in the transference. I thought the patient allied with one part of the split. It triggered hostility about misunderstanding in the analysis and allowed grievance to come out more clearly and be explored more deeply. We could work on her narcissism, the sense the patient held onto feelings of being attacked or exploited. Another patient who had a very deprived upbringing was moved that I could use my mind to think of him and about him in depth. He was never treated with such care. Does it make the patient feel special? Maybe. Sometimes patients fantasize that they are the only ones you write about. The boundary issue has to be carefully maintained. If the analyst is drawn into his own motive, there is a danger. I tell patients, part of my work is to write about patients in order to treat other patients and understand these problems. I might ask at some point if they'd help. I say, "I'll show you what I've written and you'd be free to say if it's all right or not. We don't understand a lot about human beings—anything that can be made clearer would help."

Reading as a Painful Reliving

The reliving of previous pain by patients when they read about themselves was emphasized more by the international clinicians than their United States colleagues. One reason for the difference may be that a number of examples from the international analysts were of patients who had read material when they were no longer in treatment.

They were either being asked permission or had given it previously. Therefore, these patients may not have been diverted by the anger we have sometimes seen stimulated when patients discovered an article and experienced it as a betrayal of trust by the analyst. They also would not have been diverted by a current meaning of the content as it would have been had they been in ongoing treatment. As a result, a leading edge of feeling was focused on their previous experience.

ANALYSTS WRITTEN ABOUT BY THEIR OWN ANALYSTS AND WHO READ THE PAPERS

Eight analysts in this sample were written about by their own analysts and read the material. The reactions of these analysts will be presented in the third section of the book.

DISCUSSION

While fewer international analysts than analysts residing in the United States choose to show patients what they write about them, the attitudes and experiences of those international analysts who do are not different from their United States colleagues.

Comparison of Analysts' Reactions in Both Samples to Patients' Discovering Papers

When comparing the current examples with the United States analysts' illustrations, I was struck that fewer of the international analysts who provided accounts of patients' discovering material about themselves when the analyst had not asked permission, tried to rationalize their behavior or minimize the pain caused to the patient. One reason for this difference may be that the analysts in the current project had the questionnaires and could think out and prepare their responses in advance. All of the responses of the international analysts in this sample were first written, even those accounts that were followed up in interviews. In contrast, the United States analysts had no preparation for my questions. Their accounts were given spontaneously and only verbally; they had no chance to look over what they said and reflect on how they thought about what had occurred. In addition, the fact that the United States analysts knew me may have further contributed to their wish to justify what they had done in my eyes as well as their own. It should be made clear, however, that many of the United States analysts were equally reflective, sensitive, tactful, and took ownership for what they had done, as were their colleagues who live in other parts of the world.

In most respects, the discussion of the perception of the United States analysts about their patients applies as well to the international analysts.

USING WRITTEN MATERIAL AS PART OF ANALYTIC WORK

An interesting finding in this project is that some traditionally trained analysts use written material as an active part of analytic work. These analysts not only listen for patients' associations to the writing but also make it a part of the dialogic process. Two analysts from the United States, one analyst from England, and one from Canada offered examples of productively weaving the issues stimulated by the request to write about them into their patients' analysis.

I will provide another anecdotal account that nicely illustrates this process.

An analyst asked her patient for permission to use an example from their work in a paper. The patient, who was a mental health professional, considered many negative fantasies, such as the analyst would reveal that she disliked or disrespected the patient, that the analyst would reveal a view of the material which had not been shared with the patient and catch the patient by surprise, or that someone reading or hearing the paper would have a formulation that was pathologizing in some unexpected way and she would learn about it, and so on. Nonetheless, the patient believed that writing papers was important for the field and hoped to do so herself at some future date; she agreed to the analyst's using her material. The patient went on to muse about what the analyst might say, wondering when and where this paper would be given, and thinking about her wish to attend and hear it. The analyst said that it sounded like the patient wanted to know what the analyst would be writing. If this were the case, the analyst would want the patient to read the paper and have her input about the material. The patient was flabbergasted. Having given her permission, it never occurred to her that she continued to have any say about what the analyst would do in relation to it. The analyst then interpreted that this reaction of abdicating her own views and needs and giving herself over to another's authority in the context of attachment was exactly what they had been discovering in many other areas of the patient's life. The affective experience of having this conflict enacted in the transference made a powerful impression on the patient. She brought in many other past instances where this had occurred and was alert to, and reflected upon her continued inclination to relinquish her own authority. Patient and analyst began to gain a better understanding of the origin of this behavior.

Even when analysts have not consciously decided to make use in analytic work of patient's reactions to being asked permission or to reading the material about themselves, the way the dyad processes the reactions that follow this exchange may be very productive analytically.

Another point emerges from these interviews. While analysts would never, of course, wish that patients' discover they have been written about when their permission has not been asked, the observations noted here illustrate that the consequences are not always detrimental to the patient or to the patient's feeling about the analyst and the analysis. The analyst whose patient refused to give consent similarly was able to work with his patient's response in a manner that he believed did not result in detracting from their work. Several analysts provided examples where they dealt sensitively and respectfully with patient's feelings of betrayal. The manner in which the analyst deals with the patient's reaction, while certainly not the only factor in how the patient is affected, is a crucial variable in the impact on the patient.

In the next chapter, I will describe the perceptions of relational analysts when their patients read about themselves. The theoretical assumptions of this group led them to some different perspectives on the impact of writing on patients.

9

Effect on Patients— *Psychoanalytic Dialogues* Authors[1]

Many analysts described how reading about themselves focused patients on central transferential issues and brought them to center stage in the treatment. Sometimes what became highlighted was the patient's perception of the analyst's countertransference. And sometimes it helped the analyst to become aware of the accuracy of some aspect of the patient's perception; this, in turn, may have made it easier for the patient to understand the transference part of the perception. The psychoanalytic literature on this topic, described in the first chapter in this section, is written primarily by analysts who identify themselves with relational theory.

Since relational analysts view the patient–analyst relationship, in its conscious and unconscious forms, as both the source for unearthing difficulties and the place for resolving them, they encourage heightened transference/countertransference interactions, a stimulation that some more classically trained analysts, like Stein (1988a,b) and Furlong

1. The second half of this chapter, "Writing as a Stimulus in Analytic Work," has been previously published as an article in *The Psychoanalytic Quarterly* 2005, 74:365–395, © The Psychoanalytic Quarterly, 2005. I am grateful to the editor for his permission to republish it in this book.

(1998, 2004), view as possible impediments to analytic work. Many of these relational analysts felt freer about asking permission of their patients because they believed their patients benefited from reading what their analysts wrote about them. This approach seems consonant with their view of the therapeutic action of psychoanalysis taking place in an interactional context where meanings are co-constructed.

In the first part of this chapter, I provide examples of analysts' perceptions of patients' reading about themselves that parallel the material in the last two chapters where the perception of United States analysts and international analysts were recounted. The second part of the chapter describes and illustrates how some relational analysts intentionally introduce their writing about a patient as a stimulus for analytic work.

I. PSYCHOANALYTIC DIALOGUES ANALYST-AUTHORS' PERCEPTIONS OF PATIENTS' REACTIONS TO READING ABOUT THEMSELVES

Papers Shown to Patients

Eight relational analysts in this sample always asked permission and showed the patients what they had written. Another sixteen analysts in this sample preferred to ask permission and showed patients the papers if they made this request. Of the five analysts who preferred to disguise but had on some occasions asked consent, two made it clear that they had shown the patients the material about them.

Papers Discovered by Patients

None of the analysts in this sample described patients discovering material written about them. Of course, this may have occurred and the patients may not have returned to tell them. But since most of these analysts were committed to sharing what they wrote with their patients, the likelihood of this occurring was considerably lessened.

Timing of Request

Most relational analysts in the sample asked permission during treatment because they wanted their patients' reactions to be alive in the analytic work.

During Treatment

Most of these analysts reported that their patients responded positively to reading about themselves. The patients apparently felt that the analysts' descriptions fit their experience. The majority of these analysts did not believe the writing remained a central topic for long and they saw no untoward consequences. But one analyst stressed the individuality of response.

> One patient feels appreciated by both being asked and in the content of the writing itself; another feels exploited by it and the third felt that I accurately wrote about her and us and took it as a wholesome interest.

Positive Reactions

One analyst stated that all his experiences asking consent had been positive.

> Sometimes reading something formulated, they get the point better than they do in sessions. Sometimes people have fantasies we'll become famous in the world together, something exhibitionistic. I've never had anyone regret it. Invariably it gets into the transference, e.g., wanting to be partners, a public performance—wanting to get publicity.

Unlike many analysts previously quoted, this analyst did not seem concerned about the enactment and gratification of exhibitionistic wishes. It was precisely these concerns that have led other analysts to decide in favor of disguise alone or, even more often, to choose not to write about this category of patient.

Another analyst stated that initially a patient said she didn't care what was written and she did not even want to read it.

Ultimately I didn't feel right about her not reading it and I had her read it. She found it amazing—like a photograph from another time.

While the patient had a positive reaction to what she read about herself, the analyst overrode the patient's wish not to read in order to make this happen. The patient and analyst may have explored the patient's reaction to the analyst's pushing her to read the paper against her consciously expressed wish not to do so, but this was not described in the interview.

Negative Reactions

Other analysts reported patients' negative reactions to reading about themselves. One analyst stated:

One patient was distressed by the "light" tone I took. She is herself a writer. She understood the problem of voice, tone, and style which are quite key to my work, in which I try to find a mix of personal, professional, and political so as to say things that are not otherwise sayable or come to insights that conventional academic or scholarly or professional language might otherwise not allow. But, of course, her life is deadly serious to her, not a deadly game, and so she protested.

Another analyst related the usefulness of patients' reading articles even when their reactions were negative:

The only negative reaction I ever had was one patient who after reading said, "Oh, I didn't know you thought that about me or reacted like that. How come we didn't go into that more?" But then I explored the transference and her underlying fantasies. It opened up, a critical, detached, internal object. So it was useful.

This analyst is pointing out that, though the patient was distressed about what she learned about her analyst's view of her, the material stimulated by her reading her analyst's paper aided her treatment.

Patients' Reactions Change over Time: Negative to Positive

One analyst reported:

One patient I hadn't spoken with in advance. I'd published a couple of vignettes about her. Later, she was looking at my bookshelf and wondered if I ever wrote about my patients. I wondered if she was wondering about her. She said yes. I offered for her to read what I'd written. She was flattered that I had carried her in my mind between sessions and by the way I seemed sympathetic in some respects. But she didn't like the way she appeared to me early in treatment. She thought I presented her as colder and less available than she liked to think of herself. I talked about how my feelings about her had changed over time. It helped me formulate and articulate my thoughts. It created more intimacy between us. It opened up our relationship, which then deepened. It helped her see her fears about being seen as aloof and cold, and that helped her to be more open with me and others in her life.

For this analyst, the patient's reading what he had written during treatment helped him to better conceptualize a countertransference response and then to explore the characterological aspect of the patient that stimulated his reactions. Reading the written material, in this respect, served as a new interpretation to the patient that was then expanded. Similar to other examples in this chapter, the interpretation was not consciously given; it was discovered through an inadvertent self-disclosure. The analyst had not written what he did with the conscious intention that the patient read it. The analyst was not troubled by the self-revelatory aspect and viewed what occurred as helpful for the analytic work and therapeutic change. However, this analyst did not report on the patient's reaction to being written about without permission.

Positive Reactions Changing to Negative

Another analyst stated:

> The patient initially felt positively about what I wrote. She readily gave her permission, but years later she was not happy about this and regretted she had done so. She did not know the further meaning of what she had exposed originally, but when she grasped it many years later, she felt embarrassed about what she had exposed. The example became part of a larger issue than the example itself. She felt I should have protected her as a parent in the transference. At first she had felt flattered to be written about but then she felt shamed by it. She came back to talk about it, but the issue was never satisfactorily resolved.

This example highlights the need for analysts to remain aware that, especially during treatment when the meaning of material may not yet have been sufficiently explored, patients' consent and positive reactions may transform[2] to negative ones. This patient felt unprotected by her analyst in this respect. She thought he should have known to take care of her and have known that she was not able to adequately protect herself at that time.

After Termination

One analyst raised concerns about what conflicts may be stirred and reawakened when the analyst contacts a patient after termination.

One patient I wrote about on three occasions. The first time I had a lot of trepidation about doing so; I almost didn't. The reason was that leaving was a major theme of analysis; he had a mother who he felt wouldn't let him go. It was a nine-year analysis and he felt I wouldn't let him out of my grasp. He felt all the time that he might as well leave next week because the analysis could go on forever. So while we had significant working through of issues, he could feel I was grabbing hold of him again. But I decided we could deal with it, that he could withstand it. I selfishly wanted to use his material. I called him and he responded to my call as if he had been waiting for it. He said I had his permission and he didn't have to read it. I said I'd be more comfortable if he read it. I sent it; he read it and I asked if he wanted to discuss it on the phone, come to the office, meet for lunch. He chose lunch. Reading it evoked the richness of the experience of working together again for him. It brought back the intensity of those years, things not fully resolved, conflicts about how and when we ended. He felt I'd let him end too soon. Though in subsequent conversations he said he didn't really feel that, it made me anxious about boundaries. We were having lunch—like an invitation for me to hold on to him. The tenor of our conversation was warm. I view my writing, and my work with patients in general, as collegial enterprises. Sometimes patients remember things differently from what I wrote, but usually nothing that is very significant. He was gracious, helpful, facilitative, but it didn't reach the depth of a clinical hour. With

---

2. Lacanians describe this transformation as occurring in apres-coup revisions.

him, and patients in general, I follow the patient's lead and I don't probe all that much more.

This analyst's view of treatment as a "collegial enterprise" enabled him to feel more flexible about the parameters introduced in relation to his request for permission. Most analysts would become uneasy about what they would have introduced in offering to meet outside of the office to discuss the issue. It seems this analyst took such a stance, at least consciously, to make the patient feel that he, the analyst, was not trying to pull him back to treatment. When the patient's reopened old worries about incomplete work, the analyst was led to worry about the meaning of his invitation to the patient. This analyst does not believe that it was ultimately problematic for this patient to be asked permission after termination, but the possibility of mobilizing old conflicts leads other analysts to take a different position about contacting patients post-treatment to request consent.

The second analyst provided an example that supports this apprehension. This analyst asked permission after termination on only one occasion. It had been a bad experience that he did not want to repeat.

> I wanted to write something in detail about a patient no longer in treatment. I called and asked her. She said probably okay. But then I wrote it and she read it and then said no. She found it upsetting to even think about it. She realized she felt betrayed to even think I thought about writing about her and it wasn't something we could explore. I wouldn't do that again.

Another analyst described requesting permission to publish some potentially embarrassing material, the kind that many analysts state they will not publish for fear of shaming their patients; this analyst believed her patient would respond positively to her request because it overlapped with a transference fantasy.

> It was about two to three years after analysis terminated when I asked the patient for his permission to write about him. I didn't write until I asked him. During analysis, he had a fantasy that we'd do something together, write something together or that I'd write about him. So maybe that influenced my choice. I did fulfill his fantasy. He had come back to see me two to three times a few months after ending, but this request occurred much later. The exchange was all by e-mail. I asked if he wanted to come in and talk with me about it but he didn't.

I was hesitant about asking him because it was a case of perversion. He was a creative and flexible man. It was hard to know where flexibility and defenses began. He could embrace everything, a manic defense. I started the paper describing where he had come to, how he had changed. But then I described the first part of the analysis as very difficult. He was surprised because he didn't know I had had such a hard time with him. He accepted this. It was a long analysis. He felt it had changed his life. He was a bit hurt and sobered but not angry, but he knew he had changed. Part of his pathology was that he was not aware of how he affected people. We did a lot of work on this in analysis. He asked me to change only one detail and one thing he said he didn't want me to write about, so of course I didn't, but neither was central to the narrative I wanted to convey. I thought he'd be fine about my writing about him, but I did think he'd want to come in and talk about it but he said he'd learned a lot from reading it and that it was fine. I asked several times. I was surprised he just accepted it, but I did start the paper with where he is psychologically now, which is a good place.

This analyst is aware that she has enacted and concretized a transference fantasy. She understands that this was a gratification. In contrast, her paper has also confronted her former patient with information about her difficulties in relation to him early in the treatment; this was something of which he had been unaware. The patient was spared negative countertransference during treatment only to be exposed to it afterward in the article. So the analyst's article offered some narcissistic gratification and some narcissistic challenge. Nevertheless, he granted permission to have this published. The analyst framed her concerns about gratifying a fantasy and confronting him with her negative countertransference. Neither action, as such, seems exactly the concern. Rather, the question is whether doing so affected his well-being.

The paper included material that might have shamed the patient; nonetheless, she felt that it was important for knowledge in the psychoanalytic field. Increasingly, analysts are concerned about publishing material on perversions because of concern they are shaming. The patient seems to have accepted the analyst's writing about him without untoward effects. But I will emphasize again that we need to remain conscious that what we do not know is how reading this paper will affect his feelings over time. The analyst stressed her surprise that he did not want to come in to talk with her in person. To pursue this would be a further intrusion. Perhaps he could only consent if he did not delve into his reactions too deeply. He wanted, perhaps, to believe it was okay.

In previous chapters, I have illustrated how more classically oriented analysts make use of their patients' reactions to reading about themselves. With only a few exceptions, the more classically oriented analysts have worked with their patients' responses as they would with anything else that they introduce out of their needs, such as going on vacation, being late, missing an appointment for personal or professional reasons, or making mistakes. In other words, they are responding to the consequences of something that they have imposed, with no notion that it would benefit the analysis. They write to serve the needs of the profession and their own professional and personal needs.

While most of the analysts who publish in *Psychoanalytic Dialogues* may also view asking permission and showing patients what they write as primarily serving their own personal and professional needs, others in this group view it as an action that benefits the patient. For analysts who take a view that reading what the analysts write is therapeutically beneficial, the writing becomes something that is then introduced with the conscious intention of it becoming an active part of the work. It is a stimulus for analysis, not a potential interference that needs to be worked with. This position is complex and controversial. In addition to providing information about patients' reactions to reading about themselves, examples where writing is utilized as a stimulus for analytic work permit us to explore clinical implications of relational theory and technique.

II. WRITING AS A STIMULUS FOR ANALYTIC WORK

Nine analysts in the sample who published in *Psychoanalytic Dialogues* have shifted from the classical position of providing an account of a patient to illustrate a theory or technique to viewing and using their papers about their patients as a tool for the treatment. As stated earlier, their conscious rationale for this practice is that the therapeutic action of psychoanalysis occurs in the context of conscious and unconscious engagement of patient and analyst where the meaning that occurs is co-constructed. As such, these analysts welcome, and may even create through the introduction of their papers, heightened transference/countertransference interactions. While this view is consonant with their theory, other motivations, both conscious and unconscious, may be ignored.

It must be remembered that these reports are based on relatively short interviews. As a result, the analysts' accounts may lack depth and complexity as an artifact of the brevity of my interview with them.

In most instances, these papers were not written with the conscious intent of furthering analytic work, but it is the view of these clinicians that the effect of their patients' reading these papers has had this positive outcome. As in many papers about clinical work, countertransference factors have been the stimulus for writing. The unconscious wish to communicate something to a patient outside of the usual channels would appear to be an additional motivation once it is expected that patients will read the analyst's paper about them. When patients read these papers, the papers become a kind of meta-communication between analyst and patient. If the analyst has made a conscious choice to communicate in this fashion, it may be an intervention that is similar to sitting up the patient for some sessions; in other words, it may be intended to break an impasse in the work that the more usual interventions have failed to accomplish. At least one of these papers was shown to the patient with this intention. In other instances, whether this agenda was the central conscious motive for writing the paper was not explicit. Unfortunately I did not ask this question. When the analyst has not tried more conventional interventions or is unaware of a motivation to move something in the patient's awareness or response, then the analyst's motivation for avoiding more direct communication needs to be considered. I will highlight the differences in conscious intent as I have understood them.

Countertransference Recognition

One analyst reported that his written material unconsciously communicated something to a patient that had not been explicit in the treatment. Consciously, he had shown it to the patient to ask her consent. Unconsciously, he may have wished her to know something about his countertransference.

The patient's father kissed her good-night which she experienced as eroticized. In the paper, I put in my reaction to her, something I'd not specifically told to her in the treatment. [The analyst leaves the specificity of his reaction to the patient unstated, but the implication is that it is his attraction to her.] It led to an explanation from me. I wasn't consciously intending the paper as a communication but it was. Then it became part of our work.

In this instance, what was revealed was specific to the analyst's countertransference to this particular patient. The analyst in this context was not unaware of these feelings. What he was not aware of was that he was using his request for permission to publish to reveal these feelings to the patient. The analyst, it seems, was conflicted about directly revealing an erotic countertransference. Many, probably most, analysts would share his concern. In this respect, by giving the patient the paper to read he bypassed a prohibition, communicating his feelings without consciously deciding that he was going to do so. He then needed to work on this revelation with the patient. The ramifications of this discovery were not presented. One needs to presume that the analyst was in a state of denial not to anticipate the impact of the paper on the patient. Countertransference reactions are inevitable as are unconscious intrusions. However, while it is courageous of the analyst to reveal to the patient as much as he did, it is also important for analysts to maintain an awareness of the need for self-scrutiny.

In the next example, what the patient picked up from the shared material was a more general attitude on the analyst's part, rather than a specific reaction to the patient; however, the analyst's attitude had particular pertinence to the patient's background. This analyst's conscious motive for showing the patient his paper was also to request her permission for publication.

One patient's concerns were organized around social class issues and feelings of being disrespected. When she read a paper I wrote about her, she found evidence of disrespect in what I wrote and called my attention to it in a playful, but slightly sadistic, way. She reacted to my wording that she had "kicked alcohol." I could see what she meant. It really called my attention to how she perceived me. It brought into focus the different things she saw as disrespectful which she hadn't formulated that way before, for example, my taking vacation when I wanted to and her having to pay when she went on vacation. My saying that the rules were for my benefit helped because she thought I was hypocritically covering up and pretending it was for her benefit. All this became clearer after she read what I wrote.

In this case, the written material provided supportive data for the patient's perception of the analyst's attitude of disrespect and sensitized the analyst to her point of view. It would appear that he confirmed the accuracy of her perception about what she had detected in his paper; she then felt freer to voice her complaints about other areas where she believed his disrespect showed. But this in turn enabled the analyst to clarify that she had attributed disrespect to details of the framework where it did not exist; he did so by clarifying the motives for these rules. It is not clear whether he also encouraged the patient to associate and to elaborate on this perception of disrespect since this was not the focus of his communication in the interview with me. In accordance with his theoretical beliefs, he openly communicated his own views and new self-awareness. The written material does not seem to have brought about new insight to the patient; it only confirmed her perceptions. It was the analyst who learned about himself more clearly and then used it for further clarification with the patient. The patient, in this respect, had served as his supervisor.

Another analyst offered a similar example. He also focused on the beneficial nature of his increased appreciation of countertransference reactions that a patient had perceived and addressed after reading the analyst's paper. He too consciously intended only to ask for permission.

> When patients read something I've written, sometimes they appreciate being portrayed sympathetically but when they don't feel this way, it leads to tensions and sometimes ruptures in the work. We explore how they feel misperceived or misunderstood. Sometimes this leads me to see my biases or limitations, the factors in me that have kept me from seeing something about them. For example, one woman was ambivalent about treatment versus being part of a cult. She saw my writing about this as reductionistic. I had tried to see her perspective but in reading what I wrote she saw me not getting or appreciating her point of view in her conflict. Seeing this, I felt, helped me to broaden my perspective.

All three analysts described that patients' reading papers written about them enabled the patients to show their analysts something about the analyst that had not previously been conscious. As such, the patients calling attention to the analyst's attitude or feeling about them as it is manifested in the writing served as an interpretation that the analysts were able to take in. Two of these analysts indicated that their patients had previously tried to make them aware of their attitudes, but they had not grasped the validity of the patients' perception until they could see the evidence in their own written material. Again the patient functioned as a supervisor. The patients' reading, then, had been used in a temporary reversal of role where the patient observed and interpreted the analyst. If the analyst can resist being defensive, as these three analysts were able to do, then the patient can feel validated and understood, and analysis may proceed and deepen. These analysts all maintain that showing the paper to the patient facilitated analytic work. Their focus in their interviews with me was not on the question of how to preserve confidentiality—they were completely committed to always asking permission—but on the benefit to the patient from reading about themselves.

In other instances, however, the patient's perception of the analyst's countertransference may cause disruption to the work. One analyst offered an example:

> My patient was first excited that I was writing about her. She felt like Freud's daughter. But when she read what I wrote she was inflamed. I ended with a quote from Adam Phillips about flirtation: "You can play and keep things alive and not serious." She was enraged, feeling my countertransference more play than real. She couldn't tolerate the sense I was putting our work in intellectual, theoretical terms. She felt it as abandonment. She wanted it to be that I was writing about her because I was so taken with her, not because it illustrated something. For me to have an interest in theory was something just for me. It altered the developmental progress of the analysis. This was not a good outcome. I was writing about a transference that had not been fully explored both in relation to the ongoing transference and to the meaning of my writing to her.

This analyst recognized the interference that his patient's reading about her analysis posed for their analytic work. As in many other examples, the patient's reading what the analyst wrote brought the transference meaning to the fore. The analyst was both honest and self-reflective. He acknowledged that he had not carefully enough thought through the effect that reading the paper might have on the patient based on the state of her transference and the limits of her understanding of it at the time. The kind of self-reflection that he refers to is all that one can reasonably expect when analysts make their decisions. It is an illusion to think that one can ever know enough to really be sure how a patient will react. This patient did not want to know about the analyst except in terms of his involvement with her. Nor did she want what they were doing together to have meaning or use for him apart from their engagement with each other. Her recognition of the "as if" nature of the work shattered her sense of connection with him. Not every patient reacts this way. One of Bridges's (unpublished paper 2003) patients, who initially was injured in a similar fashion, ultimately attained a therapeutic benefit from the experience of reading about himself. As one analyst described in an earlier chapter, some patients can appreciate that the analyst has a professional life that is separate from the patient's personal use of analysis (Crastnopol 1999). Gerson (2000) points out that for some patients the imagined presence of this professional community as a third party, privy to their work, is reassuring. The challenge is to discern which patients will experience it in that manner and which will not.

TAKING IN THE ANALYST'S PRESENCE

Other analysts employ their writing in a much more conscious fashion as part of analysis. One analyst illustrated this process of using writing to engage his patient differently.

> I recently asked someone's permission. She's still in treatment and we could make something together of my thinking of her. First she found it exciting, but then she found it a violation, but she could stay with it in ways that are possibly good for analysis and probably not bad for her in general. She gave permission and I showed it to her. I don't know what informed consent would mean given who she is and what our relationship is. She's not in a position to say no. She was excited by the ideas I had about her and that I was thinking about her in that way, but then it felt like it was nothing about her, all about my ideas, aggrandizing my ideas and exploitative of her. This reaction is so thematically connected with the whole analysis; analysis is

for my benefit. She fights and resists the process; she doesn't want me to get the benefit of her getting better. Instead of putting the writing aside, as I would with other patients who have said they didn't want me to write. I moved forward more aggressively, making it an issue between us. I more assertively engaged her passivity. I wanted the issue alive in the work between us.

This analyst had introduced his request for permission and shown the patient what he has written with a clear and conscious intent to get the patient to think about his thinking about her. He wanted her to examine his view of her. The writing was used to stimulate her activity, to awaken her interest in their interaction. His stated motivation for the request was not about getting permission but about provoking her increased engagement in analysis. Presumably, this analyst had tried the more usual analytic techniques without success and introduced the paper as another mode of communication in an attempt to free an impasse in analysis. This example is the clearest illustration of how writing can be enlisted specifically as a vehicle in analytic work.

Another analyst also used the written material to help the patient become aware of the analyst. The paper had not been written with this motive, but the analyst believed that disclosure had a felicitous effect.

> I asked my patient's permission to present material about her for a panel. She agreed and didn't ask more about it. Later she became curious and wanted to read it. She took the paper and kept it and it became an integral part of our work. She'd reread and come in and say she saw something more. It enabled her to see more. The paper was very personal about me. She had trouble making me into a real person. So reading the paper was hard for her but edifying because she was so struck by her inability to make me a subject. She wanted to do that consciously but she'd been unable to do it and reading the paper made that emotional inability come home to her. When she'd reread it, she'd realize that she forgot that her mother had been depressed. She'd told me her mother had been suicidal, but she had never integrated that into her representation of her mother, as something intrapsychically important to her. My denial of my mother's pain was something that I had put in the paper. The fact that she learned that I had a powerful affective life helped her integrate her awareness of her defenses against knowing of that powerful affect in herself. She began to become aware of her feelings. Also she learned that I had subjective reactions in the sessions; she had walled off knowing that. Even though

there were warm moments that she acknowledged, she didn't take them in as a full experience. Reading the paper and bringing it in over time began to bring in more feeling in her and between us.

In this instance, the analyst's intention, at least initially, was not directed toward helping the patient take in the analyst's presence. The analyst did not give the patient her paper to read until it was requested. However, in writing the paper, the analyst may have acted out her frustration at not being perceived as a subject by her analysand. Most analysts agree that once permission is asked, if patients wish to read the paper they should be allowed to do so or the analyst must forgo using the material publicly. By involving the patient in reading very personal material about the analyst, an interpretation stimulated in the countertransference is bypassed and replaced by an action. It could be hypothesized that the transference to the analyst was as the patient's depressed mother. If that is accurate, then the analyst's presence was acknowledged, possibly as a danger that had to be walled off. The analyst may have been trying to defend against a very distressing transference projection. It seems likely that the patient had avoided understanding how ill her mother was because the experience was too overwhelming and she needed to protect herself from such intense fear. The analyst may have used the writing of the paper as a way to express and explore what the patient stimulated in her, an unconscious management of a countertransference that she may not have understood in respect to the patient's conflicts. The analyst did not seem conscious of considering the impact on the patient of reading it. It may be speculated that in revealing her pain in relation to her own mother, the analyst showed the possibility of affect containment—the analyst unlike the patient can allow painful memory to be conscious—that the patient can use in an identification. In this respect, the analyst may be stimulating an identifactory self- transference and thereby evading the more painful and frightening maternal transference. It was the patient who used her reading of the paper to begin to perceive the analyst as both separate from, and similar to, herself. The analyst seemed less aware of the patient's use of the paper in terms of recognizing similarity. However, possibly, what the analyst reported is only the first step in a process. In both these examples, the papers concretize the analyst as an other. Both patients seem to have had difficulty sustaining a sense of the analyst as separate from themselves.

In the first example, it seems that the patient projected negative aspects of her experience onto the analyst and did not allow him close enough to engage in the work. In the second instance, the analyst felt that the patient was not taking in an awareness of the analyst as a person with her own sets of feelings, reactions, and personal history. Whether or not my added speculations about this second case are correct, it is clear that the patient has used reading the paper to advance her analytic work.

A written paper invites the patient to use a different way of integrating information. The analyst's voice—the auditory experience of the analyst—is not in the process but his ideas are made visible and remain permanently available. The information can be returned to again and again, unchanged by memory or desire. A paper holds a reality steady for a patient to absorb at his own pace. It makes a link between patient and analyst, but it also presents them as having different centers of volition. Both these analysts are exploring a new technique. Writing has become a tool of the treatment, helping to provide reflection on boundaries, helping boundaries to be perceived. These accounts do not make it clear why the analysts thought a new technique was necessary to facilitate this perception, but both analysts seem to have subjected the action and its ramifications to inquiry that promoted analytic work.

Enhancing Attention to Ongoing Analytic Issues

The next analyst also points out how reading what the analyst has written about her disrupts her patient's construction of her analyst's attitudes and feelings for the patient. Like the previous two patients, she needs to readjust her perception. But this patient, unlike the other two, has her perception challenged more around a specific construction than in terms of her whole sense of self. The work with the paper is described as part of the ongoing analysis more than as a stimulus that introduces something new.

> I wrote about a patient who had been hospitalized and its effect. It was near termination. My patient is in the field. The patient read it and was tearful. It was a revisiting of how this experience had shaped the patient's way of being. But the experience is mixed because of

termination; it's taking something from the patient, making use of it. The patient questions whether the patient has moved fast enough, made enough progress, whether I like the patient, really cared. These questions were there. Reading the chapter made them come up more explicitly. It was mixed to re-experience something that had been so difficult and painful. It was always present intellectually; reading it made it present emotionally. In the transference, the patient feels I am throwing the patient out. Reading what I've written threatens this construction that the patient is not important to me. The article makes the patient feel specially connected to me. The patient showed the paper to the patient's spouse who says, "Only way you'll get into print." That focuses the competitive aspects both between them and with me. The trauma I am writing about . . . being left by parents, feeling isolated, abandoned, and indifference from them—termination becomes a version of that. The patient feels an embarrassment that these feelings have been so tenacious. It's humiliating to the patient that these feelings have shadowed the patient's life. But it heightens the work on these feelings in the termination and increases our focus on them.

In this instance, it seems that the patient and analyst have been actively working on the transference issues of anxieties about whether she is cared for and her fear of abandonment. The patient's reading the paper did not introduce any content of which patient or analyst was unaware. Rather it augmented the patient's experience and brought in an intensified affective awareness. It may be that the patient was better able to allow her feelings because she felt less vulnerable. The paper gave her information about her analyst's attitude toward her. It confronted her fears that her analyst held the same attitudes as she felt her parents had. Unlike the previous examples, this analyst does not seem to be saying that reading the paper was needed for this to occur. Rather the analyst is presenting this example to illustrate how writing can augment the experience in the ongoing work.

Another analyst wrote about the effect of his infant daughter's illness and death on his work with a patient. He describes how both the event and the patient's reading about it were woven into the analytic work.

This is the only time I made the material from what I was writing part of the work. I was writing a chapter in a book that concerned serious illness in the analyst's family and its relationship to the analytic work. My second daughter was born with a severe illness and died when she was one year old. This occurred in the early part of my work with someone whom I worked with for seven or eight years. The chapter involved my patient as my colleague. Around this experience there was symmetry in our relationship. I highlighted what occurred that my patient observed and how he responded to me with generosity and relatedness. It shaped collaboration, an identification between us, a symbiotic experience in the transference/countertransference. He'd lost his father when he was very young and grew up with a depressed mother; he felt he and his mother were like Siamese twins. One of his reasons for choosing me as his analyst was a feeling he had that I was depressed enough for him to feel at home. He became aware that I had a daughter who was very ill. I was missing a lot of work. I told him—I told most of my patients—basically anyone who asked. I felt the desire and inclination to do so. I felt it kept me emotionally present. Two years after my daughter's death I'd written a proposal for this chapter. I had not yet asked him for permission to write about him. He was a writer himself and was trying to get a good friend, whose first name is the same as mine, to send off a manuscript and was talking about this the same morning I was sending my proposal in. It felt uncanny. I asked about his ideas in relationship to writing. He thought I had an ambition for it but had been inhibited. I told him and showed him my proposal. He read it, described a little competitive feeling because he thought it was good. He also felt he played a role in helping me fulfill my ambition by being collaborative. I think this sense of being collaborative and helpful to me was central to changes in feelings about himself. He could do something helpful that he hadn't been able to do with his mother.

This analyst illustrates a belief in the therapeutic action of analysis as occurring through an experience of the analyst as a new object (Loewald 1960). In the example, this experience is concretized by collaboration and mutuality in both the work and the writing. While the analyst generally views his patients as collaborators in the work, the specific need and connection to the patient stirred in him by his daughter's illness and death may have played a major role in his decision to share this writing with his patient during their work. It is the only occasion he did this. All other writing has been done after analyses have terminated.

Another analyst emphasizes the view that her patients' reading about their work was a vehicle for sharpening awareness and focusing attention on some aspect that is defended against. Although she does not present this motive as her only or central reason for showing patients what she has written about them, her belief that this kind of therapeutic benefit occurs makes her feel more comfortable asking permission to use material for publication.

> One patient appreciates scholarship so it enhances her trust in me when she reads what I write. It's not only how we work together but also how I think that makes her feel safe. I make a point to talk to her about her defenses and character style, how she inundates analysis with stories; it's her, not only a defense, it's her signature. I highlight how she uses the work—a structure as well as a defense. After reading this, she begins to question herself if what she is doing at a given moment is a defense or whether she is trying to communicate something. Of course it can be both; but what is its purpose right then? It sharpens her attention to what she is doing at the given moment.
>
> I also used some terms in relation to her husband, on whom she is hyper-dependent, in ways I might not say them directly to her. I described her idealization of him and their hyper-dependency on each other. It becomes something she can be more aware of. I hadn't been that explicit about her idealization of him in our work. At the time she read it, she said, "Hmmm. We're very close; maybe there's some idealization." It didn't hit her over the head as it might in an interpretation. This was more of an aside. But some time later she came back to it as something she realized more. The writing focused it and brought it more to the center of her awareness.

In this example, unlike the others, the focus is less on the transference/countertransference relationship and more on the patient's taking in awareness of defense against intrapsychic aspects in the patient. Like the previous analyst, this analyst emphasizes that the written word helps to focus the patient's attention on an issue that was already part of analytic work.

Reflections on Patients' Reading Their Analyst's Writing as a Stimulus to Analytic Work

Relational analysts have pioneered a new way to think about the introduction of the analyst's writing into analytic work. All these analysts provide examples of writing as facilitating. They are convinced that the patient, analyst, or both, and presumably both in the long run, benefit from this process. Based on some of the examples, it can be shown that some patients may benefit from the concrete expression in writing. They are able to better absorb something through reading than they can take in from spoken words—perhaps because they can hold these ideas constant by reintroducing them into their awareness when they begin to slip away. It may be that the written material provides a kind of transitional object, creating an object constancy for these patients that the real person of the analyst does not. Relational analysts may be illustrating the benefit of this technique for particular kinds of patients for whom usual analytic techniques are insufficient. But not every patient needs this.

The theory that the therapeutic efficacy of analysis occurs in conscious and unconscious interactions, co-constructed by patient and analyst, provides relational analysts with a justification for this method. As analysts, however, we are aware that decisions are rarely, if ever, based only on conscious rationales. Analysts wish to publish their papers; this wish is most often their leading, conscious reason for writing. There is nothing ignoble about personal ambition as long as it does not lead to insensitivity or disrespect for others. Unconscious factors also fuel wishes to publish. I have previously discussed the role that narcissistic and exhibitionistic needs may play in writing, as well as unconscious use of patients. I wish to underscore again that the conscious and unconscious motives for writing are not unique to psychoanalysts, and that all scholarship likely has some similar dynamic underpinnings, though individual variations make generalizations simplistic.

The fact that psychoanalysis as a field not only benefits from but needs published clinical illustrations is indisputable; this makes analysts' personal ambitions and unconscious needs useful for the advancement of knowledge as well as the benefit of future patients. Relational analysts are now suggesting that the patient written about may also benefit. Even if both the state of knowledge and present and future patients also gain in the process, nonetheless, self-interests more than altruistic motives are likely to be the impetus for writing.

Once analysts believe their patients gain something from their writing about them, the conflict between writing to benefit the field and the clinical effect on the patient dissolves. Certainly, when analysts believe this is true it takes them out of the terrible dilemma of conflicting loyalties. Analysts' personal ambitions can then also be fulfilled with less angst, and unconscious self-interests stir less conscious conflict. But there remains the question of when is the reading really benefiting the patient and when does the analyst only wish this to be so.

Reading about themselves distresses many patients. As will become clear in the next section, some patients who do not mind being written about, also do not want to know about it, much less read what their analyst has written about them. Asking permission is not a safeguard against patients' negative reactions; in a number of interviews with former patients, requesting permission to write about a patient was the first step in the loss of differentiation of roles between analyst and patient. The patients who report these experiences found this blurring of boundaries very detrimental to their analytic experience. Of course, such transgressions do not always happen, but when analysts rationalize their actions they are more likely to occur. On the other hand, in support of the relational analysts' position, certainly there is benefit to patients when analysts can see and acknowledge their contribution to conflicts between them. I am not referring to analysts' disclosing these contributions to their patients but simply knowing them. Undoubtedly once analysts become aware of the personal aspect that has intruded, analysts gain new knowledge about themselves that can also make them more sensitive and effective in their work.

But if patients do know their analysts' conflicts, thoughts, and feelings, what are the long-term effects of patients *knowing* because their analysts have confirmed their fantasies about how their analysts feel about them versus knowing in a more ambiguous way? When does knowing that one has had an impact on one's analyst solidify a belief in one's perceptions and feeling respected by another and when does this become a burdensome sense of having too much power? We are all now aware that there are a myriad of ways that patients discern many things about their analysts' attitudes, values, beliefs, even their character and conflicts, without the analysts ever making any of these explicit. But what I am maintaining is that there is a difference between what is implicit and explicit. When it is implicit, patients may think they "know"; nonetheless, this "knowing" remains in an area of ambiguity. This area is the analytic space of "as if" and play. As Chused (1992) stated, even if what a patient perceives about the analyst is true, it doesn't mean it is not also transference. What is the effect of collapsing this space? Might this reinforce patients' defenses and resistances? Inadvertent enactments can be informative to both patient and analyst, but to intentionally act in this fashion seems different.

Another question is what limits does concretization place on analysis? Can patients as freely pursue and explicate their fantasies when they know how their analysts really feel about them? And what does "really" mean? We know that patients' feelings about their analysts evolve and change during the work. Wouldn't we assume the same would be true for analysts? And what about the analysts' unconscious? Analysts can only write about what they consciously know, and it is unlikely they will write all of that fully. Once something is written it is there forever, but the feelings that have been recorded and transcribed may not have the same permanence. This last point needs special consideration since the writing is used as part of the work, and it is being done during the process, not after the process is ended. After termination there is more perspective and a clearer sense of what one feels and the meaning of what has been felt. Analysts may be aware that they are describing something that reflects only the current moment, but will their patients share this awareness? Is it reasonable to expect that of them? For those who can and do, will reading foster intellectualization? For some patients that may be helpful, providing a distance to more freely explore without becoming flooded by affect, but for others it may serve as defense against the very affective experience that they need.

When does an acknowledgment of an erotic countertransference provide an elevation of self-esteem that allows a patient to more freely love and be loved in the world, and when does it create an interference with the development of loving others? It is not always clear when the analyst is revealing these feelings for the sake of the patient and when it is for himself or herself. Unconscious factors push these decisions. How can one be sure?

The examples provided mainly focus on the benefits of patients taking in more about how their analysts "really " are and "really" feel about the patient. The assumption seems to be that this action on the part of the analyst is for the sake of the patient and the treatment. As analysts, we all know that motivations are more complex and multi-determined. In most of these examples, the darker sides of the analyst's conscious and unconscious motives are given little consideration.

Sometimes showing patients what the analyst has written about them may have less kind motivation behind it. The motives for writing and showing patients what is written are always multiply determined. Revelation of feeling that a patient is special or loved may have to do with the analyst's need to bind the patient to the analyst. Conscious or unconscious anger or sadism may be revealed.

There are dangers of analysts revealing these feelings, not just to their patients but also to themselves. As one relational analyst said, speech is a performative act. It may not be so much a danger that the patient knows what the analyst feels as that the analyst may begin to lose his or her own sense of being the analyst. We have learned that boundary crossings and violations are far more frequent than we had known.

The effect of knowledge of positive feelings, even when they are not so charged, is also not so clear. It is possible that patients' knowing that their analysts have definite positive feelings for them may stimulate fantasies of being special that open material to be explored, but it may also close off other material. Some patients describe a fear of revealing material that might change the analyst's positive view or increase it. Every countertransference perception is janus-faced for patients. Feeling unimportant or too important each has a cost.

And what about negative feelings or even hate in the countertransference? Some of the relational analysts state that these reactions to patients are processed in the work before they are written about. An analyst's anger if visible would need to be processed and understood. But if there is countertransference hatred unless both patient and analyst could really understand this as projective identification, how could this be absorbed? And why would the analyst choose to reveal it? Can any patient really integrate that as a fact, not an unconfirmed fantasy, that they have been hated? Maybe. But again over time, what will this mean? It seems likely that at times of stress or self-doubt, this concretization would be returned to and turned against themselves. There are times when patients do benefit from explicit confirmation or disconfirmation from their analysts, but which occasions call for this response needs to be carefully considered.

In an earlier chapter, I raised concern when analysts turned away from struggling with conflicts about employing only disguise in their published papers. The avoidance of deeper self-reflection and considerations of complex motivations that might mitigate the use of their preferred stance were troubling in some examples. Similarly, some analysts who invariably ask consent and show patients what they write may be avoiding the struggles and conflicts with the opposite solution. Asking permission when there is a chance that patients may find articles and recognize themselves seems essential, but sometimes the question may be whether these articles should be submitted for publication. Sometimes involving patients in one's writing may be detrimental to their treatment.

A further question is why this new technique is needed. In the last example, the analyst made it clear that the patient did not need the writing to do the work, but reading the writing facilitated the process by amplifying her awareness of preconscious aspects of herself. The analyst viewed it as a gentler way of confronting her. The data support the analyst's view that the patient benefited from reading about herself, at least in the present moment. Many relational analysts argue that it is these engagements that promote psychological change. It is the philosophic underpinning of their theory. But if the patient does not need this prod—the analyst in this case states that it was not necessary to introduce something through action for this patient to reflect about herself—then what is gained by introducing it, rather than letting the patient more gradually come to recognize her conflicts? Does such a decision reflect a lack of patience? Some analysts would argue that analyses take too long and anything that speeds the process is of value. But we do not know the consequences of making the analyst and the analyst's thoughts and feelings more transparent.

These examples make clear that analysts may be revealing attitudes, beliefs, and countertransference affects of which they may be unaware. They need to be open to what their patients may perceive that was unintended, as many of these analysts were. Relational analysts believe this is all part of the work. And many times it may be very effective. Just like the decision to ask permission or only disguise, the decisions need to be individualized. Self-reflection is essential for analysts as well as patients.

Data on the long-term ramifications of this technique are not yet known. What we do know is that transferences are sturdier than originally they were presumed to be. Knowledge of facts about one's analyst rarely interferes with transference proclivities. As some of these examples illustrate, some patients continue to strongly defend against taking in the individual characteristic of their analysts. These relational analysts used their writing to reveal countertransferences to their patients and/or themselves, to make themselves known and to help the patient know themselves as separate, and to highlight issues or transference/countertransference conflicts. More classical analysts have different theoretical views and more standard technical approaches to these problems. The method of the relational analysts is an ongoing experiment that may teach us more about analysis itself.

But there is another consideration; analysts' decisions to involve patients with their publications potentially may have an effect on the readers of psychoanalytic literature. As stated in the opening chapter, Levin (2003) argues that no matter how therapeutically or clinically useful it may be to have a patient involved in the analyst's report of clinical material, it should never be done. His concern is that once it is common practice that psychoanalytic papers have been read and approved by patients, the readers of the literature will no longer believe that the analysts are free to express their views. Rather readers will believe that the clinical picture that is presented will be censored by the narcissistic needs of the patients.

Based on my interviews with analysts in this study, there is reason to believe that many analysts are selective in the material they published even prior to asking patients for permission based on their concern for patients' sensitivities. It should be noted that a number of analyst-authors who never ask permission and only disguise also share these concerns and restrict their writing about areas they believe would be shaming to their patients. Levin's position presupposes that all analysts will begin to involve their patients in decisions about publication of their clinical material. While the current trend is an increase in the direction of seeking patient's permission, many analysts, even 23 percent of the relational analysts interviewed, still rely on disguises and do not, except in rare circumstances, ask consent. As long as a sizable literature exists that is not dependent on patient approval, I do not think psychoanalysts need worry about the loss of credibility in what they write for the public based on patient censorship.

The danger is not so much that the readership come to distrust what analysts write, but that if all papers were shared with patients and dependent on their approval the literature would exclude many important topics out of concern for patients' sensitivities. In many instances, analysts are probably quite accurate in assuming their patients would be hurt, hopefully not by their tone or any lack of respect, but by the embarrassment of making public something that is intensely private and possibly humiliating to them. Under these circumstances, unless analysts can be quite sure their patients are not identifiable and will not themselves seek out these papers, they need to sacrifice the benefit to the public to protect their patients. But often this is not a necessary choice and analysts can find a way to preserve their patient's confidentiality and contribute to the field of knowledge without involving their patients when they believe such an involvement might be detrimental.

My turning the focus to the topic of disguise-only versus asking patients' consent is because the method found by the analyst-authors presented in this chapter is compelling. As stated earlier, if analysts believe they can benefit their patient as well as themselves and the field by writing about them, the conflict of loyalties disappears. It would then be easy for this practice to become the community standard and for those who continued to use only disguise to be viewed as, and come to view themselves, as behaving in an aberrant fashion. Over time, aberrant behavior could come to be viewed as unacceptable behavior. If this standard of patient involvement with publication then became normative and was seen as the only acceptable behavior, Levin's concern would be warranted. It would also be granting patients an inordinate amount of power that likely would not be to their benefit. It surely would be detrimental to the literature in psychoanalysis.

Using written clinical material as a vehicle for therapeutic work is a creative innovation. There are many patients who may benefit from its introduction. But it needs to be employed reflectively and judiciously. And we need to learn about the long-range ramifications of employing it. It does not suit every patient or every clinician. Nothing can substitute for individual clinical judgment and sensitivity. We need diversity in our methods for preserving confidentiality and doing clinical work that are tailored to the particular patient–analyst pair.

Having learned how analysts view patients' reactions when they read about themselves, in the next section of the book I will provide patients' perspectives.

III

PATIENTS' ACCOUNTS OF THE EFFECT OF READING ABOUT THEMSELVES

10
Philip Roth's Discovery

"A successful Italian-American poet in his forties entered into therapy because of anxiety states experienced as a result of his enormous ambivalence about leaving his wife . . ." this had to be me. Only I had not been in my forties when I first became Spielvogel's patient; I'd come to him at age twenty-nine, wrecked by a mistake I'd made at twenty-six. Surely between a man in his forties and a man in his twenties there are differences in experience, expectation, and character that cannot be brushed aside so easily as this . . . And "successful"? Does that word (in my mind I immediately began addressing Spielvogel directly), describe to you the tenor of my life at that time? A "successful" apprenticeship absolutely, but when I came to you in 1962, at age twenty-nine, I had for three years been writing fiction I couldn't stand, and I could no longer even teach a class without fear . . . to disguise (in my brother's words) "a nice civilized Jewish boy" as something called "an Italian-American," well, that is to be somewhat dim-witted about matters of social and cultural background that might well impinge upon a person's psychology and values. . . . And while we're at it, Dr. Spielvogel, a poet and a novelist have about as much in common as a jockey and a diesel driver. . . . And so it went, my chagrin renewed practically with each word. I could not read a sentence in which it did not seem to me that the observation was off, the point missed, the nuance blurred, in short, the evidence rather munificently distorted so as to support a narrow and unilluminating thesis at the expense of the ambiguous and perplexing actuality. In all there were only two pages on the "Italian-American poet," but so angered and disappointed was I by what seemed to me the unflagging wrongness of the description of my case that it took me ten minutes to get from the top of page 85 to the bottom of 86. [pp. 239–240]

Philip Roth's outrage, expressed through his protagonist Peter Tarnopol, eloquently conveys many patients' reactions to similar discoveries. Tarnopol objects to the characterization of his father as "ineffectual" and Tarnopol's relationships with women as "masturbatory sexual objects." The sense of confusion and betrayal are intense: "How can you who have done me so much good, have it all so wrong?" (p. 243). But then there is momentary relief when he realizes that the disguise, though malforming, conceals his real identity since Dr. Spielvogel goes on to describe and diagnose graphic details of his sexual activities. However, the next paragraph strips away this protection for Spielvogel recounts a childhood incident that Tarnopol himself had written about in more detail and published in *The New Yorker* as an autobiographical story the month before. He placed his name as author of the story. He had talked about this story in analysis. Dr. Spielvogel knew this incident was included in his published narrative. His sense of betrayal escalates.

Tarnopol shows the paper to his girlfriend. "This straw fucking patient is supposed to be me!" (p. 246). She reads it and is alternately shocked by what she learns about Tarnopol and outraged by his analyst's betrayal of his confidence. Encouraged by his girlfriend, he calls Spielvogel who agrees to extend his day to see him since he is "so distressed." After a week of hearing Tarnopol call him "untrustworthy," "unethical," "wrong," and vent his fury about the analyst's misperceptions about his family and himself, Spielvogel tells Tarnopol that he has to forget about this article or leave treatment with him. Tarnopol is more shocked by this than even reading the article. He has an investment in this analysis, doesn't consider himself recovered, and is scared to be on his own. He has felt enormously helped by Spielvogel, but that does not mean he can forget the article. The argument continues. Spielvogel claims he did nothing wrong. Tarnopol pursues his anger over Spielvogel's not changing or leaving out the incident, or withdrawing his article once Spielvogel read his story. His analyst had failed to protect his privacy. "What's more important, publishing your article or keeping my trust . . . mightn't you at the very least have thought to ask my permission, ask if it was all right with me . . ." (pp. 249–250).

Spielvogel proffers the defense that scientific papers such as this could not be written and shared with colleagues if analysts had to rely on permission and approval of their patients. Patients might want to censor material that they found "unpleasant" or view as distorted things they did not like to face about themselves. Spielvogel asserts that it is not his loss of privacy that distresses Tarnopol but the fact the he feels his analyst has "plagiarized and abused" his material.

In this fictional interchange, Roth has vividly portrayed the experience of some patients when they discover they have been written about: the anger about the disguise that malforms their conflicts or seems to reveal the analyst's misunderstanding of them, the hurt about being viewed as a specimen, reduced to a syndrome and talked about in technical, pathologizing terms, the sense of betrayal that their confidentiality has not been adequately protected, and the violation of trust that permission was not asked. The analyst's defensive response continues the injury and makes it worse. He takes no responsibility for his actions and offers no empathy to his patient. Worse still, he wants to hear no more about it and tells his patient his choice is to forget his outrage or leave. He has injured and then threatened to abandon his patient. The patient wants to remain; his dependency and conflicts keep him caught in this terrible situation.

Of course, all of this is told from the patient's vantage point, as will be all the accounts in this section, and just as we could not fully know—and sometimes could not know at all—the patient's view in the earlier sections of the book, so in this section we cannot know the analyst's. But Roth also allows this analyst, who is portrayed as grossly insensitive and self-serving, if not worse, to speak the arguments of many analysts who defend the merits of employing only disguise: a scientific literature that is subject to patient permission and approval will not be viewed as credible (Levin 2003).

As it turns out, the account of discovery of the article in the novel is not fiction. Like Tarnopol's *New Yorker* story, Roth has suggested that this part of the novel is autobiographical (there are different versions of his life as a man in the book); this section is called "My True Story." But Roth's indirect and still ambiguous acknowledgment would not be sufficient data to do more than suspect it as a veridical account of his experience. However, convincing evidence is provided by Berman, a professor of literature at S.U.N.Y. Albany, in his book *The Talking Cure: Literary Representations of Psychoanalysis* (1985). Berman shows that Tarnopol's and Roth's biographies parallel each other in the factual details that one would put on a curriculum vitae as well as in the details surrounding Roth's first marriage. But even more compelling is Berman's demonstration that line for line Roth puts words in Spielvogel's article that appeared in an article by Dr. Hans J. Kleinschmidt (1967) called "The Angry Act: The Role of Aggression in Creativity," in the Spring–Summer issue of *American Imago*. Kleinschmidt's article used material that Roth published in *Portnoy's Complaint* (1969)[1]; this material, Roth-Tarnopol maintains, has been previously revealed in analysis and Kleinschmidt-Spielvogel knew it was included in his book. Roth's book *My Life as a Man* (1970) includes Roth's creative, angry response to his analyst.

In his article, Kleinschmidt presents his Italian-American poet in all his perversity and with all the technical and detached terminology that infuriates Tarnopol in the novel. The article's premise is that artists have had childhoods in which they have felt special and different; they are overly dependent on their mothers whom they idealize and defend against this by relying on a primary narcissism. The result of this narcissism is that the artist feels indifferent to the needs of others and is chronically angry. To create a "near perfect artistic object means to have committed the crime, the angry act" (Kleinschmidt, p. 116). Most of the article is devoted to Kandinsky and Thomas Mann, but there are two clinical cases presented at the end, disguised in the manner Roth describes in his novel. Roth's fictionalized account exposes his analyst as he himself felt exposed. It seems an elegantly executed act of revenge. In the heated fictionalized exchange between patient and analyst, the analyst defends himself by saying that his patient was continually exposing intimate details about people in his real life that were identifiable. The patient retorts that it is not the novelists' professional responsibility to protect others' privacy. His point is, of course, correct. However, the consequences in both treatment and life when people find

---

1. Kleinschmidt claims he never read Roth's novel before writing his article.

their privacy has been invaded and used to serve another's aim may be far-reaching and untoward in its effect on the relationship.

Should any doubt remain that Kleinschmidt was Roth's analyst, Berman's interview with Kleinschmidt (Berman 2001) dispels it. Before publishing his book *The Talking Cure* (1985), Berman sent a copy of the chapter about Roth to Kleinschmidt and asked for his comments. Kleinschmidt was irate; in a telephone call to Berman, he denied that Berman had proven anything, said the article would irreparably damage his reputation, and threatened to sue him if he published it. Berman successfully argued the legitimacy of his right to use this material since it was all from published, not confidential, sources. Kleinschmidt withdrew his threat and asked Berman to make some revisions. Berman agreed to do so. Kleinschmidt in a follow-up letter again denied that Berman had proven anything and threatened to sue. Berman reiterated his justification for publishing. When he brought the revised chapter to Kleinschmidt at his office, Kleinschmidt at first continued both his denial and threats, but finally admitted that the facts were correct and provided additional information. He had declined to read *Portnoy's Complaint* while Roth was in analysis and had been shocked when he did read it to discover that the material in it was the same as in his article.

Like some of the analysts that patients describe in this section, Kleinschmidt's boundary crossing was not restricted to writing about patients with inadequate disguise and without asking permission. Adam Gopnik, who was also Kleinschmidt's patient (Berman 2001), reported that Kleinschmidt talked about his famous patients by name. In a *New Yorker* article Gopnik (1998) recounts his experience of disappointment and disillusionment with psychoanalysis. "He talked about them so freely that I sometimes half expected him to put up autographed glossies around the office" (p. 114). According to Gopnik, these creative people and gossip about them were the topic of his hours rather than a focus on him and his difficulties.

Failure to protect patients' confidentiality in this blatant fashion, assuming Gopnik's account is accurate, is totally unacceptable. Roth, through Spielvogel, claims that to him the bigger violation may actually be that he believes his analyst has plagiarized and abused his material. While Tarnopol, as Roth's mouthpiece, has really lost his privacy, some analysts (Furlong 1998, 2004) argue, similarly to the fictional Spielvogel, that what really distresses patients is the discovery of the analyst's use of the patient in the service of the analyst's interest and desires.

One may ask why Roth or Gopnik or any of the patients who have been treated so poorly remain with these analysts. Roth addresses this question. In his novel, he says a dependency becomes established and patients are reluctant to leave even when they realize they have been treated badly. Transference is powerful. It also seems that for all his outrageousness Kleinschmidt had a charismatic charm and warmth. Even Berman (2001) acknowledges a momentary wish to be his patient.

Fortunately, such outrageous behavior is not characteristic of most analysts, but it does occur. Often it is not possible to assess what part is the patient's perception, colored by transference, and what the analyst has actually done. Analysts' account are usually assumed to be more veridical since they are the ones in positions of authority and assumed to be more objective (Joffe 2003), but documented reports of boundary violations (Gabbard and Lester 1995) make it clear that this assumption is not always correct.

Apart from Philip Roth's fictionalized, but nonetheless autobiographical, response to his analyst's writing about him, I have been unable to find any other written accounts of patients' reactions to their analysts' writing about them that have not been solicited by the analysts. The result is that this section has a very abbreviated literature review.

Reports of patients' responses to their analysts' request for their written reactions, which the analysts then included in the article about them, were cited at the beginning of the second section of the book. Although these first-hand patient accounts are important, the fact that they were written in response to their analysts' requests makes them different from Roth's reaction. All these accounts are produced under the sway of emotion, be it pleasurable or painful, but while Roth is addressing his former analyst indirectly, the other former patients are consciously and unconsciously still actively engaged with their actual analysts and the communication is written to them, as well as to an outside audience.

Roth's material, although also an angry communication to his former analyst, in this respect is more similar to the material that will appear in the next chapters where former patients tell me, not their analysts, their reactions to reading what their analysts wrote about them.

In the accounts that follow, patients report a range of experiences from gross and subtler betrayals and insensitivity, to helpful, attuned, and sensitive interactions with analysts. The reader will have the opportunity to appreciate these different ways of thinking about and dealing with the very complex and difficult issue of the effect on patients when their analysts write about them.

11
Patients Who Are
Not Analysts[1]

Strong emotional reactions to one's analyst, such as portrayed by Roth, are common in intensive treatments. Over the past two decades, analysts have become increasingly focused on the effect they have on their patients. The ways patients react are a mixture of transference stirred by intrapsychic conflicts and responses to actual characteristics and behaviors of the analyst. Most analysts now accept that their characteristics and behaviors play a role in the work. Oddly, until recently, the effect of analysts' writing about patients was not included in most analysts' reflections. This extra-analytic activity was thought of primarily as scientific, separate from the analytic work itself. And in respect to the patients' reactions, provided patients never knew that their analysts had written about them, these activities could be separated. But the research detailed in this book makes clear that there are, and at least for several decades have been, some analysts who have

---

1. Material in this chapter has previously appeared in slightly different form in the *Journal of the American Psychoanalytic Association* (2005) 53:103–129, © 2005 American Psychoanalytic Association. All rights reserved. I am grateful to the editor for granting permission for the material to be reprinted in this book. The permission was conveyed through the Copyright Clearance Center, Inc.

asked their patients' permission to publish and shown their patients what they wrote about them. Others also solicited patients' input. In addition, some patients have discovered that they have been written about and read the papers. Once patients read what their analysts have written, these papers can no longer be considered as totally separate from their impact on the patient.

Just as it was necessary in the earlier part of the book to keep in mind that the accounts I am reporting represent only the analyst's perspective, here it is necessary for readers to remember that the narrative is solely from the patient's vantage point. In both instances, the other party might relate a different story. Research data support this skepticism. In interviews conducted with patients and analysts following the termination of analysis, the views of the participants about various aspects of outcome of psychoanalysis did not always show a high degree of agreement (Kantrowitz 1987, Kantrowitz et al. 1986, 1987, Schlessinger and Robbins 1974). Clearly if analysts are to learn what their patients think and feel about having been written about, it is essential to have patients tell their reactions themselves.

The accounts that I am about to present reflect patients' conscious reactions; the deeper, unconscious layers may remain hidden, though sometimes they may also inadvertently be revealed. Nonetheless, having patients recount their experiences to a person who is not their analyst provides information that can aid analysts in more carefully considering how and when writing about patients may influence patients' representations of themselves, their analyst, and the analysis itself.

I am not suggesting that accounts to a third party are transference free (Pfeffer 1961, 1963). However, there are several notable differences. First, the former or present patient does not necessarily bring the history or even necessarily the fully developed transference that accompanied the experience with their analyst. Second, the interviewing analyst does not usually have the same personal characteristics that contribute to evoking specific aspects of the transference and is not subject to the same countertransference issues, and lastly, does not have the same publishing agendas as the treating analyst.

I hope that in reading these illustrations of egregious, hurtful, neutral, and facilitating experiences analysts will deepen their reflections on their own ways of dealing with this dilemma and learn from patients of their colleagues about the effect of reading about themselves.

Eleven patients, who are not themselves analysts, volunteered to be interviewed for this project.[2] Eight former patients and one current patient were referred to me by their former analyst or by an analyst friend or relative. Most of these analysts who responded to my request to interview patients had found it on the online psychoanalytic bulletin board. All but one of these patients initiated the contact with me. Another two former patients heard me talk about my work on this topic and contacted me.

The two patients who contacted me after hearing me talk had very negative reactions to reading about themselves. Three of the other patients were mixed in their reactions. Six patients had primarily positive reactions. Two of these six patients described how the written clinical example became an active focus in the analytic work with a positive outcome.

NEGATIVE EXPERIENCES

One former patient heard me give a lecture on the topic of confidentiality. Her former analyst was also present. She had not seen him since she left the analysis twenty years earlier. At the meeting, he offered some comments on the topic, supporting ideas about the importance of maintaining patients' privacy. This former patient called me afterward. She stated that what her former analyst said and what he did had little relationship to one another and she wanted the discrepancy made public.

> I was a patient over twenty years ago. My former analyst presented a paper, a lecture, in which he used my material. He was young and so was I. While I was seeing him I sent my husband, my house manager, and [someone with whom she worked closely] to be his patients. He told me if my husband weren't in analysis our marriage wouldn't last. Then I sent [another relative] who decided to pursue training as an analyst where my analyst taught. He must have seen me as a "cash-cow." I virtually filled the practice of this newly trained analyst. My analyst gave his paper at this same training center. My [relative] and [the person who worked with her] were both at the lecture. They both

---

2. All quotes in this paper are with the patients' permission.

came back and said it was clear he was talking about me. I was shocked. I had seen him for twelve years. I confronted him. He said he had a right to do that. I said I didn't think so and said I was leaving and that I wanted to see someone else. He refused to give me a name and said we could work it out. I said I didn't care what he thought. I wasn't staying and if he wouldn't give me a name I was going to talk with [the director of the training center]. He said okay, he'd give me a name. My [relative and co-worker] both sued him for other breaches in ethics and they won. Then there he was at the [recent] meeting and speaking as if he were a moral, ethical person, which he is not. At the meeting, I had the urge to out him as he [had done to] me, but that would be inappropriate and I'm not that angry anymore. I'm in a very good treatment now. But people should know that he was talking out of both sides of his mouth . . . that even analysts can do that.

If this patient's account is accepted as representing what actually occurred, the example is dramatically egregious. The clinical publication is merely part and parcel of a grandiosity about boundaries that informed the analysis from the start. The original problem is boundaries even more than confidentiality. The patient was, of course, young and, for many years, seems to have remained "blind" to the powerful influence of transference. Nonetheless, the analyst abused his authority in many different ways. In addition, the analyst's public comments about confidentiality, unless he has been transformed, reflect a hypocrisy that goes along with this unethical behavior. The analyst, of course, may have a different version of what occurred.

The second former patient had been asked permission for the use of her material, but had not been shown what was written. She found and read the example some years after the termination of her treatment.

My analyst had asked permission to use a dream I told him. It occurred when I had been in analysis about two or three years. I was pleased it was interesting enough to him to ask me. He did not show me what he had written. I saw him for three and a half years. I think it was a failed analysis. About eight years after I left analysis, I came across this example by chance in the bookshelf of a psychiatrist friend. I recognized the dream. He gave the dreamer a pseudonym that I looked up in the index. What affected me was not his using the dream but his take on me as the dreamer. It confirmed everything I thought he was thinking about me. It had been a very classical analysis. He had said very little in analysis but I sensed his negative judgments about me. In the book he said that my professional ambitions were part of my competitiveness with my brother. I was not married at that time and had an active social life. In the book, he called me "promiscuous." He said that as an adolescent I was uncontrollable and unmanageable. I felt he was very judgmental and non-empathic. Very early in the analysis, my marriage had broken up. He never asked me anything about it or how I felt. Everything I felt dissatisfied with in the treatment, he said was negative transference. With his insistent non-responsiveness who wouldn't react that way! It was upsetting that he felt this way about me but it validated my view of his view of me and validated my reasons for having left the analysis.

This second example reflects an apparent insensitivity and arrogance about "knowing" on the analyst's part. Hidden assumptions about "a woman's place" may have informed the analyst's assessment of pathology. The presentation in the published material shows disrespect for the patient. As she stated, reading it validated her intuitions about what her analyst thought about her and confirmed the rightness of her decision to leave.

MIXED REACTION

Three former patients conveyed their mixed reactions to the experience of reading what their analysts wrote about them. The first former patient was referred to me by a friend of his who is an analyst.

My analyst did not ask my permission while I was seeing him. He sent me the paper a year or two after termination. He wrote and asked my permission and asked if I wanted to come in and talk about it. Reading the example felt strange. I didn't recognize the dynamic he described. What concerned me was how much he was involved with me and how much with the paper. I didn't understand the theory— but I'm not a psychiatrist. What he said about me in general seemed right. I didn't know my story was so special and unique that it warranted a theory. I didn't think my analysis was that successful. I wasn't that connected with him. I think the paper had been presented at a meeting before he showed it to me. The disguise was pretty good; only family would have recognized it. I didn't have that much feeling about it—just surprised. I was a little put off that he presented it before discussing it with me but I don't know how these protocols go. I wasn't insulted. It made me feel I was a little special, in a positive way, because he made a theory out of my example. I don't spend a great deal of time thinking about this. It just comes up now and then.

There is a contrast between the patient's impression of the analyst's "involvement" with him as expressed in the paper and the lack of "connection" expressed by the patient about the treatment. This incongruity is not explained and possibly was not conscious for the patient. What troubled this patient was that there were some aspects in the account that he could not identify with and a concern that his analyst may have been more interested in a theory than in him. However, these negative feelings are balanced by his sense of being special because his analyst singled him out for this attention and that the analyst thought he warranted a publishable theory.

Another former patient, referred by a friend of hers who is an analyst, described mixed reactions to her experience of being both written about and tape-recorded. Her experience is unique in this sample because she received a low fee analysis in exchange for permission to use her material for research.

> I was a graduate student in [a field unrelated to psychoanalysis]. I sought an analysis at a low-fee clinic. I was told that a senior analyst would be willing to treat me if I would agree to have my analysis audio-taped and written about for research purposes. I thought a senior analyst sounded better than a trainee so I went. I said it was all right with me as long as the research was not on father and daughter relationships, my particular area of conflict. He said if at any time I decided that I didn't want my sessions taped, we'd have to do it differently. I was paying very little. The taping never bothered me. The tape didn't work two times and I felt something was wrong. It had just become so much a part of the set-up that I was used to.
>
> I learned a lot. But at times I thought he was working out his ideas and trying them out on me at the expense of my treatment. It enraged me. When I'd confront him about this, he'd back down and I'd feel guilty. But I was appalled when I learned that parts of my sessions were played for psychiatry residents. I wasn't told that was part of the deal. I was told that if anything was written, I could read it in advance. I'm in a chapter. I felt I sounded tongue-tied. Nothing that I said troubled me. I thought it made him look a lot worse than me.

Once I decided to change fields and become [field related to psychoanalysis], he said he wasn't going to use any more of my material, but he did continue to tape it. Then I moved. I asked if I could have access to the tapes if I ever wanted to. He agreed and said they would be in a secure place. He was very dear to me and on balance it was helpful. . . . I was still in analysis when I read the chapter. Before I read it, I said, "If I don't like what you've written, I can tell you not to publish it, right?" He said, "Wrong." I said, "So what's the point?" But it didn't come to that. His comments were about the process, not about me.

It wasn't a perfect analysis. Would it have been without the research part? I doubt it. Later he said he was sorry about his interests intruding. That affected me. But he didn't do a great job helping with father–daughter issues. He just became like my father, not inappropriately, but he was as pleased about my deciding to go into a field related to his as my father had been earlier when I started out in his profession as a graduate student . . . that didn't get analyzed.

In this instance, the writing is part of a larger bargain between patient and analyst. The patient is not sure how much this bargain limited her analysis. She knows she gained a lot but is aware of what didn't get analyzed. Of course, not everything gets analyzed for patients even when no such bargain has existed. She also minds that her analyst seemed more interested in his ideas than in her; however, his apology for the intrusion of his own interest mitigated her anger. This example, however, highlights the point that when consent is obtained, patients and analysts may have different ideas about the nature of the agreement. Thus, there is the problem of truly "informed" consent in this kind of work.

Another former patient, referred by her former analyst, retained very positive feelings about her analyst but the experience of being written about created some negative reactions.

I had a four-year analysis and then a later short return. I was having trouble getting pregnant. That's what my analyst wrote about. He called and asked how I'd feel about his writing about me. It was a year after this second stint. He said I could come in and discuss it. I had a strong response. I felt very positively about him, but this wasn't how I had expected this to happen. I thought he'd call me and we'd discuss it before he wrote it. He'd say what he saw and ask what I thought, that it would be collaborative, because the analysis had been collaborative. So I was shocked. I felt left out when he said he had a rough draft written. I told him that when I went to see him. I said that he'd taken what we had done together off to a high-powered publication, intellectual and professional and away from me. And I also had concerns about confidentiality. I had told a friend in the professional community things that could be identified in what he wrote. We met for two or three sessions to talk about it. I was also extremely protective of [relative about whom sensitive material was revealed in the article]. He understood and worked to disguise it. We talked together about how it could be done. I thought the revision was very good and felt protected.

I don't think I fully discussed with him my narcissistic hurt about factual information that was incorrect. I'd mentioned it in our first meeting about the paper, but it wasn't changed in the second write-up. I was bothered by that, but I was probably trying to please him. I should have said something. It related to a central trauma in my life. He got the details wrong in terms of the age that it happened. I felt very differently at eleven than at thirteen, which was when he said it happened [she describes the traumatic event]. He also said that other children had helped me, but really they ran to get help and I was left alone. In my analysis I felt so supported and not alone and he never shut me up, so it was a shock to me when he didn't recall it correctly. I felt left alone again. I told him the details were wrong but probably not how it made me feel. Then it wasn't changed in the second draft. I think I didn't want to deal with it. It hurt that this was in the second draft when I'd already told him. I was protecting my narcissism; I didn't talk about my hurt that he got it wrong. My most major concern was protecting the confidentiality of [her relative] and that came out fine in the second writing. It didn't change the dynamics.

I think I decided to put it aside. It was not important in the larger scheme of things. I've never felt not valued by him; though I had a negative transference, it was always worked out and I felt close and trusted him and that I could always go back and talk with him. Maybe I wanted to be more of a colleague [she is in a related field]. Maybe if I realized that in analysis I would have delved into it more, but I didn't want to be back in that dependent role and revive all that. So it was a narcissistic blow but not terrible. I still feel my analysis is the best thing I ever did. So one narcissistic pinprick won't undo it. I still feel valued, understood, cared about, and I'll go back when something comes up. Maybe after having talked about this with you, I will tell him then.

This patient was able to put a distance on her hurt and disappointment that her analyst both misremembered, and then did not correct his error in his revision. She does not allow this experience to disrupt her overall positive sense of her analysis or her analyst. She did, however, experience some de-idealization of the analyst in the wake of reading. The long-term effect will not likely be detrimental, but she was left with a hurt that probably could have been addressed and lessened had her analyst been aware of it. They clearly had a relationship where repair could occur. Her explanation that she avoided further elaboration because she did not want to open up the more dependent, regressive feelings, seems credible. Discussing her reactions in the interview appears itself to have lessened the lingering feelings of pain.

POSITIVE REACTIONS

Six patients reported primarily positive reactions to reading about themselves. Two patients of the same analyst, both referred by the analyst, had been shown the written material about them. Here is the first patient's account:

> I was in analysis for about six years. Sometime in the last year, my analyst asked about writing about me. She sent me the article sometime after I terminated. I was flattered. She said she'd camouflage it. She told me she was writing for the psychoanalytic community. I think she said she was writing about two patients. I don't remember a lot of discussion about it. She said I could see it before it was printed to see if I had any objections.
>
> I found it interesting and was rather moved by it. The language was more technical so I didn't fully understand it. . . . It was interesting to read about oneself in an objectified way. I might have had more mixed feelings about it. I took parts of it as kind of negative. But we talked about it and then I felt differently. It was a self-conscious experience. . . . In some ways it made me feel rather special; in most ways it was positive. I believe she felt it was a successful analysis.
>
> Q: Do you recall what bothered you?
>
> I really don't remember . . . maybe like she wrote and said I was . . . trying to remember . . . I'm not sure if she said something more problematic about me or characterized some pattern I didn't acknowledge or see. But she clarified it and that made it all right.

Q: Did you ask her to change that?

Oh no, I wouldn't ask her to change things. It was her piece. I experienced it mainly as a special and satisfying experience. She took an important moment in the analysis and at the time it seemed important to me too. It was a long time ago and I don't remember a lot. But at the time it informed something important about the analysis. After, when it was published, she sent me a copy. I went to talk with her about it. I don't know if it was an excuse to go back. All this was at least three years ago. Recently I went back to see her again, once a week for a couple of months. She asked me if it would be all right to talk with you about this experience. I was happy to do it. I'm curious by nature and interested in what you would ask. We had good rapport. I think it was a positive, intense experience. I found her writing about me validating. Now as I'm thinking about it, I think I may have compared myself with the other patient and thought she thought the other patient's analysis was more successful. Maybe that was competitive of me. But she said I had misinterpreted what she had written. Then I felt better.

This former patient's account of reading what her analyst wrote again demonstrates the importance of the analyst and patient discussing the patient's reaction to what is written. The patient's initial inability to recall what had troubled her suggests that she may not have totally laid this reaction to rest as she thinks. However, in the course of reviewing her basically positive feelings about her analysis, she is able to let it become conscious again. The primary impact of reading was a positive, validating one. Nonetheless, had the analyst not met and discussed her reactions, the patient might have been left more troubled by her competitive feelings. Of course, this suggests that the area of competition remains a vulnerable one for her. But no analysis deals with all areas as fully as others and no conflictual area ever completely disappears.

The second patient was unequivocally positive about her experience.

I was touched [that the analyst] was thinking about my analysis a year after I had finished. She contacted me and asked how I'd feel about some of my analysis being written about. She said she would be careful about confidentiality and leave out volatile material or anything I might find damaging to my reputation. She outlined what she had in mind to write and then sent me a copy. She asked if I wanted to change anything. I didn't. I thought it was terrific. She had asked if I wanted to write something about my analysis and I had. I wrote about some parts that she didn't include. That was fine because they weren't to the point she was making. What she wrote was completely accurate. It was fascinating to see her reactions. The analysis had been 100 percent focused on me. It was so different to see her reactions and what was about her in the material. She described having a screen memory of recalling loss. My analysis centered on the loss of my father. It was very powerful to see my analysis made her sad and go through pain as well. I had assumed something like that, but it was different to actually know it. I thought I was significant to her but this made me see it was true. She disguised me as [a profession that related to writing]. I knew she was a writer so it made me feel like family. I don't know who reads this. I assume it's used to train other analysts. I think it would be helpful. The highest compliment was to think what I said was worthwhile and might be something for others to learn from, and that she had ruminated about my analysis after-wards . . . so loving, so thoughtful, so kind. I suppose someone could think of it negatively. If the analyst's views were different from the patient's or if it wasn't a good analysis, but then why would you ask them? It's hard to imagine what would make someone feel negative. I guess if you weren't carefully concealed, that you could be identi-fied. That would be something to worry about. But the substance of what went on does need to be what happened.

I terminated about seven years ago. One issue was that I was afraid about becoming a parent. I married at the end of analysis. About a year and half later I went back to work on this issue. Then I adopted. I named my little girl after my analyst. My analyst was shocked—she is very self-effacing, but she was so important to me. I did not want to abuse the relationship, but I brought my daughter to meet her and we had tea.

This patient holds continued positive, possibly idealized, senti-ments about her analyst. Finding out that her analyst was writing about her and the account as validating, confirmed her feelings that her ana-lyst held her in positive regard. The inclusion of the analyst's revela-tion of her countertransference response to the patient, a shared feeling triggered by loss, and disguising the patient in a manner that made her similar to the analyst, made the patient feel closer to the analyst. Per-haps these factors contributed to the patient's naming her child after the analyst—"like a member of the family"—and bringing her child to meet her former analyst. This patient seems sensitive to boundary intrusions. She does not want to "abuse the relationship." The positive feelings have lasted over many years. The post-analytic tea visit with the daughter is an expression of this. Perhaps negative feelings have not been looked at as fully. The patient tries to consider what they could be. She can't find ones that apply. But she has raised the concern in her mind. While having tea at the analyst's with her daughter in a follow-up visit does not make their relationship into a social one, it does shift the boundary. For this patient and analyst, this form of post-analytic contact does not seem to have become problematic, but for other patient–analyst pairs it might have been.

Other former patients have also felt validated by what they read about themselves.

> My analyst told me he was thinking of writing something from my analysis as part of a paper. He said he would show it to me before it was presented and later published in a book. I read it in a session. It was like seeing myself in a mirror. There was an embarrassment of recognition about how I had been, but much more a sense of flattery to be written about—whether that was real or not—it felt like getting attention. There was some sense of my most embarrassing moments being put out for the world to see [laughter] but really there's not such a wide readership. I didn't think I'd be recognizable. I was made anonymous enough. My partner is the only one who could recognize me and that was okay.
>
> I think I had some sense of sadistic revenge that my mother was conveyed as [extremely aggressive]. There was a moment my analyst reported where he made a relaxed joke about something I had been taking very seriously. He told me that some analysts in the audience where he gave the paper were outraged that he didn't analyze that moment. But to me the way he handled that moment was such an indication of his judgment. I tended to overanalyze things and become self-critical. His being relaxed was wonderful for me. The analysts in the audience were off the mark.
>
> I didn't remember everything exactly as he did, but there weren't major differences. He left out details or didn't get the sequence right. I'm overly fussy about such things. But reading about myself made the significance of some events become thrown into starker relief. In the analysis I didn't necessarily step back and look at it like that. Reading it summarized things and brought them together. It felt lighter. I had mixed emotions—disappointment and regret that I had

made such a big deal or let things have such a big impact but also relief that they weren't such a big deal anymore, that I didn't have to keep letting it get me down. After I terminated analysis, he sent me a copy. It was gratifying that he was that involved with what went on between us and that he saw it as important enough to write about.

This patient underscores the perspective that can be gained by looking back on analysis and seeing it in summary form. Like many patients, he is also flattered and gratified by his analyst's interest and involvement with him that he feels writing about him reflects.

The next patient related a similar experience of validation and gratification in her analyst's willingness to respond to her specific needs and to believe that it was important to write about the effect of having done so.

My analyst asked if she could use me for a topic in a paper about five years into analysis. I was flattered that I was interesting enough to be written about! I was concerned about disguise because my background would be identifiable. She did it very well and what she wrote about were not things that disturbed me. I wanted people to hear my story because I had been pushed to do behavior therapy. I was very symptomatic. I had severe obsessive-compulsive disorder. I couldn't leave my house. But I couldn't do that until I felt that I was understood. My analyst was very patient. After two and a half years, I felt she understood and I trusted her enough to do it, but only with her. So she integrated psychoanalysis with behavior therapy and I'm 95 percent cured. She described this in the paper. So when I read the paper, I felt enormously moved. It summarized and pulled together my analysis. The way she wrote it was sensitive. It showed she really got it. There were things she said that I didn't really want to be that bad, but they really were and it was put in context. It was one thing to feel it in the room between us but to see the same empathy in writing really drove it home. There were a few statements where I felt her empathy even more, such as when she wrote "as if half awakened from a nightmare and not able to do behavior therapy until she wakened from it." I think the paper consolidated how much she got it, how much she cared to pull it together. The writing made me even more appreciative. She was very open. She gave me a rough draft. My husband and I made a few changes and she accepted them. I think she just assumed I'd want to read it, just openly offered it and I definitely wanted to read it. I would have asked if she hadn't offered.

That would have been grist for the mill. But her offering made it an open process. I'm sure I told her my gratitude about having the treatment summarized even though it was painful and humbling to see where I'd been.

I wanted to be truly portrayed. I wished my true self known, but I also didn't want to be exposed. She got my essence without making it specific; she left out the major things that would identify me. I left in one story she told because I took pride in the burst of "wickedness" it revealed. She chuckled about it, but we didn't talk about the pleasure I took in it. There's a little anxiety about some of these personal things but I was keen that others see the message about needing a personal story told before behavior therapy—really no one would do it. I'd seen so many psychiatrists and they each wanted to go right to behavioral work and wouldn't listen to my saying what I needed! Only the psychoanalytic world seemed to understand and appreciate it. But this wasn't in the literature.

I was surprised and a little concerned about the confidentiality, exposing myself more by talking to you. But now thinking about it and talking to you, I don't feel that way. I trust her enough to trust her connections. I trust you to report this discreetly [a great deal of personal detail related during the interview, not pertinent to the topic of this chapter, has been eliminated from this example].

This patient emphasizes that reading about what she had experienced in her analysis had a validating impact, an impact that reinforced and strengthened the original experience. In this respect, the process of reading had a consolidating effect. This patient and analyst pair did not actively analyze this process. Other examples follow where the effect of reading became directly employed as part of the treatment.

READING PAPERS AS PART OF THE THERAPEUTIC PROCESS

Two patients believed the introduction of writing about them and its reverberations had beneficial therapeutic consequence. The first of these two patients had been referred by her former analyst.

I was in analysis for some time when my analyst said he would be interested in writing about my treatment. He said he wouldn't do it if I didn't want him to. It would be disguised. I said fine; I'm a scientist myself. I said I'd like to read it. When he wrote it, he gave me the paper to read. I made a correction of a quote. We disagreed about some interpretation. He corrected the quote but did not change his interpretations. We "agreed to disagree," which is okay. Overall I was flattered he was sufficiently interested and motivated to write it. It was a case study on an experiment around the use of Prozac. I talked about why I wanted to try it; he told me the reservations he had. I did it for a specific length of time—a trial. I thought Fluoxetine (Prozac), our shorthand for the chemical drug effect of Prozac, was more useful and he thought the non-drug, psychological effect of his prescribing the chemical Prozac more so. We didn't disagree about what happened. Just whether the psychochemical or psychological factors had more weight. We were in agreement that both aspects were important. We discussed it all as part of this experiment. The fact that he was willing to be open to the idea of me doing it, that he'd write about being willing to do it meant to me that he was taking me seriously; he was looking at me from my point of view. He put what I thought I needed ahead of his beliefs and training. It made a huge difference to me. It was out there from the beginning that he didn't use drugs with analysis. Four years later we did this experiment and it was reassuring that he looked at his ideas, examined them, and shared them.

I read it once and then again when the article came out, which was after I had terminated analysis, about six to twelve months afterwards. I had read the first draft before I terminated. I don't think he started writing until he asked my okay. I have every reason to think he wouldn't have written it if I'd said no. It was a very positive experience and I talked about it in the analysis.

He called to ask if I'd talk to you. It's totally consistent that he'd ask me first. I have no issue about it. I'm open enough to say I was in analysis, not something to be ashamed of or secretive about, just private. I felt he was protecting my privacy; I had a right to say no. But I think people must have a window into the profession. It's done with trust, respect, and honesty. It was an active demonstration of what he said: that he could be trusted. It was a turning point. I really felt that my saying yes or no was the goal of the discussion and that he hadn't asked me as an afterthought.

This patient then reflected on the importance of publications.

With any medical profession, there's intensive training. You learn what's known at the time and with practice you get more skilled, but you also get more isolated from the mainstream of what is being taught.

You only get that update at meetings. That's dangerous for patients. What is seen is filtered through old training. The doctor makes a hypothesis and becomes enchanted with it. It is conceivable that if there is no opportunity to have a check by others, as thoughts in writing provide, what is thought can move further and further from reality and gradually slip from reality itself. Ongoing discussion and papers with colleagues are so important for everyone, but maybe especially for analysts because they work so privately.

While a number of patients describe what their analysts had written as validating, this patient emphasizes that it was the analyst's willingness to take the risk of following her intuition despite his misgivings and his interest in writing about it that solidified her trust and respect for him. Similarly to the patient whose analyst was willing to follow her treatment plan (though in that case, it was to do analysis before behavioral interventions, a plan that would accord with the analyst's training), this former patient is moved by her analyst's taking her seriously and putting her perspective ahead of his accepted ideas. Both his acceptance of her "experiment" with Prozac and his willingness to bow to her decision about publication consolidate her trust and respect for her analyst. Since she refers to this moment in the analysis as "a turning point," I am assuming that the ability to trust that fully had been an issue in treatment. For this patient, it was the act of writing about the experiment, rather than specifically what was written, that provides the therapeutic benefit. In this regard, an action was symbolic; it served as an integrating agent.

The analyst had been active in articulating his interpretation. Nevertheless, he allowed the patient to disagree and did not impose his point of view. He allowed his point of view to be questioned and bracketed. The way he dealt with the request for permission was similar.

The next and last patient illustrates how her analyst's use of the paper that included her clinical material led to new analytic understanding as well as being therapeutically beneficial. This patient was referred by an analyst (not her own) who was aware of my research.

The background: A woman, whose husband is an analyst but who herself is in an unrelated profession, was disrupted by her analyst's abrupt cancellation of an analytic hour. The patient had been in therapy with this analyst for two and a half years and then in analysis for another two years when this incident occurred. The patient sensed this cancellation as different from any other. After it she felt the analyst was preoccupied and different from her usual self. The patient thought and talked about this occurrence and her reaction over a period of time. Then the patient dreamed that her teenage daughter had cancer. Both the patient and the analyst kept coming back to this dream. Eventually, the analyst disclosed to the patient that the analyst's child had cancer. In the hour of the disclosure, the analyst answered all the patient's questions about her son's disease. Following that hour, the analyst returned to her usual, abstinent, analytic stance. From then on, the patient stated that she was affected by knowing her analyst's son had cancer. But she was also affected by both the fact of the disclosure that made the patient feel very "special" and by the subsequent return of a "just analytic" stance that hurt her feelings.

A few months later she, my analyst, asked if she could include this experience of her disclosure and its ramifications in a paper she was writing about the effect of her son's illness on her work. I was thrilled and felt very special again. Early in analysis I had read a lot of analytic papers and had had a fantasy of being written about by my analyst. I readily agreed. I can't remember if she said she'd show the paper to me or not. But she did show me the excerpt about me. She gave it to me during an hour and wanted me to read it in her presence. She was really clear that she wouldn't publish it if it were not okay with me. That moved me.

Reading the paper, seeing what she said in black and white was different from the fantasy of being so special. She went into details about my fantasies some of which were embarrassing to me. Early in the analysis I had been very curious about her and done everything I could to find out about her. She referred to this as "extra analytic detective work." I felt that didn't take into account my internal processes and was a put-down; it made me feel bad. I asked if she would remove the phrase. She had no problem with removing it. I basically felt fine about what she wrote.

Later, she told me the paper would be presented at [a national meeting] that I was going to with my husband. I felt like a star. At the meeting I was totally focused on her giving the paper, when it was, what had been said. During the whole meeting I never saw my analyst, but just after she gave the paper, I passed her in the hall. I knew from the program when it was given but naturally I didn't go. She didn't acknowledge me. I was really hurt.

The following Monday my analytic hour was scheduled for an unusual time. When I got there no one answered. I was very upset. I thought I had violated her boundaries and she was pushing me away. I called. The reality was that she was there, but had fallen asleep; I assume that she was really suffering from jet lag as I know I was. But it was a real turning point in my analysis. I began to comprehend that I wasn't special, that I wasn't going to be her friend, that I wasn't the star of this paper. It got me into a darker side of me. I'd been a happy child who never got angry. I learned a lot more about other parts of myself. It was painful but very important.

Later when the paper was going to be published, she added a section about the process of writing and how she had thought about it, how it had affected our work together. She told the publishers that she could not publish it without conferring with me before doing so. That really touched me. She wrote about some reasons she was reluctant to tell me about her son, my initial seductiveness with her and trying to find out about her. And then her reluctance to write about me because she thought that I had come to think of myself as a "co-author!" That was true, but the exclamation point hurt me and I asked her to remove it and she did. It felt like she was looking down on me, being sarcastic. What initially I was looking for was evidence of how much she loved me, to be the best and the brightest. I saw she did care about me and had made me special in that there were five or six cases and mine was the most elaborated, took up the most pages. She had felt my dream was a gift to her, that I had intuited something of her situation. I was filled with my sense of my importance, specialness. I really thought that paper was about me. But all that became a reference point in my analysis after which I began to understand things about myself differently. The issue of the paper itself faded as important in itself.

I reread the paper this morning for the first time since I read it before its publication. I found it amazing because I knew I used to think the paper was about me and now it is so clear to me that this wasn't true. It made me realize how much I've changed since then. That was three or four years ago. I don't think until I read it this morning I could take in my analyst's way of processing things and thinking. She was writing about why she did and thought what she did. The paper was about her, not about me. She wrote about how she didn't think it was a good idea to disclose to me.

The experience of reading the paper really made me deal with my feelings of being the most important, the favorite. She had to be really clear that this brief disclosure was not what our relationship was going to be like. It was tough her keeping the boundaries and at the same time keeping her loving connection with me. We ran into each other a lot at analytically related events. So there was a lot of work on establishing appropriate boundaries. I really pushed boundaries to make her my special friend and momentarily I thought I had won. Ultimately I'm so grateful she was so clear because I wanted and needed to learn things about myself that I couldn't if she hadn't stayed so analytic. I used to think, and sometimes still do, that to terminate one of us has to die. That was one way I interpreted the dream about my daughter having cancer as a separation. I think I'm afraid of getting too close because if I do I won't ever be able to terminate. I think there were moments with regard to her disclosure and with knowing about the paper that I felt seduced, but she really made me work with it. That made working on this issue central. And it was central for me, but I hadn't known it until then. So I really learned something.

This example conveys many mixed feelings of the patient that occurred in the process of reading the paper. The request for informed consent was an external stimulation of conflicts that are part of the patient's character. The patient's capacity to focus and articulate her experience conveys the overall beneficial effect of reading about herself. This patient–analyst pair was able to use the analyst's paper for the growth of the patient by working with the ramifications of her reactions to it over time.

DISCUSSION: LIMITATIONS OF SAMPLE

First, it is necessary to consider the limitations of these examples. The sample is very small. Generalizations from only eleven illustrations need to be made cautiously; they cannot be viewed as more than suggestive of trends. Then, there is the question of who volunteers and why. Patients and former patients are motivated to report experiences when their affects in relation to them are strong. It may not be surprising, therefore, that these examples mostly fall into polarities of anger/disillusionment/condemnation and appreciation/idealization/tribute. Most analyses will eventually traverse both extremes. Often only one part of the analysis is being recounted. Neither glowing accounts nor outrage is likely to reflect all that occurred, though there may be good reasons for both emotions. Complexity and range of affect and experience are what characterize deep and meaningful analyses. So when patients present examples that seem more uni-dimensional, one needs to question the factors that account for such representations. Perhaps the material displays a current state of experience; if this is indeed the case, the portrayal may change over time. Also as I stated in the introduction to this chapter, these reports are the patient's current, conscious experiences; there may be many different and contradictory layers of emotion and thought that are not in awareness.

REACTIONS AS SYMPTOMATIC OF LARGER ISSUES

When patients feel betrayed, it is unlikely that the publication itself is ever the only issue; it is more likely symptomatic of a larger problem. Unhappiness with the publication must then be understood in the context of unhappiness with the treatment itself. The incident crystallizes the nature of the patient's concerns about how he/she is being treated in this analysis, for better or for worse. Being written about, with or without permission, when it is without sensitivity to the patient— his issues, privacy, and need for respect—is likely to reflect either a countertransference issue or a character issue of the analyst. Sometimes patients have been mistreated. On other occasions, the analyst's request may be an enactment in which patient and analyst issues converge; it may bring to the fore previously unrecognized transference/countertransference constellations that can become the subject of analysis, provided they are recognized.

At other times, the analyst's writing agenda is less influenced by unconscious factors and the reaction stimulated by the meaning of the content, or the fact of the analyst's writing, is more related to the patient's conflicts or characterological issues. The balance of the contribution from patient and analyst undoubtedly varies in each dyad. When patients' particular narcissistic issues or central conflicts are mobilized by their analysts' writing about them, a previously unrecognized or underestimated problem may be exposed for analytic inquiry. The dyad's explorations of these reactions, negative or positive, may then segue to deeper material condensed there.

DIFFICULTIES IN DEFINING EFFECT

Whether a patient is disturbed or pleased by what they have read does not in itself inform us about the effect on the treatment and its outcome. Considerations of what is harmful, neutral, or beneficial in the experience are essential, but how each of these outcomes is operationally defined is complex. Harm, benefit, and outcome may each be thought of differently at different times and from different perspectives, such as that of the patient, analyst, friends, family, or other sources of outside observation. Halpern (2003) offers a definition of "harm":

> Given that the goal of psychotherapy is psychological healing, harm is that which interferes with this goal. Harmful events are thus not identical to painful events. There are times that psychotherapy is both painful and therapeutic. Similarly, just because a patient may feel bad while he or she reads about his or her case, it does not mean that this interferes with his or her therapy. On the other hand, a patient could feel fine about what she or he reads, yet find herself or himself blocked in treatment. [p. 119]

The accounts in this chapter differ from the earlier ones in the book in that they furnish *first person* information rather than the *perceived effect* of this experience according to the analyst-author. They provide a window into clinical repercussions that may not have been shared with treating analysts and that are not ordinarily available to the psychoanalytic community. The impact of patients' reading about themselves depends on many factors, the most important of which seems to be the nature of the relationship between patient and analyst and their ability to process what occurs. The subjective experiences presented in these examples highlight areas of patients' sensitivities that may help analysts when thinking about how they write and how they work with the ramifications of patients reading about themselves.

NEGATIVE REACTIONS

If the tone in which the analyst writes is disrespectful or judgmental, there is no doubt the patient will be offended. This observation is so obvious that it should be unnecessary to address it. But unfortunately it is not. Often when analysts assume that patients will not read what they write, they do not take sufficient care in the presentation of patient material. Sometimes even when clinicians give their papers to their patients, their sensitivity may remain insufficient (Brendel 2002, 2003, "Carter" 2003).

Concern that the analyst is more interested in his or her own theory or agenda than in the patient was a reaction often expressed. The patient may not voice this feeling to the analyst, but it is a frequent enough response to the request for permission that analysts should be alert to it as a possibility. Some patients were narcissistically injured by this thought. But according to my interviews, the opposite reaction to a patient's recognition of the analyst having an interest outside of the patient also occurred. As we have seen, some patients felt flattered or special to have their material warranting this extra attention. Also, when patients understood that what was written about them provided information that could be generalized to other patients and therefore useful to the analytic community, it was reassuring for patients insofar as they were persuaded that it was not the private analytic relationship that was being divulged. The challenge to analysts is to appreciate which patients will respond in which fashion.

Not being told in advance of the full implications of their consent also disrupts patients' sense of trust. The patient who had a reduced-fee analysis had not understood taping her material for "research purposes" to include residents hearing her tapes. Another patient even felt upset by the fact that the analyst began writing before asking her permission.

Patients may make positive or negative comparisons when they are one of several patients used as illustrations in the analyst's paper. In one example, a patient confirmed her sense of being special because her example was longer than the others. In another example, a patient experienced competitive feelings when she thought her analyst viewed the other patient described in the paper as having had a more successful analysis; she believed her competitive issues had not been sufficiently explored in analysis. The patient was conscious of this reaction but did not tell the analyst.

POSITIVE REACTIONS

As previously stated, patients often report that they are flattered or feel special when their analysts ask to write about them. The analysts' selection of them boosts their self-esteem. Many analysts, who do not believe in asking consent and use only disguise in their clinical examples, believe that this gratification is detrimental to the treatment. In the present examples, it is not possible to assess whether this concern pertains. In the last example, however, the patient conveys in detail that this feeling of specialness, first stimulated by the analyst's self-disclosure and then further strengthened by being written about, became the subject of analytic scrutiny with beneficial results. This patient is the only one still in treatment so that a retrospective evaluation of her experience is not yet possible. However, even if other reactions emerge over time and other complications ensue from this interaction, it seems that this patient and analyst were able to examine the double self-disclosure of the analyst (first in revealing worry about her son and then further revealing her countertransference in her article) to address a central, previously unexplored character issue.

Patients also report experiencing their analysts' writing about them as validating. One patient describes reading about herself as a "consolidating" experience. Reading about oneself in this respect seems to be experienced like an interpretation where the patient is able to grasp and hold on to the analyst's view. Gratification that may interfere with some patients' treatments may be healing for other patients who have suffered from insufficient attention and need this validation before they can tolerate in depth self-exploration. Patients' seeing the same empathy in writing that has been experienced in treatment was also described as enhancing their sense of trust in the analyst's genuine care for them.

Other patients talk about the importance of feeling they have been taken seriously. The two patients whose analysts employed adjunct therapies—medication and cognitive-behavioral techniques—both felt their analysts' willingness to do something that was not their usual practice and then to write about it augmented their sense of being respected. Both treatments sound as if they were extremely beneficial to these patients. These patients are likely to believe that they had a significant impact on their analysts. Whether this belief became the subject of analysis is not reported. A potential downside of retaining such an unanalyzed belief might be patients' conscious or unconscious overestimation of their own power.

PRE-PUBLICATION DISCUSSIONS

When analysts ask patients for consent after termination, even if they meet and talk with their former patients, patients may not tell the former analyst some reactions, particularly when they are ones of upset. Though patients may recognize the stirring of familiar feelings or be surprised and hurt, unless the experience is deeply disturbing they would sometimes rather bear it silently than again open more regressive places. One patient described the wish not to return to the state of being a patient.

Comparing the reaction of one patient in the wake of having something important misremembered with the patient who felt so valued because her analyst remembered her well, it becomes apparent that showing a patient what is written about them—even when the analyst meets with the former patient, as both these analysts did—is not a guarantee that patients are always forthright about their feelings. Unless the analyst persists in asking for the patients' reactions, former patients may cover over the meaning it has had for them. Whether positive or negative, the non-verbalized response may have unexpected reverberations over time.

Since it is the analyst's request, not the patient's life, that has occasioned the interaction that stimulated this reaction, the sense of upset has been iatrogenically introduced. As previously stated, the dilemma becomes whether the analyst should simply respect the patient's manifest acceptance of what has been written and consented to, or whether he/she should be actively trying to detect and explore unacknowledged positive or negative reactions. Sometimes these interviews helped set these residual feelings to rest. But there were also patients who sought out other analysts to deal with their distress about what they had read.

When consent is asked during treatment, patients may or may not ask to read what has been written. Some patients do not want to know that they have been written about. Analysts need to consider carefully this possibility before asking—as well as be aware that their assessments in either direction may not be correct. If the analyst is convinced that the patient would not want to know, then disguise may be preferable. But then the analyst must consider how each patient would react to discovery of an article.

Often, however, in discussions, both during and after treatment, when patients read papers prior to publication, they did express their concerns. When these reactions are revealed to the analyst, there is opportunity for negotiating what is included in the paper and for doing reparative work. Some patients expressed positive feelings about "knowing" their refusal would have been accepted.

Some analysts in this study stated they informed their patients about their intention to write, giving them the right to refuse permission, but not to modify what they write. But unless patients know exactly what is written, they do not know the meaning of their agreement. The analyst who gave a reduced fee in exchange for research participation did not feel it was incumbent on him to negotiate with his patient. It should be noted that though she was angry about his arbitrary refusal, she retained positive feelings about him and their work.

IMPLICATIONS FOR KNOWLEDGE OF THE FIELD

One implication arising from this study is that published clinical material may be skewed in the direction of positive outcomes. The five analysts who referred subjects for this chapter all chose patients who they believed had considerable therapeutic benefit from their treatment and felt very appreciative of their analysts. In the larger study, many analysts stated that they only ask permission to write about patients when they believe they have a good alliance and a positive state in the transference. Although some analysts then write about times of discord or impasse, they write once this disharmony has been overcome. Previously I reported Levin's (2003) concern about the perception of a literature censored by patients if consent is always asked, but there are also data that analysts become self-censoring in anticipation of patients' reactions. Since there is an increasing trend toward asking permission, a danger exists that negative or equivocal experiences may lose representation in psychoanalytic literature. Colleagues and the larger community could then have a distorted picture about the breath of analytic practice. This topic will be more fully discussed in the final chapter.

In the next chapter, patients who are themselves analysts or analytic candidates recount their experiences when they read about themselves.

12
Patients Who Are Analysts[1]

Both analysts' and patients' accounts make clear: writing about patients poses many problems. When the patient is someone who is, or is training to become, an analyst, another dimension of complexity is added. On one hand, people with analytic training are apt to be both psychologically minded and able to express their self-understanding in complex ways that illustrate points that the writing analysts wish to make. On the other, they are also the group most vulnerable in regard to preserving their confidentiality. Colleagues and friends are more likely to recognize them.

The 141 analysts whom I interviewed held differing views about the use of candidates' material. Many stated they would never write about candidates, even if they believe they could successfully disguise them and had permission, because there is always some potential that they may be exposed. In contrast, other analysts believe that candidates,

---

1. Material in this chapter has previously appeared in slightly different form in the *Journal of the American Psychoanalytic Association* (2005) 53:131–153, © 2005 American Psychoanalytic Association. All rights reserved. I am grateful to the editor for granting permission for the material to be reprinted in this book. The permission was conveyed through the Copyright Clearance Center, Inc.

if they can be successfully disguised and give consent, are the best group to write about because they would value publications and want to contribute to the development of the psychoanalytic field.

Analysts and analytic candidates who want to write have double identifications when their analyst is a writer. They also hold a dual perspective on their analysis and their analysts' writing about it. They are both patients and the subjects of papers; simultaneously they learn through the process to become analysts and their reactions to being written about contribute consciously, or unconsciously, to their own attitudes and practices when they write about their own patients. They are inside and outside the process. A potential for intellectualization to interfere with affective experience exists. For this reason, showing analyst-patients what is written about them creates yet another problem. Not to do so, however, is risky. They are certainly likely to recognize themselves and may be recognized by others and then feel exposed. They may also experience it as very disrespectful and feel betrayed if they are not asked. These patients are the current or future colleagues of their analysts.

In this chapter, I will describe and discuss the reactions of patients who are themselves or are becoming analysts. Twenty-six analysts described their experiences. Eighteen[2] of these analysts reported their reactions to reading about themselves as part of interviews I initiated; these interviews were part of the larger study. Two other analysts reported by e-mail that they had been written about by their analysts but did not elaborate on their experience. Eight other analysts contacted me in response to a request that I placed on the psychoanalytic bulletin board on the Internet for volunteers. All quotes in this paper are with the patient-analysts' permission. Again, we need to remember that the analysts of these analyst–responders might have different stories to tell.

ANALYSTS I CONTACTED

Eighteen analysts told me their reactions to having been written about in the context of communicating their attitudes and practices in

---

2. Six analysts interviewed after the *JAPA* article was written were added to the sample.

regard to writing about their own patients. Their accounts of being written about were reported as asides. As a result, the amount of material given by each has considerable variation. Eight of these analysts had been asked for their consent; ten discovered the material.

Permission Asked

Two analysts recounted that when they were patients they had been asked for permission, read the material, and found it innocuous. However, one of these two patient-analysts emphasized that, though confidentiality had been maintained, it did not assure anonymity.

> A former analyst of mine wrote about me and asked permission, disguised me. I gave permission. I mentioned this to a colleague who said, "Oh, you must have been John." He was right on. He'd read it and remembered the paper. I felt a little embarrassed but nothing in the paper was that troubling. But it's a cautionary tale. I think we underestimate the perceptiveness of the readership.

The third analyst, when a patient prior to analytic training, was asked for permission before his analyst submitted the paper for publication. He had been very upset by the analyst's insensitivity to preserving his confidentiality.

> Before I was a candidate, my first analyst, though in other ways abstemious, wrote about me without asking me. He gave me a copy of the article to read while I was in the third year of analysis for me to approve it. It wasn't disguised enough so that if it were to appear that my friends in the field not recognize me. I refused permission for it to be published at that time. I said I might feel differently later. Ten years later I did feel differently and told him it was fine to publish it. But by that time he had lost interest in it and it was never published. But at the time, it shook me. I felt what he did was wrong. It breached analytic confidentiality at a vulnerable time of analysis around material not fully explored and closed off those issues with a conclusion about the material; that was a foreclosure of work that had not yet been explored enough. It was inexplicable to me that he would do this. I got a lot from this analysis; it was very helpful and I was able to talk about and explore what he did and how I felt about it. He was very open to hearing my complaints, understood, and said he hadn't realized I'd be

recognized and felt that was something he needed to explore in himself, and agreed not to publish unless or until I gave permission.

The fourth analyst-patient in this group had been asked by her analyst if he could write about a dream of hers, but he never did. She asked if she was correct in her assumption and he said she was. She was "very disappointed but didn't tell him." Her "idealization" kept her from expressing "anger and disappointment to him." It was not until her second analysis that she worked this out. As a result she never asks a patient's permission until she has written a rough draft.

The fifth analyst felt deceived.

> He showed me what he wrote. But he had previously said that his notes were so he could remember and not for writing. I was totally recognizable. He let me change it, but it still wasn't right. That's the way it was published.

The sixth analyst-then patient was initially unable to object to her analyst's use of her in words but felt a strong negative reaction to his having done so. When she was able to voice this, she felt she remained totally ineffective in conveying her feelings in a way that stopped her analyst from writing about her. She was unable to extricate herself from what she experienced as a hurtful situation.

> He told me he was going to do it. He didn't ask. I wasn't in a place in my analysis where I could have felt free to object. I did object later and did so strongly. I was so embedded in the regression I couldn't leave. At the time he first wrote about me, and he wrote about me repeatedly, he said it wouldn't stop him if I didn't agree. He said being in analysis implied consent. At the time in [her community] that was a common view. The first article he wrote about me made his career. He tried to disguise me but all my friends recognized me. It was humiliating. He then wrote papers I heard at conferences—a retraumatization of the narcissistic issues that brought me to analysis. I was livid. I told him I wanted him to stop. I think he genuinely believed he was doing me a favor by telling me at all. He did show me the first paper and I changed one word, but it wasn't a question of my permission. Even when I could object, I couldn't leave. I stayed with him for both my personal and training analysis.

These last two analyst-patients still retain anger and hurt in relation to their analysts' insensitivity toward them. One never voiced his feelings; the other felt unresponded to. In this last instance, the problems in the analysis seem far greater than issues limited to being written about. Again, of course, this report is only from the patient's perspective; her analyst might offer a different view. But it is clear that they were never able to work out her sense of being overpowered.

Informing a patient that you will write about them is not the same as asking their permission. These last three examples also point out the difficulty in the meaning of a patient being "informed"; in one example, the patient's idealization interfered with any possibility of refusal or later exploration of her hurt. In the other two, the patients were clearer about their feelings, but their analysts were not responsive. In one of these examples, the patient was even less able to act on her own behalf or work out the difficulty in the treatment.

Permission Not Asked

Ten analysts interviewed as part of the larger project were not asked for the use of their material. They all found and read what their analysts wrote. Four considered what had been written about them as totally benign. One was amused and delighted to discover an article in which his former analyst gave an example from his childhood. He was charmed to think that something he had thought relatively insignificant was viewed as valuable enough to be reported by his analyst in a publication. The fact that his permission had not been asked did not trouble him. He considered not being asked for consent as standard professional practice at that time.

Two of these analysts seemed to be unperturbed by discovering material had been written about them. One of these two said, " It occurred, no big deal"; the other offered a somewhat, but not much more, elaborated reaction.

> One of my analysts made a one-sentence description of something between us. I found it. He didn't ask me. It was innocuous and didn't bother me. It was while I was in analysis but didn't identify me at all and he didn't ask my permission.

The fourth analyst was told by her analyst that she had been written about some time after her termination and just prior to her graduation from the institute. In other words, she was informed that he had written about her, but he was not asking her permission.

> My former analyst told me he had written a paper about incorporation and introjection and asked if I'd recognized myself in it. I hadn't read it. When I did, it never crossed my mind that he would have my permission. He had used only a dream of mine. I had been curious to see how he evaluated my dream. When I read it, I was relieved to see that he saw my dream as a more mature way of processing, that he saw it as more healthy than sick. I think he was right not to consult me; it was just a dream and nothing else. No one other than I could have recognized it as me. When he told me it was a communication colleague to colleague and never analyzed. I was gratified I'd made a dream that signified a step forward in my analytic experience. Theoretically, if he had written about me and seen me as less mature I would have felt exposed to myself and felt badly. But knowing the kind of man my analyst was, he wouldn't have written it in that case. This instead was a positive acknowledgment of analytic work. I saw no problem with it.

These four analysts were all totally accepting of a hierarchical relationship. Two of the analysts were also flattered by what their analysts wrote about them.

In contrast, six other analysts-then patients interviewed in the study were very upset by their analysts' use of them. These analysts were not disturbed by the fact that their analysts had not asked their permission nor that they had written about them; nonetheless each experienced a particular kind of injury from the experience. One of these analysts stated that the illustration about him was "highly distorted and had several factual errors." He had never objected but was delighted to have the opportunity to do so as he reported this to me. The second of these analysts was hurt by the disguise her analyst used; she believed it revealed the analyst's unflattering view of her.

The third analyst elaborated the experience of discovery as an intrusion.

> This intrusion happened to me as a patient. I think my analyst used material about me in a classroom situation and may have written about me. It wasn't the issue of my analyst doing it but my knowing that was the intrusion. In my own analysis, I felt a disappointment and a sense of being misused; being an object—I don't think I really worked

it out—but maybe she would have disappointed me in some other way. It was hard to start another treatment. I knew I felt betrayed.

The last two analysts, although an aspect of their analysts' writing about them had upset them, did not view the writing itself as central to their analytic experience. The first patient believes her analysis to have been very beneficial and informative; the second patient sees her distress about exposure as a place that gave her the opportunity to express an internalized sense of disappointment in the transference. Again, these analysts' overall acceptance of their analysts' use of their material may reflect the fact that this was common professional practice at that time.

But three other analysts were very distressed and many years later still retained their anger about how they had been treated. In all three instances, their analysts' writing about them without asking permission was only one of the many ways they felt they had been betrayed and boundaries had been crossed in the treatment. One of these analysts describes her experience.

> My permission was not asked even though the analyst was the editor of the journal in which the article appeared and the journal states explicitly that patients must be asked explicitly. This was not the only betrayal in that treatment.

From the reports of these eighteen analyst-then patients, it is clear that whether or not permission was asked was not the determining feature in their reaction to being written about.

ANALYSTS WHO CONTACTED ME

The second group of eight analysts contacted me in response to a request for volunteers that I posted on the on-line psychoanalytic bulletin board or through being informed about my work by colleagues. Unlike the first group, they did so specifically to describe their experiences of reading what their analyst had written about them. Seven of these analysts were asked for permission; six of them had negative reactions to the manner in which their analysts handled writing about them. The seventh, asked for permission after termination, reacted positively and believed reading what her analyst wrote was therapeutically beneficial. Only one analyst in this group was not asked for permission and discovered the paper while still in treatment. She reported taking pleasure in being written about and saw it as no issue that her permission was not sought.

NEGATIVE REACTIONS

Permission Requested: Reading during Treatment

Six analyst-patients reported being asked for permission by their analysts during the course of their analysis. Five of these patients, candidates at the time, had negative reactions to their experiences. One analyst-then patient had at first felt negatively but changed her view over time.

In one instance, the candidate had selected her training analyst because she had been impressed by something she had read by him. She herself wanted to write. During the course of her analysis, her analyst mentioned that he was writing and she suggested that he include her material in it. He asked if she were serious.

> I said I was serious as long as I could read it. He wrote it and I did read it and edited it. It went back and forth and we talked about what it meant to me to have it written and that he wanted to do it. That was all fine. I thought it would be okay because we were doing it collaboratively. But subsequently something else happened. I had a forced termination with him because a charge was made against him for abuse of a patient and he was dismissed as a training analyst. Later he lost his license. I stayed in analysis with him for six months after this. I knew I was going to have to change training analysts. The book didn't come out during that time. I wish I had been more cautious. The book will come out with my material in it and I won't be able to talk with him about it. I'm stuck with this and can't discuss it, except in my current analysis.
>
> I think there was an element of a boundary problem for us too. I was emulating him as a writer, idealizing him. The writer and the analyst part got mixed up. I don't think either of us recognized that. I read other things in addition that he was writing, not just my example. I started to feel like a collaborator in the writing. We got excited about it as a process. I was excited to be seen as a colleague and a writer. He

said he knew people would say it was not a good idea to do this while I was in analysis, but this situation was an exception. Well, why did I need to be an exception? But it was very gratifying to both of us. I was an interesting case. But the exhibitionism and the feeling I was a colleague . . . I couldn't see all that then, but I wish he could have. I was the only current candidate in analysis with him when all this happened.

The way he presented me had such a positive spin on it, everything working out; it all looked so good. There were parts of what I worked out in analysis that did go well, but then things slipped. I don't know if it was because of all these messy events. I'm in analysis with another training analyst now. I have mixed feelings about it. But it has helped me to see that there were these small boundary issues, not gross ones. But I feel my stuff as a patient was neglected.

Another candidate, whose training analyst was also in a personal crisis at the time of requesting to write about him, recounted his experience. A year and a half into his analysis, his analyst asked permission to present some of his material at an analytic meeting. The analyst gave the patient a copy of his report of the sessions as well as the discussant's comments.

It was disconcerting to me that he chose these particular sessions because they were not characteristic. They showed us at odds with each other. The discussant's comments were overly pathologizing. What was said was sort of glib. The discussant thought that as a patient–analyst pair we were "heavy." I thought we were more vital than that. I felt having people write about my personality was intrusive. I thought when I gave permission I was being helpful to the field. I didn't think carefully enough about what it would be like to read about myself. These sessions were presented at a panel discussion at an analytic meeting.

But what happened didn't end with the issues about being written about. Something bigger overshadowed that. My analyst offered for me to read what he presented but in the folder containing this material was also enclosed a note, clearly from his lover, not his wife . . . dearest so and so. I tried not to read it once I realized what it was. I returned it the next day. That was a turning point. I realized my analyst was having troubles and this was a clear example of my analyst being out of control, an inability to contain his own struggles.

I think it's not a good idea to write about someone while they are actively in treatment. It told me too much of what my analyst's thinking and feeling were. If I were writing I wouldn't do it while someone was in treatment. I thought what he said about me presented me in a way that was not very sympathetic. The sessions he picked were ones where he was put off, frustrated. He didn't think I was thinking in a useful way. He was irritated and bugged by me. After I read this I became more anxious and tried to please him. I told him it was disturbing, but that didn't really go anywhere. I knew he was in an extramarital affair. He didn't believe me that I stopped reading the letter. He felt I did something that he thought made it so it couldn't be analyzed. I was describing feeling sort of dissociated. I described it as etherized. I went to see another training analyst for a consultation. Later, after my analyst told me he was relocating, I then went back to this consultant as my new training analyst. I left this first analysis extremely confused about how we didn't work it out. With my new training analyst I came to understand why I stayed so long and idealized my first analyst at that time.

At one point [in this first training analysis], I had thought of moving and transferring my candidacy to another city. My analyst had been very hurt, it seemed. Then it turned out he was leaving and moving away. He had recently been made a training analyst and he didn't have any other candidates in analysis yet. [Prior to being a candidate] I had gone to a conference where he was a discussant. He had a lightness and freedom that I admired.

When he asked about writing about me, he thought because I was a candidate I would understand the value of writing. I think he confused our relationship. He was treating me as a mature colleague who wouldn't react. The potential for writing about a patient that can be hurtful has to be carefully considered. It can even be a boundary violation.

Actually I realize more was going on for him. He'd fall asleep during the three to four months that preceded this incident. I'd talk about it, but I didn't have the courage or strength to really confront him. I'd get angry but I didn't consider getting a consultation or anything. We terminated eight months after he told me he was leaving. He took a long trip after telling me and after that I told him off, sitting up, but then I found myself back on the couch. I feel very grateful to my second analyst for helping me understand my part in all this and make some sense of this experience.

The third candidate was in analysis several months when his analyst asked his permission to write about him. This candidate, unlike the former two, states that he felt positively about his analytic experience, although he felt negatively about his analyst's having asked his permission to write about him. He knew his analyst wrote and would have preferred not to be told about his material being used. The candidate himself is a writer and has clear views on how writing about patients should be done.

I write and never ask permission. I was on the couch when he told me he had written about me. I asked what he had written about. He gave it to me to read. He had disguised me as a woman! I thought it was bizarre—bizarre that he thought that he had to ask permission for this very small example using my material—and bizarre that he had to let me know that he thought of me as a woman. Why did he have to do that? I didn't want to go there.

I knew from something that he said in a class that his analyst had died three days after he ended his analysis. I think maybe he saw me as threatening because after his termination, his analyst died. I would bring that up, but whatever his disguising me as a woman brought up . . . whatever this hit about my bisexuality or fear of being a woman, I couldn't deal with. We dealt with homosexual feelings but it was creepy to think he thought of me as a woman. And when you inform patients as he did, it's not very analytic.

In general, I thought my analysis was very helpful. But I know there were things we didn't get to. There was a whole level of regression where he was not willing to go with me. I had a dream of a hand in a toilet. I thought this was like a psychotic part of myself. I was interested in learning about it. I don't think I'm psychotic and I wasn't worried about becoming psychotic, but I wanted to understand that regressed level in me. I regressed on the couch but not when I got off it. He told me that when he was a candidate he had a patient he had to hospitalize and that the analytic community not only was not supportive but also condemned him. He was afraid to go more deeply. I had to threaten to quit on three different occasions because he refused to reconstruct. I'd relate it to stuff in my childhood. Finally he'd related it to my past and what he said was brilliant and helpful. But he wanted to keep everything in the here and now—relational school exclusively.

I was his first training analysis and he told me he was in supervision and asked my permission to discuss my case. I said of course. He asked if I wanted to know who his supervisor was. I said no but I did eventually ask. I think a layer of my unconscious didn't get exposed. We didn't get to any female identification.

The way he brought that to my attention wasn't analytic. I have no interest in my analysis being used for scientific purposes. If my analyst wanted to use it for that, that's fine. That's my analyst's life and desire, and I feel it's better for patients not to know. I'd have been happier not to have been asked as long as it was well disguised. I just didn't want this issue of his in my analysis. He and I debated about this asking permission. I said how I felt obligated to only disguise and he said he felt obligated to ask permission.

Another example of where he brought himself into the analysis where I thought it shouldn't be occurred: One day he left the foot cover off the end of the couch. He asked if I'd noticed and I hadn't. He asked if I wondered why. I hadn't. He said he had forgotten my session. I didn't need to know that. My father died when I was thirteen. I didn't need that. Really I think this interrupted and disrupted me by an issue of his. It was his issue thrust on me.

Basically I feel positive about my analysis and thought for the most part he was excellent, but these are areas where I think he screwed up. I think everyone does about something.

While the first two analysts crossed boundaries and, I presume unconsciously, intruded their issues into their patient's treatment, the analyst in the third example consciously intended that his patient know his thoughts. The patient, while maintaining that overall this analysis was useful, strongly objects to these intrusions of the analyst's personal reactions and the limits he thinks this created in his analysis. Inexperience may account for some of the analyst's behavior since this patient is the training analyst's first candidate; however, it may be that this training analyst maintains a theoretical belief in the usefulness of these disclosures; though clearly, the candidate does not agree. As in other examples I have given, the behavior in relation to writing seems just one in a series of other behaviors that were disruptive to the patient.

Many analysts, who believe in only disguising their clinical examples, state that to introduce writing about a patient during the course of treatment is always an intrusion and should not be done. These three patients agree. The last wishes he had never been told. None of these patients object to having been written about; their quarrel is only with the way it was done. But different procedures are not guarantees of more successful outcomes. Attunement to the specific patient's reaction and its exploration seem the more relevant factors.

Reading after Termination

When analysts write clinical examples, they need to be sensitive to patients' reactions and attend carefully to boundaries after treatment as well as during it.

An analyst-then patient, whose views changed over time, had begun her analytic training but was not yet in a training analysis. She received a letter from her then analyst during a summer break, asking her permission to write about a dream. She wrote back giving her consent.

> Because of where I was in the treatment, I did not ask to see what she wrote. A couple of years later, a friend read and recognized this dream as mine and told me about it. I felt exposed but I never went to read it. I was no longer in this treatment and I didn't want to open up things. I was in a different phase of my life. I felt shamed and betrayed because of the way my friend told me my dream was used. My analyst was making a point she and I never addressed. It wasn't in our work.
>
> The most productive and major theme in my analysis was to be upfront and deal with my aggression and envy directly. I had my analyst as an idealized figure so my aggression and envy in relation to her were not brought out into the open. In a dream right before termination I brought up what had gotten swept under the rug. I wish she had asked me to read it but I wasn't in a place where I would have asked. This analysis was helpful to me in many ways but we both agreed there were issues we hadn't been able to deal with. That dream she used in writing was about how I couldn't deal with my anger. Her article was about that. Over the years, I came to appreciate that she was working on her difficulty in helping me with this in the treatment. At first I felt bad about myself and idealized her, but over the years I realized we both had our difficulties, not just me. Also I realized everything cannot be done in a single analysis. It gave me empathy for her and me.

This analyst had been upfront in her request of her patient, but seemed not to realize that the same inhibited aggression she perceived in the treatment prevented the patient from being direct, or sufficiently aware of her need to protect her own interests. No longer in this treatment and in a different psychological place, the analyst-patient does not want to return to confront or explore her later reaction of betrayal from feeling exposed—both to her friend and to the analyst's views that had not been explored with her. Her sense of shame, however, changed over time as she realized the limitations were not only hers but her analyst's as well, and of any single analysis.

A former patient, who many years later trained to be an analyst, offered another example in which the analyst failed to attend sensitively enough to the patient's concerns for confidentiality and the maintenance of adequate boundaries. This patient was asked about having her material written up four years into a six-year analysis, but the actual paper was not written or read until about two and half years later when the former patient had moved away.

> When she asked me if she could write about me, I was flattered and said sure. There were at least two papers presented at the local analytic society. I don't think they were ever published. My former analyst left a message on my answering machine saying she hoped I didn't have a problem with this being presented and asked if I wanted to read them and I did. [Former analyst] sent the papers for me to read. I called and said I sort of did have feelings about it and I wanted to talk about it. I never said no because I felt guilty about it; the papers were written and the meeting was already set. I was sure that I was recognizable and hadn't been well enough disguised. I had been analyzed in a small analytic community and had a relative who was an analyst. I was sure I would be recognized. [Former analyst] disagreed, saying that the disguise was pretty good. I disagreed but I didn't say don't read it. The paper was read and my relative who is an analyst called and said it was pretty clear that my material had been presented. It was no surprise. A lot of people in the community knew this was the person I had been in analysis with. It was very painful.
>
> I thought I was being helpful to my analyst and to the analytic community. The synopses given of the treatment were pretty good but some were oversimplified. Very personal things were included like sexual history and transference fantasies with sexual content. Since I could be identified it was very painful. [Former analyst] didn't pick up on the boundary issues.
>
> That analysis was very helpful but only in my second analysis did I recognize other boundary issues in the analysis. My analyst sent me not only this paper about me but also other papers to get my feedback. My analyst knew that I wanted to write. That was hard because

this was my analyst, someone I idealized. It wasn't easy for me to do. I recognized two other people my analyst wrote about. It was a small community—I knew some of the other patients.

I went back into analysis twelve years later and into analytic training. In retrospect I realize I idealized my first analyst a lot. My first analyst was friendly with my analyst relative in the place where I was analyzed. Later they went out. I was jealous and appalled but I wasn't worried that my confidentiality might be violated. It felt unfair.

I don't think anyone in analysis can really give informed consent during the analysis. The analysis itself was very helpful and my second analysis even more so. But I feel disillusioned by the boundary violations and that I can't talk about what happened and that's hard. I feared being exploited and taken advantage of but my second analyst was very helpful with this. The writing part was bad but not as bad as the thing with my former analyst and my relative. I see it now as a continuum of boundary difficulties.

In terms of what was written, the things said were very gratifying—calling me brilliant and talking about my accomplishments. I didn't feel I learned anything I didn't know before about my analyst's views about me. But I did find what was written as over-simplified and that was disappointing. But what was more disappointing was that roles got confused. My analyst was treating me more as a colleague than a patient. I'm really sensitive to this issue now and when I write I would be very careful to disguise.

Although this analyst waited until after the analysis to write about the patient, the analyst's failure to adequately disguise the material, and, even more, the failure to respond to the patient's expressed concern about the inadequacy of the disguise, reflects an insensitivity that was extremely disturbing to the patient. As the patient notes, there were other boundary insensitivities. Similar to several other patients, this patient believes there was a confusion of roles. Even though it was after the analysis, this patient did not want to be related to as a colleague, consulted about her analyst's other writings; she wanted to remain in the role of a former patient; her transference lived on to some extent. But in this instance, the former analyst seemed oblivious that their past patient–analyst relationship should inform future behavior that was connected to this patient; the analyst felt free to have a dating relationship with a close relative of the patient's; the relative also felt free to engage in the relationship; the patient felt betrayed by both of them. As the patient noted, how the analyst handled writing about her material was just one in a continuum of boundary difficulties.

Another former patient-analyst described her feelings about her negotiations around being written about with her analyst.

> I told my analyst from the beginning I did not want to be written up anywhere or presented locally or in New York. I was asked permission to be presented at an IPA meeting the first year of my analysis and I granted this. Many years later following my leaving analysis, I was speaking to my analyst on the phone. Someone read a chapter in [the analyst's] book that was in the process of being written and it was about me. I was recognized. I became a bit upset and following several discussions the chapter was respectfully taken out.
>
> This is one reason why I have not submitted a paper I wrote, because I don't want to use my patient's life story to either glorify my work or compromise my patient in any way. This is a difficult topic.

This analyst's wish to write seems to override her former patient's clearly expressed wish that she not be written about. However, the analyst does ultimately respond to her former patient's distress. It is not clear whether this more respectful resolution, compared with the previous example, occurred because the former patient-analyst was clearer and more forceful in her protest, the analyst more sensitive and responsive, or a combination of these factors.

POSITIVE REACTIONS

Not Asked Permission during Analysis

One patient while in analysis as a candidate discovered that her analyst was presenting material from her analysis when she heard it at a scientific meeting.

> In the paper, he described a dream I had. The dream related to a particular topic he was writing about. He wrote just a little about the person who had the dream. I was the only one who could have recognized it as me. I had no idea I was going to be presented. He hadn't asked me about it. Then I also heard it presented at a national meeting and read it when it came out in a journal. I got a kick out of it. I

was in love with him and thought I was special. I was titillated, flattered, and not angry.

In my analysis, it fostered my talking about my transference that I had been reluctant to do previously. He asked me how I felt about it but never asked about permission to present it again or about publishing it. I guess he took my not being upset as it being okay. I was in a very unhappy marriage and very much in love with him. It did foster my fantasy, affirmed that he was interested in me, but I don't think it was disruptive. I did tell my husband about it; he didn't think it was so great, but I think it was a gigue to me to give my husband a hard time then, to make him jealous of my analyst.

As a training analyst, I listen to candidates today and I know they'd be much more upset about it. Was I being Pollyannaish? I don't think so. You've got to remember the times. There were only three women in my medical school class. I was used to sort of being harassed.

Analysts might feel concern that this analyst-patient was so gratified by her analyst's writing about her that issues of specialness might not have been sufficiently addressed. In addition, the erotic transference seems to have been intensified by the analyst's writing about her and might have further complicated an already troubled marital situation. Nonetheless, the patient-analyst herself believes that discovering she was written about by her analyst opened up transference feelings that had not previously been expressed. Her view many years later remains that this was a positive experience that she seems to have enjoyed and does not view as disruptive.

Asked Permission after Termination

Five or six years after termination of analysis, this patient's analyst called to tell her he was writing a paper and wanted to use her material as the central illustration. He wanted to know if that was all right with her and if she wanted to read it. She said she did.

I'd had fantasies that I would be a case he'd write about. I knew he wrote. The topic he wanted to write about was a recurring issue in my analysis. We'd done a lot of work on it. About a week after he called, the paper arrived. I read the draft. He was pretty thorough. I thought it was great. I'm a frustrated writer and enough of a ham. I have a past as [a writing profession] so I ended up doing two things—

looking at style and reading about myself as a patient. On the phone he said he'd worked at disguising it and one thing he had done was change my gender. That got my goat; it's my least favorite way to disguise; it's too radical, but I wasn't going to make a fuss. I made suggestions of other ways of disguising and corrected bits of background history that he got wrong and sent it back. A few weeks later he sent back the part about me as he'd revised it and said that if that seemed okay with me it was pretty much how it would appear. There was one thing we'd both missed and I corrected that. He hadn't changed the gender back but that was okay, though it felt funny. He offered the opportunity to come in and talk with him about the material but I didn't think it necessary.

One thing that surprised me in the analysis and again in his writing the paper was that he regarded this issue as serious enough that he wasn't sure the analysis would survive it. While I just thought I was doing my thing in analysis working on it, he saw it as a major resistance. When I sent the last draft back I said I was appreciative of the opportunity to go over this again and clarify it. He was delighted. I felt the experience of reading it was therapeutic, to be going over the therapy again. There was one piece where we remembered it differently. He said he felt we'd done a bit of analytic work in going over the paper. I agreed. The clarification was that he thought this issue had remained incompletely resolved even at the end of analysis. I was surprised; I didn't feel that. I responded to that in the first draft. It was like he had made an interpretation and I clarified; then he rewrote it and then it felt more the way I experienced it and I wrote that to him.

He did something that upset me and he was surprised that it did; it happened early in the treatment around eight to nine months. It involved an unexpected, unscheduled absence on his part. His manner of letting me know scared me. It left me hanging, not knowing; it frightened me very much. By coincidence later I learned the reality and once I did I was no longer afraid. I was angry that he had handled it that way. I thought he should have, would have, understood me better or felt as much compassion as I thought he would that he wouldn't have made this mistake. He handled it as a classical analyst would handle it and that was cruel.

What he did made no sense to me in terms of the kind of person I thought he was. It was upsetting but then it subsided and then resurfaced again as a resistance, not because he did something again, but a re-experiencing of the feelings. The issue kept resurfacing. He thought it had the feeling of something irreversible. The thing became an issue because to him it was a surprise that I reacted the way I did at that time. He had to work his reaction through and thought I just got a partial understanding of it. It was much less distressing to me than he thought it was.

One bit of error of fact surprised me. I thought in talking about my history I'd been clearer. All research about memory says we edit memories, but the mistake he made in my case fit better with the theory he was using than my material actually did. He addressed this in his final note to me. He had not corrected it after the first draft so I pounced on it as important and said again the way it really was in my history. In the letter he wrote when the paper was all done, he specifically addressed it. He referred to it as something he hadn't previously grasped and indicated he'd address it in the paper. So if it comes out as something he hasn't changed I'd be very surprised. He told me where he was submitting the article. If it comes out, I suspect he'll send me a reprint.

In a way, it would have been good if he had asked me about writing this while I was in treatment. I wouldn't have been surprised or offended. I have fantasies of how then he would have been sure to get this right. To read it during analysis would have been helpful. Writing about anything in depth has its own transformative analytic aspect. I think it would have been good and helpful to have it happen then. The disadvantage of it was that I could have gotten into a lot of intellectual bullshit. But I think by the time I was in analysis I knew myself enough to know when I was getting into that. If there had been a problem, it would probably have been along the lines of trying to make the relationship too intellectualized. But on the other hand, it would have made the treatment more collaborative around this particular issue, which would have been a positive thing; it would have smoothed the process out.

It felt empathic to me that he worked on what happened in the paper. It brought home to me how surprised he really was by my reaction. The manner of my reacting hadn' t seemed that surprising to me but it was clear that it was a real shock to him—much more than I ever realized. Realizing that and his working on it and writing this paper made me feel that he was empathic in the way I had originally thought he was. It was therapeutic to see the paper and to clarify things through it.

This former patient-analyst illustrates, as do many patients who are not analysts, how reading an analyst's accounts about the treatment can have therapeutic benefit. In this instance, the paper serves to clarify an affectively charged issue that remained more alive for the analyst than for the patient. Its clarification influences the representation that the analyst-patient had held of her analyst over time; she sees him as empathic in a way she has not since the early days of her analysis. While she had come to accept and tolerate her disappointment, reading the paper provided a reworking of this disillusionment and transformed her internal representation of her analyst. This analyst-responder's reaction may also be influenced by her theoretical position, which seems to be, at least in part, intersubjective. Not all patients, whether or not they are analysts, want to know their analyst's thinking. Other analyst-patients in this sample described how collaboration slipped into loss of clear definition in the roles of patient and analyst, which they found detrimental.

It should also be noted that unlike two other patient-analysts, she believes that the opportunity to read the paper during analysis would have been beneficial. Her reaction highlights how the meaning of being written about, and the specific content of the paper, is individual and idiosyncratic to the particular patient–analyst pair and the nature of their relationship. What can be concluded is that the meaning to the particular patient needs to be understood. A stance that benefits one patient may not benefit another.

DISCUSSION: DIFFERENCES BETWEEN PATIENTS I CONTACTED AND THOSE WHO CONTACTED ME

Six of the eighteen former patients-now analysts that I contacted in relation to the larger project did not report distress in relation to reading what their analysts wrote about them, whether or not their permission had been asked. Another four of this group of analysts, while troubled by some aspect of what the analyst wrote or the way it was dealt with, nonetheless retained positive feelings about their analysts and their treatment. In contrast, most—six out of eight—of the former patients-now analysts who initiated contact with me related experiences of mild to severe upset in relation to their analyst's use of them and their material. All the nonanalyst-patients in the previous chapter, who contacted me, expressed strong emotions about reading about themselves—though in their case, a number of the reactions were extremely positive.

While the number of analysts in both groups (reported in this section) are small as well as not comparable in number (eighteen patient-analysts contacted by me and eight patient-analysts who volunteered), the differences between the groups suggest a different dynamic may exist when people initiate contact. Since most of the former patients-now analysts who actively sought to recount their experiences were distressed, it may be that when negative affects are stimulated there is a pressure to tell and a relief in the retelling what occurred. Similar to people who have experienced trauma, recounting a narrative in which something unexpected and painful occurs helps to discharge some of the negative feelings. Especially when the person feels safe in the situation of reporting such events, there is likely to be some sense of deintensifying the negative affect from the initial experience. In the retelling, the person is neither alone nor helpless as in the original situation.

Telling provides an opportunity to have someone understand what was misunderstood as well as validation for the reasons for pain and distress. In addition, these negative experiences will be publicized supplying another sense of vindication for the sense of having been misused. All the analysands who volunteered had intense reactions, be they negative or positive. People who actively volunteer may be motivated by an intensity of reaction that is different from those who are answering the same question in a different context where they have not themselves sought to report the experience. Therefore, these two groups may not be comparable. For this reason, I presented their reactions separately.

Nonetheless, there is some crossover in the groups. In the group I contacted, one person was as distressed as most of those who contacted me. Five others expressed varying degrees of upset about how they were characterized; for one person, just knowing she had been written about, not the fact of writing or the content per se, was experienced as an injury that was difficult to recover from. And in the other group, two patients-now analysts who initiated contact with me did so to report positive experiences. One person who had enjoyed being the subject of her analyst's paper enjoyed displaying this again.

Another person provided an illustration of the beneficial aspects of reading about oneself.

QUESTIONING PREVIOUS ASSUMPTIONS

Analysts' accounts of their experiences of reading what their own analysts have written about them make several points clear. It cannot be assumed that analysts-as-patients will necessarily be distressed if their analysts write about them without permission. An historical perspective is also necessary. One analyst who had this experience accepted it with no distress; she did think that her bland response might be due to it occurring in an era when those in authority did not think permission was necessary. As reported earlier in the book, until the 1980s (and probably even longer), 70 percent of analysts writing for *JAPA* and *IJP* employed only disguise. When this practice was considered normative, fewer patients were apt to be distressed by it.

Currently, with the issue of patients' rights as a focus throughout the world, patients, perhaps especially when they are training to become analysts because they are more likely to be identified, may think differently and not so easily accept their analyst's writing about them unless he or she asks permission. As the interviews in this book have shown, at present it has become a more common practice to ask patients' permission, show them what is written during the course of treatment, and to negotiate changes about factual material and omit material that they wish not to appear. It is not surprising then that patients now are more apt to be distressed when they discover they have not been part of this process. But the material presented in this chapter also makes clear that some patients, even patients who are training to become analysts, do not want to know if their analysts write about them.

It should also be noted that another change in practice is that patients are more likely to be asked during treatment, rather than after termination. The advantage is that patient and analyst are able to process reactions. An important disadvantage is that how the patient feels about the analyst's request and the publication of this material may change over time. Of course, some patients who gave permission after termination also came to regret this decision.

The practice of asking and obtaining permission is no guarantee that patients, in this case patients who will become analysts, will continue to feel that their consent was a wise decision. A number of the analysts-then patients in this study came to regret their consent. Some of them stressed the fact that informed consent was not possible under the sway of the transference. As stated previously, many analysts also have raised this concern (Aron 2000, Gabbard 2000, Goldberg 1997, Stoller 1988, Tuckett 2000a). However, other analyst-patients did not regret their decision to grant permission. There are no simple answers or generalizations. The sensitivity of patients to disclosure and of analysts to patients' vulnerabilities and to their own ability to respect and maintain boundaries varies. It seems also to depend on the particular patient and the particular patient–analyst pair.

INTELLECTUALIZATION

The concern that patients who are, or are training to be, analysts are likely to intellectualize the treatment process when reading about themselves is not supported by the conscious reactions of these patient-analysts. Perhaps those who expressed little reaction were employing this defense, but there are no data that clearly indicate intellectualization as a response. Rather, many of these who shared their experiences expressed intense affect about being the subject of their analysts' writing. However, the sample size is small; it may be that for other patient–analyst pairs intellectualization does turn out to be an impediment to deepening the analysis when patients read about themselves. However, it is likely when this is true that intellectualization is a defense that appears in many other contexts as well and would likely come to the fore as a defense to be analyzed one place or another.

WRITING AS HURTFUL

The material provided by these twenty-six analyst-responders echoes and reinforces the data provided by the eleven patients who are not analysts. Some generalizations about what does not work out well will be repeated and summarized. First, in those instances when the request to write about a patient-analyst is part of a pattern of boundary crossings, and sometimes violations, the patient-analyst has suffered from a generalized abuse of authority where the paper was only one instance of this problem.

Although the patients who reported these cases were upset, many of them still maintained that other aspects of their analyses were helpful. This may well be true. However, it would seem that despite their distress they were not as outraged as might be expected. These reactions may reflect the same transference-related attachment that was noted in the Philip Roth example. Four of the seven analysts who were written about by their own analysts when they were patients do not feel this was harmful to them. A fifth objected only to the timing of publication and the sixth only to the disguise. A seventh did not object to the material being used but wished her confidentiality had been better preserved and that she had never learned about it. However, this analyst describes longer-term untoward consequences: the sense of betrayal engendered by the experience made it hard for her to enter another treatment. Her experience is perhaps an argument against actively pursuing information about a patient's reaction to the analyst's writing.

It is noteworthy that a relatively large number of analysts in this sample had themselves been the subject of a paper by their analysts. It may well be wondered whether other analysts who discovered they had been written about felt more troubled by the experience and, as a consequence, have chosen not to write about patients. I know of no data on this topic. The question of the power of the transference remains.

Second, as previously stated, when the written material contains descriptions that are unflattering or pathologizing, patient-analysts are invariably hurt. The same is true when clinical illustrations reveal something that has not been communicated or negative countertransferences are portrayed that have not been analyzed as part of the analytic work. One analyst, interviewed for another part of this project, described a former patient who had previously given permission rescinding it after reading the material. One of the patient's comments was, "I thought you liked me." As has been noted, other analysts emphasized that they would never write anything that might shame a patient or expose something that might cause a disruption in the patient's life if it were to be recognized.

Another potential problem created by patients', even former patients', reading about themselves is the loss of their role as the patient. These interviews highlight the slippery slope involved in patients' reading and making clarifications about their material. Most analyst-patients welcomed the opportunity to review and correct factual errors, misunderstandings, or disagreements about what had occurred; in some instances, this process was therapeutically and analytically very useful. However, the interactions about the written material could, and sometimes did, slip into a more collegial exchange. The patient-analysts then frequently expressed their upset that their analysts had lost their role as analysts and their appreciation of their patients' roles as patients. Even after the termination of analysis, at least one patient-analyst minded being engaged with her former analyst in this fashion; for this particular former patient, the distress was part of a much wider insensitivity to boundaries. Not all former patient-analysts share this feeling. Some former patient-analysts welcome a more collegial relationship after termination, but others do not. Again it is necessary to try to be sensitive to these individual variations.

INDIVIDUALIZING

These caveats apply to all patients, not just patients who wish to become analysts. What is also clear, and should not be surprising, is that what is shameful, hurtful, intrusive, or exposing varies for the particular patient. Sensitivity about how clinical material is written and how the patient will experience it varies as much as any other aspect of the clinical process.

The reports of analysts who were asked by their analyst for permission to write and publish their clinical material gives a particular window on these experiences. Part of what needs to be considered is that the majority of the reporting former patient-analysts are also people who themselves write. A number of these analysts, although very critical of their own analyst's behavior in relation to writing about them, believe that they have a better way to approach this issue. However, some of the solutions they have found are ones that have proven unfortunate choices for other patient-analysts. The fact that particular approaches work with some patient–analyst pairs and not with others may have less to do with the issue of writing per se and more with either the dynamics of the pair or, at times, a more general problem the particular treating analyst has around boundary issues.

In the fourth and final section of this book, I will discuss what readers and the larger community view as acceptable practices when using patients' examples from slightly different perspectives. The topics of writing about oneself in disguise and ethics in clinical writing will be considered.

IV
OTHER CONSIDERATIONS IN CLINICAL WRITING

13
Self in Disguise

When analysts write about clinical material, they most often write about ideas that have been stimulated by their work with patients. But often, intellectual interests also relate to personal concerns. Under these circumstances, they sometimes write about themselves. When they identify themselves as the source of the material, the papers usually relate to self-analysis (Eifferman 1987, Gardner 1983, Jacobs 1991, Silber 1996, Smith 2001, Sonnenberg 1991), personal experience in analysis (Guntrip 1975, Hurwitz 1986, Little 1981, Simon 1993), and countertransference awareness (Casement 1985, Crastnopol 1999, Ehrenberg 1992, Pizer 2000, Schwaber 1992, Spillius 1994, Yanof 1996). Sometimes, however, it has been concluded that analysts have written about themselves in disguise (Deutsch 1973, A. Freud, 1922, Freud 1899, Kohut 1979). Since they have concealed their identity, the fact of their subterfuge comes to light only if they or someone else later reveals it. As a result, it is not possible to know how frequently analysts do actually use their own material as clinical illustrations. There is a history of writing about oneself in disguise that goes back to the earliest days of psychoanalysis (Freud 1899).

In this chapter, ideas about the use of disguise of the self in clinical illustration will be considered in relation to personal privacy, professional aspiration, and scientific validity. Problems of objectivity, the influence of subjectivity, misunderstanding, disguise, and misrepresentation are discussed in relation to contemporary attitudes and practices of analysts in this sample who have written about themselves in disguise as well as in relation to case examples from the psychoanalytic literature where it has been presumed that analysts have disguised themselves.

The method for obtaining this information was the same as for all material in this book: telephone interviews or e-mail exchanges with analysts who published papers containing clinical examples primarily in three psychoanalytic journals (*JAPA, IJP,* and *Psychoanalytic Dialogues*). In the course of the interviews, they were asked whether they had ever written about themselves in disguise and their thoughts about this practice.

Nine of the thirty United States analysts who published in *JAPA* between 1995 and 2000 had written about themselves in disguise on one or more occasions. Ten[1] of the thirty-six international analysts who published clinical material in *IJP* during this time period had also written about themselves in disguise. Ten of the thirty-one North American analysts who had published in *Psychoanalytic Dialogues* had also employed disguise when writing about themselves.

ATTITUDES TOWARD WRITING ABOUT SELF-DISGUISE

The majority of analysts in all the samples who wrote about themselves did so because they thought their personal experience contributed to an appreciation of the ideas they were trying to illustrate. One analyst stated this succinctly:

> I wrote about myself from something in my analysis because I thought my illustration made the point better than anything else I'd heard from patients.

Some analysts who had not used their own experiences in this manner found the question about doing so an occasion for reflection

---

1. These analysts resided two each in Canada, England, and Italy and one each in Brazil, France, Peru, and Spain.

and a possible change of view. To quote an analyst who published in *JAPA*:

> I've never written about myself in disguise. I have written about myself in terms of countertransference. I'd be skeptical about the truth-value of doing that [writing about self in disguise]. On the other hand, a lot is written to support ideas. So, in a way, why not? I'm not a great fan of self-revelation, though when supervising it really helps when the therapist tells what is going on for them. But in writing? I don't know, but maybe it could work if it were done in a way that highlighted some idea.

A few international analysts who stated they had not written about themselves in disguise, like the American analyst just quoted, also said that if their own material seemed relevant to the ideas they were writing about, they would present them in this fashion.

Preserving Privacy

Five American analysts who published in *JAPA* and one relational analyst expressed no conflict about using themselves in disguise for the purpose of illustration. They made it clear that the reason for the disguise was to retain their privacy. In the first example, the issue of privacy is more implicit; in the other five examples a concern about the personal nature of the material is made explicit.

> I have written about myself and disguised it. I did it only in a small vignette and then once again in an unpublished article. When I gave the paper I wrote it as if I were a patient, but when I wrote it I made myself a respondent in a study.

> I wrote about myself from my own analysis on four occasions. Two times I stated it was my analysis and two times I disguised it. I showed all four vignettes to my analyst because it was about what he had said. Two vignettes he did not remember, but it was fine with him to use them and he said I didn't need to show them to him, but I wanted to. I don't know why I disguised two but not the other two. It occurs to me in the two in which I identify myself the emphasis is on my analyst's interaction with me and its positive effect. Whereas the other two are more revealing of conflict in me. I'd be embarrassed to have others know these internal workings in me, the more regressive conflicts.

I wrote about myself in disguise because I wrote about the treatment relationship and how it evolved. I wanted to describe what a terrible analysis I had. My analyst was sadistic. I stuck in there too long. I camouflaged myself as a man. I'm sure making it a man changed something, but I would have felt too exposed. I only told one friend I did that.

On one occasion I wrote about myself. The material was narrow enough in terms of the point I was making that it didn't matter. When I presented the paper at a meeting, I said it was me but for publication I made it a young [names another profession], which is what I wanted to be as a child. I disguised it probably because I didn't want anyone who read it to start reading into it.

I have used material from myself disguised by putting it in the third person. Though I haven't done this in recent years, I'm more comfortable being personal now.

Years back I used anecdotal examples from myself disguised as a patient. Now I find other ways to write about myself and my ideas that feel less private.

Change in Attitude about Privacy

Another analyst who had previously written personal examples in disguise expressed even more emphatically the comfort the last two analysts now feel about self-disclosure.

I have used myself disguised as a patient. Actually recently I wrote something directly autobiographical but the editor didn't think it was appropriate so I wrote it in the third person and described it as a mental health professional. I've used things from my analysis and written it as from a mental health professional patient.

The changes in attitude in what analysts report between "then" and "now" may reflect a change in the social climate regarding the acceptability of countertransference reactions and of self-disclosure. Until the 1980s, in the United States and in many, but by no means all, international psychoanalytic groups, countertransference responses were viewed as reactions to be contained and mastered rather than as sources of information to be learned from and not necessarily eradicable. Many relational analysts, as I have illustrated in Chapter 9, view self-disclosure as an intrinsic part of the work. Most of the relational analysts in the sample state they increasingly feel more comfortable about being self-revealing and now write about themselves in the first person. Many other analysts, who previously might have chosen to disguise themselves, now may be more likely to offer their experiences in first-person accounts. But as illustrated in the example just cited, not all analysts share this view and some editors may believe self-revelation to be "unprofessional," "titillating," "exhibitionistic," and "distracting from the issues being discussed."[2]

Discomfort about Having Presented Oneself in Disguise

Most of the twenty-one analysts publishing in *JAPA* who had not written about themselves in disguise merely stated this fact without any affective charge. But three analysts expressed a kind of outrage at the idea, saying, "NO" with emphasis or "Never." Five international analysts, like some of their American colleagues, expressed anger and were very critical of the idea of presenting their own material disguised. They viewed it as "deceitful" and creating "misrepresentations." One of these analysts stated it was "not fair play." The ten relational analysts who reported having written about themselves in disguise stated they had done so on only one occasion, early in their writing careers. In almost every instance, the example they wrote about was their own analysis and they had disguised themselves by writing in the third person, that is, "An analyst who. . . ." and so forth.

Throughout the groups sampled in this book, some discomfort was expressed about writing about oneself. The discomfort was most striking among analysts who resided outside the United States. They described that they wrote about themselves only briefly and some of them specified on only one occasion. None of the international analysts in the sample elaborated on this question.

Discomfort was also apparent in two analysts publishing in *JAPA*, who used their own material as part of a composite case. The cases were written to illustrate specific dynamic constellations. In both instances,

---

2. Quotes are from colleagues with whom I discussed ideas about self-revelation.

the personal material was blended into an illustration that primarily focused on another, in one instance a patient, in the other a supervisee. The analysts stated that they were cautious about what they have done on these occasions.

> I once wrote a very small thing about myself, something I understood from my own analysis when I wrote about a patient and blended it in. I don't know how it would be possible to write a whole case that way.

> It never even occurred to me to write about myself in disguise. But wait, not as a patient, but I did include myself in a composite picture—using an example mostly based on a resident I supervised, an element in the composite was from an experience when I was a graduate student that was woven into the example.

The first analyst emphasizes the "small"ness of the part that was self-disguised material and the impossibility of writing a full case in this fashion. The second analyst at first did not even recall writing using self-disguise. Both believed their use of the material was relevant, but neither of them seemed really comfortable with having used it.

A relational analyst, similarly, emphasized how little material about himself was presented in disguise:

> I have written about myself in disguise for a line or two, not a whole vignette, but I took it from when I was a patient. I quoted things that I said or thought to illustrate something else I was writing.

The doubts of another relational analyst were more specific. As we can see below, this analyst raised concerns about objectivity and "believability" when writing about oneself.

> I once wrote a little anecdote from my own analysis. It was broad, general, and small. I spoke it rather than writing it. I don't know how I think about that. It bothered me with Kohut [referring to "The Two Analyses of Mr. Z.," 1979]. It didn't have the convincing power as if it were about a patient. There is no objectivity. If I were to do it, I would write it and share it with some people to see what they thought. If it made the point or not.

Another relational analyst was very critical of himself:

> I wrote about myself one time and never did it again. It was an experience from my analysis where I was the patient and I wrote it in

the third person. It feels deceptive. It felt compelling and illustrated my point well, but I feel I don't want to do this. It has to be ethical. It feels weird to write about oneself that way.

It is clear that many analysts fear that they are being deceptive when they write about themselves without acknowledging that they are doing so. Self-descriptions do lack the objectivity of an outside observer even if they are revealed; however, they make a contribution in that they supply more immediacy of experience and sometimes explicate its subtleties more fully. This claim cannot be made for composite examples where some deception is an issue unless readers are informed. Moreover, composites can only illustrate phenomena that lend themselves to generalization, not the more nuanced appreciation of psychological concerns that a single psychoanalytic case study can reveal. Problems with composite examples will be discussed more fully later in this chapter.

Ethics

Being open about oneself was valued by many relational analysts interviewed for this book. Yet there were some, like the last analyst above, for whom the use of disguise to protect personal privacy did not seem acceptable. Not all analysts concur that there is something unethical in disguising oneself in the third person. Many analysts merely view it as a necessary convenience for protecting privacy. But clearly, there is controversy about this topic.

Objectivity versus Subjectivity

The reactions of these analyst-authors bring into focus the following concerns: Are examples employing self-disguise believable? Useful? If so, under what circumstances? Examples about the self cannot be entirely objective since no self-report can be. On the other hand, analysts now are aware that their subjectivity also influences all their case illustrations. While one could argue that it is reasonable to expect more "objectivity" when describing another person than when describing oneself, the reader cannot be expected to be aware of the multiple conscious and unconscious biases brought to bear by the author when reporting case material. Therefore, it is quite possible that the reader is no more likely to detect distortion in one instance than the other.

To some extent, clinical illustrations may always be semi-fictional accounts (Spence 1991). To cite a personal example, when I was a candidate in analytic training, one of my supervisors asked if he could write about my case telling me that he would show me the material before submitting it for publication. When I read the illustration, the patient was totally unrecognizable to me, though previously I had thought my supervisor and I had a very similar understanding of my patient. A parallel example is provided by one of the analyst-authors in this project. The analyst reported that when several patients read material written about them they failed to recognize themselves! In these instances, it may be that the analyst had discussed these patients in abstract, theoretical terms, distant from the patients' base of knowledge. Nonetheless, if examples are depictions that are intended to make ideas vivid and alive so that they can be generalized to other cases, then they need to be rooted in a personally recognizable form.[3]

Patients not informed that their analysts have written about them and who have come upon their own clinical examples hopefully will not think, "Oh, that's me!" But if they do not think, "That could be me" or "That's someone who sounds like me" or "who struggles with problems like mine" or "reacts like me" or some other form of self-recognition, then the analyst's subjectivity has sufficiently changed the example so that the illustration is supported more by fiction than by fact. Can such illustrations be viewed as any more "objective" or "valid" than self-reports? If patients do not recognize themselves is this due to the analyst's misunderstanding of the patient, or due to the disguise, or due to a difference in understanding between the patient and the analyst? There may be no clear generalizable answers to these questions. Only the examination of specific instances can be informative.

A difference between these unrecognizable examples and disguised self-reports is that the reader feels less betrayed by the former. Everyone knows subjectivity distorts; it's a matter of degree. Perhaps omit-

---

3. An exception to this assumption may occur when a clinical point of interest to an author was not central to the patient's difficulties and scarcely mentioned in the analysis.

ting information, just like omitting information as a means of disguise when reporting patient material, would address this concern. Another solution is to write in the third person, for example, "an analyst who" or "a patient who. . . ." This device leaves the situation ambiguous as to whether the analyst referred to is the author or some other analyst who gave the author the illustration.

Incidents of Suspected Self-Disguise in the Psychoanalytic Literature

Differences in the manner of disguise among the examples in the psychoanalytic literature can be distinguished. Four papers are thought to be portrayals of analysts represented as patients: Freud's (1899) "Screen Memories," Anna Freud's (1922) "Beating Fantasies and Daydreams," Helene Deutsch's (1921) "On the Pathological Lie (Pseudologia Phantastica)," and Heinz Kohut's (1979) "The Two Analyses of Mr. Z." In all four papers, a single case example is used to illuminate a clinical phenomenon.

In "Screen Memories," Freud presents himself as the analyst of the patient whose age and profession is slightly altered to disguise and distinguish him from Freud. He then reports the case as told by the patient. Freud uses his customary style of posing and then answering questions, but on this occasion they are interspersed in the dialogue with the patient instead of being directed to the reader. The self-analytic capacities demonstrated by "the patient" are impressive but they are also credible. It is not a full case history. Freud only recounts the features that are relevant to illustrate the nature of screen memories. The changes in age and profession do not distort the material. The issue of objectivity does not seem relevant since the point of the paper is to describe a phenomenon and the case example serves as an excellent illustration.

Anna Freud's stance in "Beating Fantasies and Daydreams" is slightly different. She refers to her father's paper on beating fantasies and states that one daydream is particularly well suited to illustrate the point of her own paper. She never specifies her role in relation to the material presented. The fantasy life of a young girl is traced from age five or six into her teenage years. It is told as a narrative in the third person. Her method of disguise is to omit rather than alter information. This paper also does not present a full case history. Only data related to the development and function of these particular fantasies are provided. The fantasies are elaborated in a plausible fashion and objectivity again does not seem a relevant concern.

Paul Roazen (1982) believes that Deutsch's (1921) paper "On the Pathological Lie" is autobiographical. He bases this view on quotes from her memoir about "a mythical love-experience" during her adolescence, which she describes as "the forerunner of my later tendency to fantasize" (Deutsch 1973, p. 54). Deutsch had not published this paper. It was Roazen who found it among her papers and then had it published in 1982. Therefore, it is not clear whether she ever intended to have it in print. If Roazen is right in his assumption that Helene Deutsch is the patient in disguise, then like some of the analyst–authors in this study, this experiment occurred early in her career.

In the paper, she clearly identifies herself as the analyst. Although a full case history is not given, she relates more factual history than Freud or Anna Freud did in their papers. In addition, she describes personal qualities of "the patient": "she was an attractive, much-sought-after girl, intelligent and with a lively temperament" (Deutsch 1921, p. 375). The case example illustrates her theoretical point. Her conclusion, in contrast, could be viewed as a self-deluding explanation for her own behavior. Liars, she says, "tell their stories in order to arouse the admiration, envy, etc. of their listeners . . . [and] the pseudologist merely follows an inner urge to communicate without really caring about the reaction of the environment . . . the content of the pseudology is determined internally and is not adapted to the tastes of the audience" (p. 382). Her assessment of the motive, while it may be correct, has to be treated with reservation. She is not just describing a phenomenon; there is an argument at stake here, a way in which she does not want "her patient" to be seen. Given the description she provides for the patient as being "attractive," "sought-after," and of "lively temperament," one could suspect that admiration and perhaps even envy were reactions that this analyst-author wished to evoke and that she may have denied this motive even to herself. The theoretical conclusions she reaches, therefore, do not convey a sense of total credibility once we suspect that she is both author and subject. Descriptions of personal qualities presented with an evaluative stance were not included in the papers by Freud or Anna Freud. But one must keep in mind both that the autobiographical content of Deutsch's paper is not accepted by all analysts (S. Gifford, personal communication) and that Deutsch herself did not submit it for publication. It may be that Deutsch had qualms about the paper becoming a part of the psychoanalytic literature; these reservations may have included the manner of presenting herself, if she is indeed the patient.

The belief that Kohut wrote about himself in disguise is based on statements made in the introduction to Cocks's book *The Curve of Life* (1994) that presents an edited collection of Heinz Kohut's correspondence from 1923 to 1981. According to Cocks, Kohut's son, and according to his son, Kohut's wife, believe that Kohut was describing himself when he wrote "The Two Analyses of Mr. Z." (1979). Cocks agrees with this speculation and provides parallels in the life of Kohut and Mr. Z. to bolster this idea. Over the years, this speculation has become treated as if were a fact (Gedo 2002; Rangell 2002). But there are other analysts who do not accept this conclusion (Ornstein in Strozier 2001). Lipson (2003) points out discrepancies in the history of Kohut and Mr. Z. that are significant. One example is that Mr. Z.'s father was reportedly hospitalized for several months when Mr. Z. was three and a half years old. His father was said to have fallen in love with his nurse. He did not return home until Mr. Z. was five. In contrast, Kohut's father left to serve in the Army for two years when Kohut was fifteen months. Another significant discrepancy is that when Mr. Z. sought his second analysis he was living alone and socially isolated. In contrast, when Kohut began his self-analysis he was married and had a son. A third point of contrast is that Mr. Z. was described as unfulfilled and underachieving whereas Kohut had a successful career and was increasingly prominent in his profession. These discrepancies present two men with significantly different levels of adaptation. If Kohut is truly Mr. Z., then the case provides a good illustration for Kohut's view that one can be highly accomplished and seemingly socially adapted and still suffer from a disorder of the self. This understanding of narcissistic vulnerability contributed to an appreciation of narcissistic phenomena. The case history of Mr. Z. was intended to illustrate a new analytic method for treating this disorder. If Mr. Z. is Kohut in disguise, then Kohut came to a more sympathetic view of himself even though it was misleading to couch it in terms of transference and countertransference. Whether or not Kohut is Mr. Z., many analysts find that Kohut's theory and technique have broadened their clinical understanding and enabled them to analyze a wider range of problems more effectively.

It is not my intention to join either side of this debate about Mr. Z.'s identity; rather I wish to consider the implications if Mr. Z. is assumed to be Kohut in disguise and the effect this assumption has had on many analysts' thoughts about using their own material in this fashion. I wish to highlight the differences between the other author-analysts who have presented themselves in disguise and Kohut, if in fact he is Mr. Z.

Both Freud and Anna Freud presented the clinical material through the patient as narrator. This device for conveying the data means it was recounted from an authentically subjective point of view. The analysis of the clinical material was presented in their own voice. To view their reflections and understanding of the phenomena described as self-analysis would in no way make their conclusions less credible. When analysts present their own material in the third person, as the voice of the patient, they are essentially following the model set by Freud and Anna Freud. The validation of their contributions comes from the clinical utility of those insights for colleagues. Kohut's intention, whether or not he was Mr. Z. is similar. He was proposing a new insight into a psychological phenomenon. What was different was that he imagined and described clinical interactions between patient and analyst. If he was Mr. Z., then at least some of this was fictional and not observed clinical data since he was playing both patient and analyst. On this account, the readership can legitimately claim deception even if what they learn turns out to have been valid and useful. Freud also presented a fictional dialogue but in his case it was only to relate the function of a phenomenon, not to illustrate a treatment process.

But it perhaps is not quite this simple. What if Mr. Z. is a composite of Kohut and other patients? Presentations of aggregates are an accepted practice for disguise. Or are they? Whether or not the readers have been told that this form of disguise is being used makes a difference. If they are not informed that the author has created a composite to make his or her point in order to preserve confidentiality, then they are doing what Kohut may have done in this respect. Unless Mr. Z. is a patient analyzed by Kohut, the dialogue between patient and analyst is fictional—be it from a composite or a fantasized interaction.

Clinical data can never be objective, like medical data. As stated many times before in this book, the analyst's subjectivity inevitably influences selection, presentation, and conclusions drawn. Deutsch's example, if it is in fact herself, becomes suspect only because the conclusions drawn may be seen as presenting herself in a way she wishes to see it, that is, to preserve a desirable image of herself. Since she never submitted the paper for publication, this deception, if that is what it is, is only a self-deception. She has not presented her theory to readers to convince them. But even if she had, readers would be free to reinterpret the data she presented differently, though of course knowledge that she was presenting herself might more quickly alert them to what could be seen as self-serving in her depiction and attitude.

But even when author and subject are not one and the same, the perspective of the author necessarily skews all data provided in clinical examples. The material is intended to stimulate the reader to consider a particular point of view. It is only if the author consciously withholds data that would contradict his or her conclusions that the data itself become suspect. Unconscious sources of distortion, of course, may also exist in any example, but readers understand that they cannot hold authors accountable for things of which they are not aware; however, they may perceive things that are ignored by the author and for this reason distrust the conclusions. When other analysts draw different conclusions from the data, theoretical debate occurs. Other fields also have debate about clinical conclusions drawn from data. What is different about psychoanalysis is that the actual data cannot be replicated in the same way. Even tape or video recordings, besides the inevitable effect of their presence on the nature of what transpired, do not replicate the clinical situation; they leave out the subjective experience of the analyst as well as the nuanced nature of the patient–analyst experience of each other that is not conveyed in words or images. For all these reasons, the expectation that psychoanalytic data conform to standards of other scientific data is not feasible.

What can be expected is that analysts do not consciously dissemble by excluding data that might support conclusions different from their own. It also seems crucial that they disclose when they are presenting composite pictures. Including material about themselves as part of an aggregate does not seem deceptive whereas creating a dialogue for a composite and presenting it as if it were an individual patient does. As

Halpern (2003) says, "We need to develop standards for intellectual integrity that pertain to the kind of subjective information therapists write about" (p. 133). I will return to this topic in the chapter on ethics and in the concluding chapter of the book.

What is different about Kohut's presentation of Mr. Z., if he is Kohut, is that Kohut is proposing a new clinical theory and technique based on the nature and evolution of a presumably self-analyzed transference. Since the account he presents of transference and countertransference must be unknown amalgams of self-analysis and imagination, the emergence and development of Kohut's theory would be based on self-analysis and presented as an interactive process with another; this would be an unacceptable use of disguise. In other words, the central points Kohut wants to make by using this example could not be supported because they originated from a fabrication. It is not that the self-analysis itself need be assumed to be invalid, but the "created" process might be viewed as self-serving and deceptive. Clearly, this does not mean his ideas were incorrect, only that his method for presenting them could in no way be acceptable.

The unfortunate consequence of the now commonly accepted belief that Kohut and Mr. Z. are one and the same person is that many analysts have come to equate presenting one's own material in disguise as intrinsically suspect. A rule of thumb might be to seek confirmation of one's self-insights in the material of others (patients, literature, etc.); it is likely that analysts will sensitively detect similarities in their patients that resonate with their own difficulties (Kantrowitz 1996). Under these circumstances, analysts could, of course, choose to present only their patients' material; however, as some of the analysts I interviewed state, sometimes they think their own material best illustrates the point they wish to make. I am suggesting that there is nothing inherently unacceptable about their using it, provided its use does not in other ways deceive the reader.

In the next chapter, I will explore the topic of ethics in relation to clinical writing. I hope to clarify the ways in which ethics in a "legalistic" sense is not usually a relevant perspective in this matter whereas clinical integrity is.

14
Ethics

As I have discussed throughout this book, when analysts write about their patients they have dual loyalties. They wish to preserve their patients' privacy and to contribute to the advancement of psychoanalysis as a scientific field. Of course, as has been acknowledged, when analysts write, they also serve their own professional ambitions and possibly other less conscious personal agendas. And as we have seen in the examples throughout this book, they are chancing clinical consequences for their patients if they ask their patients' consent, have them read what they have written, or if the patients discover and read the publication about them without having been informed. The primary ethical principle that guides their decisions is "do no harm." But it is not always possible to know in advance when harm may occur and which decision may cause it.

The struggle that many analysts experience in deciding whether to only disguise or ask consent as well indicates that "truth telling" is another ethical concern; many analysts become uncomfortable with the idea that they will not be respecting their patients' autonomy and will be "deceiving" patients if they publish material without their permission. However, other analysts believe these analysts have imposed legal ideas about "rights" and believe decisions should be related only to the ramifications within the psychoanalytic situation. This latter group of analysts is not consciously conflicted about employing only disguise; they believe in most, though not all, instances disguise alone is the preferred method since it imposes the least influence of the analytic situation. Both positions will be considered and discussed in this chapter. In addition, the analyst's own conscious and unconscious publishing agenda may vie with considerations of the effect on the patient, an ethical dilemma that may be skirted by denial or rationalization.

The psychoanalytic literature has very few publications of clinical material that further an appreciation of the relationship between ethical principles and the professional use of clinical material. The rights of patients certainly include the preservation of confidentiality. Legal judgment, as reported by the analysts in this study, indicates that the publication of clinical material does not necessarily require informed consent. Most psychoanalytic journals insist on adequate provision of disguise but not patients' permission for acceptance of papers. Only the *Journal of Clinical Ethics* ("Carter" 2003, Halpern 2003, Howe 2003) and *Contemporary Psychoanalysis* (Scharff 2000) mandate informed consent.

Ethical considerations are intended to protect patients. Ideally, they aid therapists in their clinical judgments. Ethicists' views, however, may not take into account many of the complexities of clinical situations and unconscious, as well as conscious, factors influencing patient–therapist relationships and their interactions. My intention is to highlight where ethical precepts inform, providing helpful guides for clinicians, and where they may be reductive, prescribing behaviors that may suit some situations well and others poorly.

In this chapter, I will summarize the current guidelines for publishing papers including clinical material, and the reports of three clinicians who specifically addressed their patients' reactions to reading about themselves in relation to ethical principles and the limitations they found in this approach. I will then discuss the conclusions reached by three ethicists who discussed one of these cases in light of what I have learned from interviewing 141 analysts and thirty-seven patients who read about themselves.

GUIDELINES FOR PUBLICATIONS

Guidelines for psychoanalytic papers were published in the *International Journal of Psychoanalysis* (Gabbard and Williams 2001). The editors addressed the need to both preserve patient privacy and present material in a manner that did not entail distortion or mislead the reader. They provided suggestions for ways of maintaining confidentiality, such as disguising of superficial details, using case material that is a composite of several patients, presenting a dialogue between analyst and patient without background biographical information, and conveying clinical material through a colleague as author. Whenever a paper includes clinical material, authors should specify which method they had employed to assure confidentiality. Requesting patients' consent was included among their suggestions, but the decision about whether this was clinically appropriate was left to the discretion of the author-analyst. Gabbard (2000) has elaborated the benefits and drawbacks of each approach. The editors eschewed standardization of any one particular method and espoused individualization based on the clinical situation.

A survey of other mental health journals conducted by Scharff (2000) reveals that most editorial positions are similar. The American Psychological Association, while having a printed code of ethics, does not specify guidelines for preserving confidentiality when publishing. The American Psychiatric Association states in *Principles of Medical Ethics* that there needs to be adequate disguise to assure patient confidentiality; specific guidelines are provided within each medical journal. The *Principles of Ethics for Psychoanalysts* of the American Psychoanalytic Association maintains similar criteria. The only psychoanalytic journal surveyed by Scharff (2000) requiring both disguise and permission was *Contemporary Psychoanalysis*.[1] In contrast to the editors of most mental health publications who do not advocate a standardized approach for preserving confidentiality, the International Committee of Medical Journal Editors

---

1. The instructions to authors of *Contemporary Psychoanalysis* state: "It is the author's responsibility to disguise the identity of patients when presenting case material and to obtain their written permission to do so." Scharff, J. (2000). On Writing from Clinical Experience. *Journal of the American Psychoanalytic Association* 48:421–447.

(ICMJE) maintains that clinical accounts of patients should not be disguised in any way and that informed consent must always be obtained from the patient who is the subject of a clinical report. Gabbard and Williams (2001) argue that this approach is not appropriate for the presentation of psychoanalytic material.

In agreement with their position, Wallwork (2005) maintains that legal applications are a misunderstanding of ethics; when ethics are applied in this fashion they act to shut down thinking. In Wallwork's view, ethical problems are really ones that fall in gray areas where there is a negotiation between high-level principles and the concrete specifics of each situation. Multiple values are in play. Moral narratives, such as the reports from analysts and patients in this book, are an essential way of learning ethics. By imagining oneself in the role of one without power as well as in the role of authority, an appreciation of an ethical position can emerge. Gabbard and Williams's and Wallwork's views parallel the stance of open exploration and individualization that has been advocated throughout this book.

While most analysts take precautions to protect their patients' privacy, I am aware of only three publications that specify clinicians' concerns as ethical when writing about their patients. I will briefly summarize these accounts to highlight the issues that are considered ethical and that underscore the limits of this approach when applied to the therapeutic situation.

CLINICAL EXAMPLES

Stoller (1988) provides an extensive quote from a patient who chanced upon a paper that included her clinical material. Years after terminating, at Stoller's request, she wrote about the experience.

> I scan the article before putting it aside for later, and my eye catches a vignette. Which I then read. I felt a kind of panic. I felt my blood turn cold. For there I was, the patient, displayed (circumspectly) on the printed page. Here I was being written about without knowledge of the fact. Confidentiality was not an issue. But I was stunned. I couldn't—and still can't very well—articulate my feelings. Later, as I read the article, I found myself devouring each word in my paragraph, searching for clues to your writing about my experience, prob-

ing the psychic space between us, trying to imagine your thoughts and feelings.

My feelings ranged from horror to outrage, from narcissistic pleasure to indignation. Even sadness welled up. I felt used. I felt particularly honored. But why such varied emotions? Were they peculiar to me and my histories? Is it akin to what a girl experiences when touched by her father in forbidden places, or is it a bit more generalizable, that there was a failure to respect our bond.

You said it hadn't hurt me, that you were justified because I couldn't be identified (I recall that slightly differently. I believe I said it need not have hurt her because she could not be identified, thereby ignoring in the comfort of *proper ethics* her more complex experience). Was that it? Was that the limit to your thoughts and feelings? How could you know that by not informing, or warning me, or whatever, that you were transgressing that sacred boundary, the infinite trust I placed in you. Why did it matter so? It was true [and], no one else knew. [pp. 381–382]

Stoller asks whether writing about a patient before termination is ever all right, whether the fantasies stirred in the patient who agrees are resolvable or not, and whether insight that comes from seeing oneself written about aids the power of interpretation or is harmful. These are clinical questions and they are similar to the questions I have raised and are raised by the analysts I interviewed. To Stoller, "Proper ethics" meant only that the patient could not be identified. His experience of his patient's distressed reaction made him reconsider this construction of his responsibility to his patients.

Lipton (1991) describes asking permission of a patient still in analysis to publish a paper in which the clinical example was about material that had been well analyzed and was no longer central to the analytic work. He assured the patient that he would be well disguised and wanted him to see what he had written and give his reactions. Lipton believed he was asking this as a question, but he later learned that his patient perceived this as offering him no choice. His patient "swallow[ed] his feelings of shock, anger and fear of exposure" (p. 971). The patient's mother had beaten him when he expressed anger and he was used to hiding his rage. He had a lifelong fantasy that his father would come to his aid and so he never allowed anger to be manifested toward him either. The transference to Lipton contained representations of both parents and prevented any direct display of the patient's anger. But it came out indirectly. The patient noted that Lipton was a poor writer. He then wondered about attending the meeting where Lipton was presenting the paper. Lipton told him the time, date, and place but added that his attending might complicate the analysis. The patient correctly interpreted this statement as discouraging his attendance and experienced it as if it were then forbidden. The patient then felt like "a child being discussed in absentia by gods who would judge him and decide his fate" (p. 971). What followed were demands for changed hours, emergency telephone calls, and reactions to imagined slights by the analyst.

"The request, so *ethically*[2] introduced out of respect for the patient, had the unexpected effect of recreating a problem the patient had always had with his parents. The request was experienced as a demand and as an unprovoked blow from a psychotic parent that had to be accepted immediately. Negative feelings had to be hidden" (p. 972).

Some years later the patient reread the paper and re-experienced his anger. He felt he was being described as crazy. Later still when the patient returned for a second analysis, he explained that he had agreed to publication of the paper because he thought the analyst would be indebted to him and that would lead the analyst to grant him a low fee in the future and be more tolerant of ways that he perceived himself to be difficult. Lipton believed the patient's entitlement could be worked through analytically, but his indebtedness to the patient for making the patient an exception was a piece of reality that would not change.

> I think now that my wish to present a paper was more noticeable and stronger than I realized at the time, and that my own needs interfered with the neutral analytic stance I thought I was maintaining. At the same time, the patient's pathology was heavily weighted in favor of his using many extra-analytic as well as analytic circumstances in a need to punish himself . . . and became grist for the analytic mill. [p. 973]

Like Stoller, Lipton is distinguishing between ethical and clinical issues. He does not have questions about the ethics of what he did, but he reexamines his clinical sensitivity and acknowledges his self-deception when making the request. The conflicts stirred up by the

---

2. Italics mine.

request process interfered partially with his analyzing capacity. There was a premature foreclosure of analytic scrutiny. Like many analysts described in these interviews, he acknowledged that his professional ambition at the time blinded him to the patient's best interest.

The third example is provided by a psychiatrist (Brendel 2002) who early in his professional career also requested permission to publish a patient's clinical material without anticipating sufficiently its clinical impact. The patient had been in an every-other-week psychotherapy for help with long-standing depression and social isolation. In less than two years, he had made considerable therapeutic gains. According to the patient, his work life, social life, comfort with other people, and self-esteem had all dramatically improved in treatment with his therapist ("Carter" 2003). The therapist had asked for his permission to publish a paper that according to the patient's understanding was to be about his exceptional progress. He was told that his material would be heavily disguised and that he could read the paper once it was published. The patient gave his consent.

When he was given a copy of the paper, a little over a year after it was first discussed, the therapist told the patient that progress he had made since the time of the writing—the last six months or so—had not been included in the paper. He also told him that he had "embellished the description" (Brendel 2003, p. 90) both to protect his confidentiality and to emphasize certain clinical features for the discussants' use of it in teaching. The patient took it home to read. When he did, he became very upset, angry, and humiliated. His therapist had described him in terms that the patient experienced as derogatory and condescending, making him feel like a laboratory specimen. His therapist seemed to have responded to him with annoyance, disappointment, and little compassion. He felt betrayed on several counts.

The paper as it was written was not what he believed he had given consent for. Rather than presenting his progress, which was what he had understood as his therapist's intended topic, the patient believed that the paper had exaggerated his symptomatology. He found it hard to understand how his therapist had not anticipated how upset he would be reading an account where he was described as so socially awkward. He blamed his therapist for not properly preparing him for the content in the article. In addition, there were accounts of his therapist's reactions to him that were very unflattering.

In the two-week space before his next session, "Carter's" reactions underwent several transformations. At first he believed the published paper represented reality and that he had distorted what had occurred. If he were as damaged as his therapist had presented him, he had to doubt his ability to trust his own perceptions. All his gains in confidence dissolved and one of his initial reactions was social withdrawal. Then he began to see that there were factual errors in the account and that his therapist had exaggerated his social awkwardness for the sake of illustration. How could he be sure which parts were false and which parts were true? Then he became angry. His trusted therapist had put him through this traumatic suffering and confusion. He considered ending the treatment with his therapist, even briefly had fantasies of suing him for emotional harm, though he did not seriously consider doing so. But after discussing the situation with friends, he decided to return and tried to clarify what had occurred.

The therapist was surprised by his reaction, and very apologetic about having caused the patient so much pain. He explained that the countertransference reactions he had written about were intended to show that these were a normal part of treatment and workable when the therapist is aware of them. He assured the patient the report was an exaggeration, that he liked and respected him and enjoyed working with him. The therapist also thought that the patient had focused only on his portrayal of him as dysfunctional and not attended to where some progress had been described in the article. The therapist proposed that they work together to clarify and repair what had happened. He also proposed that they present an account of what had occurred to an ethics symposium. He thought the situation made it evident that the *ethical guidelines* of requesting consent and thick disguise were not adequate for the clinical situation.

Both the therapist and the patient wrote accounts of their experiences (Brendel 2003, "Carter" 2003) and presented these to a panel of three ethicists for discussion at an ethics symposium. In these accounts, the therapist elaborated his shame, regret, and guilt. He wondered whether his professional ambition had unwittingly led him to exploit his patient in order for him to have a publication. He also questioned whether unconsciously he had avoided showing the patient the paper in advance for fear that he might then have withdrawn his permission to have it published.

In all three of these examples, the clinicians retrospectively became aware that the ethical guidelines were an inadequate basis for making clinical decisions in relation to publishing their patient's clinical material. Ethical principles are based on assumptions that there is a "right" and a "wrong" way that apply to all situations. Such assumptions are suitable in legal situations but they are insufficiently complex for clinical ones. Clinical integrity is different because it takes into account the analyst's assessment of the consequences of his or her decision on the patient, the analyst, and the analytic process. As we have learned, some analysts believe it is always detrimental to involve the patient while others are equally convinced it is a loss of integrity not to seek patients' consent. One group believes the analyst's request impinges on the patient by creating an awareness of the analyst's interests and reactions that can be detrimental to the process; whereas the other group believes the analyst's not making a request disrespects the patient by not granting full autonomy of choice about making public material that the patient had intended only for the consulting room. For the increasingly large number of clinicians who believe in individualizing, moral reasoning becomes an essential part of the decision-making process. Definitions of ethical principles are not invariant and the process of moral reasoning needs explication.

ETHICAL PRINCIPLES

I am presenting a range of ethical perspectives for analytic consideration. Different philosophical traditions offer different principles for guidance in moral reasoning in decision making. Lear (2003) contrasts the Judeo-Christian tradition based on absolutes—thou shall and thou shall not—with the ethical tradition from the Greeks. Aristotle did not believe that there was a rule book or law that could instill a person's character with virtues that are necessary for the achievement of happiness. The development of virtue requires sensitivity to the particular situation and changing circumstances. Applying these principles to analytic work, Lear gives the example that in some instances it would show courage to retreat and, at other times, it would show courage to keep analyzing. Lear concludes that if there is no rule book, then analysts have to trust their good judgment when making decisions about the method for preserving confidentiality when publishing clinical material. He does not, however, define "good judgment" or how it can be assessed apart from its consequences that cannot be known in advance.

Aristotle's view that there cannot be rules for ethical behavior, while flexible when compared with Judeo-Christian's ethics of right and wrong or Plato's belief that there was only one proper way to behave in a given set of circumstances, is not one of moral relativism. Aristotle maintains "there are various *correct* ways of living for different men. What is good for one person may not be good for another" (Popkin and Stroll 1969, p. 9). The *right* way for any individual cannot be determined by reason alone; it requires training and education to develop a moral character and wisdom. It also requires experimentation in actual situations. Aristotle subscribes to the principle of the mean; that is, virtue is acting moderately, choosing a behavior that lies between two extremes. Courage, for example, is the mean between cowardice and rashness. But where along the continuum each person's mean will fall is what varies. Some people can be more courageous than others, but each is proper for that person. These principles counsel moderation without prescribing one particular behavior for all, but they do not provide much guidance for decisions regarding the method for preserving confidentiality and the appropriateness of publications. The material from analysis involves two people, not one; what is the "proper way" for the analyst may not be the "proper way" for the patient. If the analyst is trying to take the patient's perspective into account, he or she may not be able to find the same middle ground.

Clifford's (1845–1879) ethics of belief offers principles that are more feasibly extrapolated to the dilemmas associated with publications. It is a more contemporary and pragmatic way of thinking about moral decisions. According to Clifford, right and wrong has to do with how people come to their beliefs. Three questions always need to be considered. First, has sufficient evidence been examined? Second, have doubts been suppressed? And third, has investigation of these doubts been avoided?

Clifford's thoughts on the inevitability of bias have a perspective that resembles those of current-day theorists about the effect of subjectivity. When a person holds a belief, even if it seems insignificant, it prepares a person to believe other, similar information as confirmatory and decreases the likelihood of believing contradictory evidence. When one holds a strong belief, or wishes to hold a belief on one side of a question, the examination of evidence on the other side inevitably lacks the "fairness and completeness" (p. 97) that would be applied when someone had a genuine doubt.

> We feel much happier and more secure when we think we know precisely what to do. . . . It is the sense of power attached to a sense of knowledge that makes men desirous of believing and afraid if doubting [but when one believes without sufficient evidence] it weakens our powers of self-control, of doubting, of judicially and fairly weighing evidence. [p. 98]

The issue is not the belief per se, but acting on it. Eventually, beliefs become strong enough to be acted upon. A person's belief does not remain merely a personal matter relevant to only him. Therefore, strongly held beliefs must be questioned. According to Clifford, even when the outcome of a given action has no harmful consequences, a person does not have the right to believe without obtaining and examining evidence on both sides of any given question; one has a duty to investigate the basis for convictions before acting upon them. From Clifford's perspective, even if there were no untoward consequences, the analyst's decision could not be considered ethical unless the analyst had pursued evidence for the anticipated effect of using only disguise, asking consent, as well as whether publication was advisable at all. In other words, moral reasoning means that the analyst has considered the possible consequences of the decision for herself, her patient, and the treatment, but it does not mean that the actual outcome can be predicted.

The question remains, even given all this scrutiny, whether anyone can be expected to overcome blind spots when convictions are strongly held. Consultations with colleagues is one way biased beliefs may be revealed, However, it is likely that those who are inclined toward a particular view will seek like-minded colleagues for these discussions and reinforce the beliefs they already hold. Influence by others in decision making depends on the balance of conviction and openness (Bernstein 1983). Discussion with respected colleagues can broaden one's perspective when sufficient openness exists, but, ultimately, there is no substitute for sensitivity to issues of the particular patient and judgment about one's capacity to deal with the clinical consequences of any given decision with this patient.

Areas for Ethical Consideration

In an ethics symposium, Joffe[3] (2003), Howe[4] (2003), and Halpern[5] (2003) discussed salient clinical decisions that confront clinician-authors: (1) ownership of clinical material; (2) when to write and whom to write about; (3) the nature of disguise; (4) the meaning of informed consent; (5) the manner of writing; (6) the impact on patients when reading about themselves; and (7) responsibility to the professional community. Most of the analysts' views have appeared earlier in this book but are repeated here to contrast or expand the ethicists' views.

OWNERSHIP

A potential clash of perspectives may occur between patient and analyst about the ownership of analytic material. Joffe thinks that it is reasonable that patients retain an interest in how their story is told even when they have given their consent for it to be published; however, he points out that giving them the power to determine interpretations could threaten the academic value and scientific integrity of articles. When a paper presents a therapy, there are two people's narratives, not just one. The patient's story is central to the therapist, but the therapist should be able to retain control over his own narrative. Therefore, Joffe proposes that there should be an "early, open, and mutually re-

---

3. Steven Joffe, M.D., M.P.H., is an instructor in pediatrics at Harvard Medical School, an attending physician in pediatric hematology and oncology at the Dana-Farber Cancer Institute at Children's Hospital, and the Hospital Ethicist at Dana-Farber Hospital.

4. Edmund G. Howe, M.D., J.D., is Professor of Psychiatry and Director of Programs in Medical Ethics at Uniformed Services University of the Health Sciences in Bethesda, MD, and Editor in Chief of *The Journal of Clinical Ethics*.

5. Jodi Halpern, M.D., Ph.D., is Assistant Professor of Bioethics and Medical Humanities in the Division of Health and Medical Sciences at the School of Public Health, University of California, Berkeley.

spectful conversation about the terms of presentation" (p. 104). When the clinician believes such an interaction would not be possible or desirable, then rethinking the ethics of presenting the clinical material is necessary. Joffe also points out that the clinician is perceived as the authority and therefore his construction of the story is likely to be viewed as definitive. He does not suggest that the patient's account should be privileged instead, but rather that claims of privilege be kept in mind in creating and reading narratives.

Goldberg (in press) delineates the boundaries of ownership. The narrative of and about the patient belongs to the patient; the analyst's ideas about the patient, his formulations of the patient's material, and his countertransference discoveries belong to the analyst. He provides a clinical example where the analyst wished to publish material, about his self-discovery and the patient was explicit that she did not want material from her analysis used in any fashion. The clash of perspectives created a stalemate for which Goldberg did not propose a resolution. The delineation of ownership does not solve the clinical fallout for the patient and analyst. Joffe's view would likely be to abandon the idea of publication, but the analyst could claim his right to publish material about his own reactions. The question, of course, is whether this would be possible without the patient being identifiable even to herself and without employing a disguise that distorted the data.

WHEN TO WRITE AND WHOM TO WRITE ABOUT

Howe states that both the timing of when to tell a patient information about himself and when to write should be determined by the patient's readiness. Requests for permission to publish clinical material should not be driven by the therapist's wish to publish. Halpern believes that patients' readiness is reflected in increased tolerance for ambivalence, decreased propensity to shame, and demonstration of the patient's ability to express negative feelings toward the therapist.

In the past, analysts had been trained to write about treatments only once they were terminated. The idea was that at this point in time it would no longer affect the patient. But now that analysts understand that transference does not dissolve with termination and can easily be revived (Pfeffer 1961, 1963, Schlessinger and Robbins 1974), this position is not so clear. Former patients' internalized representations of their analysts continue to affect them long after actual contact has ended (Tessman 2003). As previously stated, interviews with former patients indicate they may experience this later contact, as well as the content of what is written, as disruptive and upsetting, but not want to communicate or explore this with the former analyst because they do not want to return to feeling like a patient.

From the interviews in this book, we have learned that it is currently a common professional practice when writing extended case material for analysts to ask their patients for permission during treatment. Many patients seem to be appreciative of this practice; some even find it useful, but not everyone has this reaction. Some patients in this study detailed disruptive experiences. The literature reviewed in the first chapter informs us about many analysts' concerns that requesting permission and writing during treatment may intrude on the process (Aron 2000, Freud 1905, Gabbard 1997, 2000, Goldberg 1997, Renik 1994, Shapiro 1994, Stein 1988b). But we need to remember that they were also concerned that a request for a generalized permission at the onset of treatment, though advocated by some analysts who maintained this would avoid the regressive effect of the transference (Goldberg 1997, Lipton 1991, Michels 2000), was not an acceptable solution. In addition to the fact that meaningfully informed consent is impossible at the beginning of treatment (Lear 2003), Aron pointed out that analysts cannot know how appropriate it would be with individual patients until the treatment has evolved over some time. There are patients whom analysts would never consider writing about. While analysts differ about the particular characteristics they view as making patients unacceptable subjects for paper, they agree that assessment of these characteristics is unlikely to be reliable at the outset of the treatment relationship. All analysts agreed that when a patient's identity could not be sufficiently disguised, they would forgo writing about the patient.

DISGUISE

Joffe states that the standard of the International Committee of Medical Journal Editors (ICMJE) is that omitting details is acceptable whereas altering details that are not obvious to the reader is not.[6] However, he qualifies this statement. What constitutes alteration is not so clear since clinical material is always a construction altered to a greater or lesser extent by the author's point of view. This is not to be viewed as misconduct but as an inevitability of the nature of narratives, which is to be interpretative.

Howe believes whether therapists should only disguise material or request permission depends on the circumstances. When patients' identities can be disguised so others, including the patients themselves, won't recognize them and the patient will probably not be harmed, therapists should write only what they would directly say to the patients. Under these circumstances, he thinks they should *not* ask permission. His reason for this recommendation is that some patients "can read negative judgments" (p. 113) into whatever is written. Some patients may interpret being asked for their consent as the therapist "valu[ing] their own interests more than they do their patients'" (p. 114). Nonetheless, Howe believes that it is likely to be more harmful for patients to discover a paper about themselves and read it on their own than to read material in the presence of a therapist who has asked for consent.

Another concern about publications is that the material in the paper may be viewed as private by the patient. If a clinical point is dependent on the disclosure of this kind of private experience, Halpern suggests the author find another form of disguise, such as the use of aggregate cases. She also believes that use of composite cases is preferable to disguise when therapists write about psychopathology. In addition, obtaining consent would then be easier since the clinical details would be more limited and, therefore, could be processed in the treatment when it was timely. If patients did refuse, it would be less distressing to therapists since they would have other material to use.

Disguise poses certain problems for the scientific community. It may confuse readers by setting off chains of their personal associations that may actually not be pertinent to the case. At worst, the disguise may

---

6. This is the same position as the Committee on Scientific Activities of the American Psychoanalytic Association.

be used by others to support conclusions related to their own work, when, in fact, what they assume to be data are really fictional covers.

Because the nature of the data is different, analysts' views about disguise differ from many ethicists'. Ethicists generally are reviewing physicians' cases in medical reports that can be objectively presented and verified. Reports of therapeutic work are inherently different. The subjectivity of the clinician inevitably enters the account. Unlike medical reports where the patient's view is not usually relevant to the data, inclusion of the patient's account might cast clinical material in a different light. The reader must remain aware that the patient's perspective is not included. The data presented, therefore, cannot be objective in the same way as in medical cases.

Analysts and ethicists agree that patients' identity must be protected. For this reason, as previously stated, most analysts do not write about patients in the mental health field or those who have relatives in it. If they do decide to write about them, they usually ask permission and have the patients read what they have written before publication to assure the disguise is adequate. Unfortunately, however, there are times when analysts do not sufficiently attend to their patients' concerns about adequate disguise. As we have seen, many of the patients surveyed in my research have felt exposed and betrayed.

Frequently it was the disguise chosen that patients found to be upsetting. Often they felt it illuminated their analysts' countertransference or unconscious feelings about them. You will recall the male patient disguised as a woman who was distressed that his analyst chose this method to communicate his view of the patient; in another instance, a female patient felt injured that her analyst stripped her of her accomplishments by describing her as a housewife rather than as a professional. She wondered about her analyst's unconscious competitive feelings.

As stated previously, some patients do not want to read what is written about them; what is more, some patients do not want to even know that they are being written about. We now know that when some patients have found material about themselves for which permission had not been sought, they have returned to their analysts to discuss it and satisfactory resolutions have often been reached; but others were upset and did not return. Some have assimilated the experience but others have continued to be distraught.

Composites, Halpern's suggestion, may work in some instances, but there are anecdotal accounts of patients who have been furious about this device. They have felt that the essence of them has been malformed by being placed in an aggregate. When discussing recommendations for writing, Halpern addresses this very problem. She points out that patients are distressed when they feel salient aspects have been overlooked, or that they have been "reduced" in the presentation. Composites as disguise suffer from precisely this drawback, making this solution untenable for many analysts.

Informed Consent

Howe believes that when patients need to be presented in great detail therapists should disguise as much as they can, write only what they would say to patients, and ask patients' consent. They must take the time and have the countertransferential ability to discuss the written material with the patient in person before it is submitted for publication. If the patient requests that the therapist not publish the material, or if the therapist believes the patient's reactions suggest he or she may be harmed, the therapist should stop writing. Unless this careful review of material is part of the ongoing therapeutic process, the patient should not have to pay for this time. The avenue of asking consent should be employed if the therapist is in doubt about the right thing to do.

Joffe suggests that in addition to asking for consent authors should tell subjects how their privacy will be protected and should negotiate the specifics with their patients. Authors should show patients prepublication drafts of their papers to assure disagreements about confidentiality do not exist and, if they do, respect the time needed to resolve them.

Halpern (2003) believes that the psychotherapeutic relationship may make truly autonomous decisions impossible. To make an autonomous decision, it is necessary for a patient to have an adequate understanding of what is being consented to. Understanding requires adequate information. At a minimum this would mean reading what is written prior to its publication. The patient must know the purpose of the publication to be able to evaluate the work. In therapy, however, it would be unusual for the therapist to state his motives. Revelation of the therapist's professional ambitions, if this were a primary motive, would cross a boundary that might complicate the therapeutic relationship. The therapist also does not usually tell the patient who the readership will be in terms of how empathic or respectful in regard to clinical material. To fully acknowledge the variable sensitivity of readers would also seem difficult.

Halpern emphasizes that the pressures from the transference make true volunteerism unlikely. Rather, fear or idealization makes compliance likely. Therapists, therefore, should try to be aware of their own needs and try to minimize their impact on the treatment. She believes that most patients may not feel free to say no. To be able to make an informed consent, patients need to be able to deliberate about their decisions. But since therapy often involves a regressive process, the patient does not have his "most mature, competent and logical self" (2003, p. 126) available in sessions for discussion with his therapist. Discussion with friends often does not occur because many patients do not feel comfortable revealing details of therapy to them. Discussing decisions with an outside consultant would be costly of time and money, and there would not be the necessary alliance.

As stated in the beginning of the book and in this chapter when discussing problems in relation to the timing of requests, many analysts are sensitive to the problems of informed consent (Aron 2000, Gabbard 2000, Goldberg 1997, Stoller 1988, Tuckett 2000a). Like Halpern, they cite the influence of the transference making a truly informed decision impossible. Even if there can be no truly informed consent because of the influence of transference, if patients are asked for permission and the analyst believes they will want to read the paper, they should be told in advance what they are agreeing to; it is the analyst's responsibility to be sure that it has been explained in detail. Furlong (personal communication) adds that analysts need to appreciate that we deal in levels of the mind and that some parts permanently function at the level of magical thinking and dependent mirroring in the significant other. This level can be understood and partially tamed, partially redirected and sublimated, but never mastered. So informed consent necessarily involves us in a professional splitting between our clinical self as a transferential object and our rational identity as a member of a wider scientific community. Even if patients have adequate information about the field of psychoanalysis to evaluate their analyst's publication, which they usually do not, issues of transference would likely color their judgment.

Many analysts assume that patients will not be able to refuse. Although many patients may not, the finding in this study indicates that some patients do, in fact, withhold permission; as previously stated, eighteen analysts had patients refuse to grant consent. Analysts also describe their own decisions not to use material as well as rescinding permission given by patients when they believed it would be detrimental to the patient's treatment. It is likely that all of these nonpublication situations also have a clinical impact. The request, not only the publication, has an effect.

MANNER OF WRITING

Halpern (2003) provides specific suggestions for how therapists should write about their patients. She advocates using "humanizing language," addressing "strengths and growth as well as illness, and timing case writing according to patients' needs, rather than according to therapists' academic opportunities" (p. 130). She argues that therapists' subjectivity is inevitable. It is an illusion to believe that one can present clinical material objectively; this assumption both reifies patients' psychological processes and denies the influence of therapists' character, conflicts, and style on the process. Her other suggestion is that papers should focus on clinical process that captures particular meaning rather than trying to give an overview of cases. Descriptions of process are inherently less objectifying because they include contributions of feelings and vulnerabilities of both participants.

This form of writing, she realizes, may be problematic in that it exposes therapists' reactions to patients in ways that could be countertherapeutic, such as feelings of love or hate; however, she believes the exposure of "less threatening negative emotions might not be harmful" (p. 132). Halpern also believes the "medicalized" case format (p. 134) is inappropriate for reports of psychotherapy patients. Diagnostic language is dehumanizing and sets the patient apart as "sick" in contrast to the "normal" reader. To fit patients into preexisting theories or etiological accounts of disorders is objectifying. Both judgments of generalization and prediction can foreclose the emergence of new aspects of the patient, an interference with the very goal of treatment. Writing about an area of conflict or state before it has been thoroughly discussed in the process of the work with the patient can potentially foreclose the patient's understanding or, due to the nature of transference, risk the patient's submitting uncritically to the proposed constructions by their analysts. Potentially, it may also foreclose the analyst's openness to hearing other or contradictory material in relation to the specific issue.

As stated earlier, she also cautions against writing about material that the patient feels is very private. She advises against writing in a way that omits what patients feel are salient aspects of them or in a manner that "reduces" the patient's life or person for a didactic purpose.

Howe (2003) emphasizes that conformity with scientific conventions of presentation may be experienced as objectifying and demeaning to patients. He believes that the manner in which therapists speak, write, and "even think about their patients may affect how therapists feel about their patients" (p. 112) and how their patients respond. Joffe states that in addition to a truthful account, the author must be both humble in his/her claims and respectful and non-shaming of the patient.

A considerable number of analysts in the study address similar points. As previously reported, one analyst's sensitivity to analysts writing about their patients in pathologizing words or condescending tones led her to be very careful never to write in this fashion. Another analyst-author who employed only disguise emphasized that he wrote in a manner that should patients ever discover an article, they would never feel shamed or surprised by what it contained. Only material that had been discussed in the treatment would be included, and material considered private would be excluded. The tone would always be respectful. This analyst-author, as well as many others, would not write about negative countertransference. However, analysts were not uniform in this view. Some analysts, most often those who subscribed to a relational perspective, believe that if negative countertransference reactions are processed with the patient, they are an appropriate topic for papers.

Some patients may be able to accept material that is embarrassing without too much distress, but others have felt humiliated. The sense that one's mind or person had been represented in a partial way is another potential source of injury. Of course, what is shameful to one person may not be to another; nevertheless, a good starting point for analysts might be to imagine how they would feel if the material they are presenting were about themselves.

IMPACT ON PATIENTS WHEN THEY READ ABOUT THEMSELVES AND REPARATIVE RESPONSES

Howe addresses the necessity of learning from patients. When patients respond negatively toward therapists in relation to clinical descriptions, the therapist should take it seriously that the patients have been hurt; this reaction should not be viewed as primarily reflecting personal psychopathology. Since patients may also be afraid to ask questions, therapists should try to discern what might be a patient's reluctance. When therapists unwittingly hurt patients, they should try to make amends as well as try to search for hidden, negative meanings patients may have taken from what occurred. And when therapists do feel negatively toward a patient, they should try not to react based on this feeling but try to confirm that "there is good reason, whether they or these patients know it, for these patients to do whatever it is that they do" (p. 111).

Halpern believes that assessing the effect of patients' reading about themselves cannot be done on the basis of patients' immediate reactions. As stated before, she defines harm as an interference with healing. Feeling pain is not necessarily anti-therapeutic nor is the lack of distress a guarantee there will be no detrimental consequence. Halpern also stresses that therapists may be overly confident about the benevolence of their intent to protect the patient. She believes that the kind of empathy conveyed in a clinical engagement is not possible in the written material because much of empathy is nonverbally transmitted. She cautions therapists not to count on their empathic presence having the same therapeutic effect on a patient while reading what the therapist has written as it would have in the treatment situation. Nonetheless, she believes that if therapists validate their patients' perceptions and are not defensive, great benefit may result from the process.

Joffe (2003) states that therapists are accountable to their patients as well as to their professional communities. He suggests that "narratives can actually help bring together what were once rigidly separate communities of caregivers and patients" (p. 106) when they enter a collaboration about what will be presented.

As previously reported, some analysts offer examples of actively, not only reactively, using written material as part of the work. They point out that misunderstandings of which they had previously been unaware came to light and were clarified. The written article for some patients provides a mirror, as Halpern suggests, validating the patient's perception while also facilitating consolidation and strengthening of self-confidence and feelings of being empathically recognized. It can also bring to the fore certain issues that had not previously been so apparent and, at an appropriate time, may provide a "useful de-idealization" of the analyst (Lafarge 2000). In other instances, when patients read an account of themselves, it highlighted a central transference dynamic that gave a powerful reality to their current engagement or affective state.

RESPONSIBILITY TO THE SCIENTIFIC COMMUNITY

Howe points out that leaving the decision about the method of preserving confidentiality to the judgment of the individual clinician, while best for the patient, decreases the readers' ability to assess the scientific validity of what is reported. In agreement with Howe, Joffe states that if vignettes are too thickly disguised, it may present a problem for both science and education. It threatens the credibility and veracity of the published material. Joffe proposes that when disguises are employed authors should inform the journal editors and peer reviewers what has been altered or omitted in order for them to determine whether the validity of the case has been compromised. He also emphasizes that while patients have the right to refuse to have their material presented, they do not have the right to suppress the therapists' interpretations of material if they consent to the paper's publication.

As I have reported earlier, analysts also express concern about practices that may mislead the scientific community. Disguises may cause the reader to make erroneous conclusions (Klumpner and Frank 1991, Lipton 1991). Using composites may seem too much like fiction (Goldberg 1997). Many analysts interviewed suggest that authors employing thick disguises alert readers to the fact that this has been done. But this practice may, in fact, "blow" the disguise. As previously stated, Reed (1993) instead proposes that readers be aware that disguises are employed to protect the patient's confidentiality and read the material only for the point that the author is trying to illustrate and not assume the background data is factual. As stated in a previous chapter, Levin (2003) expresses the concern that patients' approval of their clinical material may also lead to the readership being suspicious about the veracity of the account since patients' narcissistic sensitivities might lead to censorship of important material. And as also previously mentioned, analysts' own self-censoring in presenting material potentially embarrassing to patients may also lead to a distorted representation of psychoanalytic work in the literature.

DISCUSSION

The ethical principles proposed by Clifford over a century ago seem relevant today. We cannot escape being biased by our own beliefs, but we can be vigilant about the fact that we are subject to this influence. A belief that one approach—be it disguise alone or consent—is invariably the correct one is belied by the findings in this study. Analysts need to argue with themselves against their own point of view. It is incumbent on analysts to ask themselves what they imagine the effect on each patient of asking for permission versus discovering they had been written about. Evidence to support asking for consent includes a patient's ability to appreciate the value of publications for the professional community, to be able to compartmentalize the personal from the professional benefit in relation to their material, to have the capacity to express and explore negative feelings and reactions in relation to the analyst, and not to be too prone to reactions of shame. When analysts decide to ask for consent and it is granted, they need to listen carefully for derivative material that suggests the patient's contradictory feelings, and explore them with patients. In other words, in accordance with Clifford's principles, analysts need continually to argue with themselves against their own bias only to disguise or ask for consent and against their self-interest in wishing to publish. It is also suggested that they subject their thinking to the scrutiny of an external observer who is more likely to be aware of transference/countertransference blind spots and biases created by conviction and self-interest.

Ethicists' commitment to protection of the patient's confidentiality and veracity of accounts is not questioned. But when the principle of the clinicians' integrity is linked to informing and gaining consent from the patient, this tenet may conflict with another ethical precept, "do no harm." Both ethicists and analysts are likely to conclude that under these circumstances analysts should not include the clinical material in their writing. But if the only published accounts are ones that patients read and consent to, the literature will be skewed in a manner that distorts the nature of the therapeutic enterprise. Potentially, it threatens both scientific integrity and learning about both theory and technique. The literature, then, rather than advancing knowledge, might malform it.

15
Conclusions

In this final chapter, I revisit and expand themes that have recurred throughout the book: (1) the analyst's process: his or her motives for writing, reflections on the use of patient material, process of decision making, and considerations of the effect on patients; (2) the impact of decisions on the patient and clinical process; and (3) the effect of decisions on the professional community and psychoanalysis as a field.

THE ANALYST'S PROCESS

Reasons for Writing

Why do analysts write? Most analysts in this study stated that their reason for writing about patients was to illustrate a concept, theory, or technique. A smaller number of analysts believe that their clinical writing reflected a more personal need to work out a countertransference. Some analysts consciously wrote as a way to work out their understanding of what was occurring or had occurred in the treatment. One analyst described feeling a need to shed "an excess of stimulation coming off the case." Writing became the vehicle to discharge the overload of stimulation.

Generally, thoughts about countertransference involve reactions stirred by the individual patient. Psychological conflicts or characterological patterns of adaptation and defense mesh or clash and awaken preconscious and unconscious aspects in the analyst. The analyst's capacity to grapple with these reverberations presents an opportunity not only to help the patient but also for personal psychological growth. Writing is a way to explore and expand self and other knowledge.

Some analysts, particularly those influenced by the French, also consider the trans-individual nature of unconscious life and its need for expression. Mauger (2003) believes that there is a need to disclose transference material publicly because these unconscious concerns are shared universally. Writing provides "a release valve" for the overflow of unconscious stirrings that are not specific to the particular patient–analyst dyad. To recast this perspective in terms more familiar to non-European analysts, all people struggle with conflicts about aggression and sexuality, even when these are not the central concerns that lead them to seek psychological help. Working intimately with another person who focuses his or her yearnings, needs, and unresolved conflicts and all the defenses against the emergence of these same issues, evokes an intensity of response and defenses against such responses that the analyst needs to contain, understand, and use for the patient's benefit.

The specifics of conflict, defense, and affect stated between patient and analyst may or may not overlap, but there is a dimension that is bigger than any particular dynamic constellation. Analysts need to have a forum for expression of this tension. Writing about patients and clinical situations provides this outlet for the individual analyst and simultaneously provides a vicarious source of release for the reading analyst. A shared sense of struggle with human vulnerability and conflict makes writer and reader both less alone. It helps them to metabolize tension and stimulation through its explication and communication.

Mauger contends that unless the cumulative pressure created in the analyst, created less by his exposure to personal histories (no matter how troublesome these may be) than by exposure to universal unconscious stirrings that are part of human experience, is given some form of expression, it may cause an impasse in the treatment. Accordingly, while there is a danger in revealing too much and breaking confidentiality, there is also a danger in revealing too little. Writing serves an affect regulatory function.

While there is, no doubt, this universal tension, I am inclined to think that different contents stimulate tension for different analysts and for some analysts more than others. Writing is likely to help analysts discharge this affect as they clarify the conflicts that have arisen. Analysts may also have specific motives, some conscious and others not, such as when writing is an act of revenge (Gabbard 2000) or reparation (Stein 1988a). My speculation is that even those analysts who profess to be illustrating concepts, theories, and techniques are also reworking both specific personal concerns and discharging a more general affective stimulation stirred and left over from analytic engagements; however, they may not be conscious of, or perhaps just not want to publicly acknowledge, its presence.

Some non-writing analysts believe that analysts who write listen to patients with a writing agenda. Undoubtedly some analysts may do so; however, this was not substantiated in the interviews done for this book. While it is likely that once an analyst is writing on a particular topic, he or she is sensitized to hearing material related to this subject and may possibly make more inquires about it than previously, this is not the same as listening to patients to find a topic for writing. Listening is inevitably influenced by the analyst's subjectivity: his or her interests, values, beliefs, and conflicts. The fact of the analyst's writing is not likely to skew his or her attention any more than other internal pulls seeking external expression. In fact, unless a particular writing agenda is continued over a very long time period, the actual writing may free the analyst's attention from preoccupation with that particular theme.

Ownership

Whether an analyst believes it is acceptable to publish what he or she has written without the patient's consent often depends on how the analyst conceptualizes ownership of clinical material; this question has been heatedly debated. As previously stated, Goldberg (2004c) tries to resolve this debate by designating the analyst's conceptualizations, interpretations, and countertransference as belonging to the analyst and the history and narrative of the treatment as the property of the patient. Mauger and others, such as Furlong (1998, 2004), influenced by some French psychoanalytic perspectives, maintain the trans-individual nature of transference (and countertransference) belongs to the analyst as much as the patient. Both Goldberg (2004b) and Mauger argue that it may be to the patient's detriment not to share material. For Mauger, this applies in a general way; for Goldberg, the benefits to the patient of analysts' communications outside of the analytic setting are more specific, such as analysts' seeking consultation about the work. While both Goldberg and Mauger help define the nature of what is owned, neither specifies ways in which analysts can communicate in writing that which they have defined as belonging to the analyst without simultaneously revealing material that belongs to the patient. It would seem virtually impossible to discuss a countertransference without a discussion of the material that stirred it.

Decisions to Publish

Halpern's view (2003) that writing should be limited to ideas that contribute to new knowledge in the field[1] seems a useful criterion for trying to publish articles. But analyst-authors know that their peer reviewers will not always agree with their assessment of the importance of the ideas they offer. Often peer reviewers differ greatly with each other about the value of any particular contribution. Often, too, value is assessed differently from one time period to another. For example, a paper I wrote in the early 1980s on the patient–analyst match was rejected by all the classical psychoanalytic journals. One journal editor told me that I had an unusual view; he said it seemed I thought that the therapeutic action in psychoanalysis was related to both making unconscious experiences conscious and the nature of the relationship and interactive characteristics of the patient and the analyst. In his estimation, I had to choose. Eventually, this paper was published (Kantrowitz 1986). Today such ideas

---

1. Topics that she considers in this category include demonstrations of new clinical techniques, demonstrations of what goes wrong in a treatment, and illustrations that challenge current clinical approaches.

are so commonplace that one would need to say much more for it to be seen as adding to our present-day knowledge.

But analysts' motives for publishing are not only for the good of the field. Personal ambition is, of course, a factor. Wish for professional advancement is not ignoble. However, when it conflicts with patients' best interests, it becomes problematic. Whether clinicians are able to properly address this conflict is also problematic. There is an inevitable skewing in favor of one's own point of view. But others may skew it in another direction by being so timid about potential negative effects on patients as to never write. Analysts may have conscious or unconscious anxieties about self-exposure in regard to feelings about the patient or some guilt about interpretations or interventions. This could be a type of exhibitionistic conflict, also related to the motives for wanting to write. As stated at the beginning of the book, narcissistic needs and guilt about unconscious use of the patient can create powerful pulls that may not be recognized.

Goldberg (2005) contends that expectations that analysts be self-less and saintly are unrealistic. Should an analyst actually behave with "unwavering goodness" it would be as much a countertransference as its opposite. Analysts will inevitably make misjudgments and evidence moral failings for conscious and unconscious reasons. What differentiates analysts from non-analysts is their use of the tool of analysis for self-scrutiny. Goldberg wishes us to question the "self-righteous" stance that can be assumed around confidentiality, toward writing analysts, and analysts behavior in general. Perhaps it is the tendency to idealize analysis itself that leads to the expectation that analysts' own self-reflective capacities should result in unambiguous moral behavior.

Those analysts who write want to believe it is all right with and for the patient; they try to make reality converge with their own wishes. This is human nature, but for clinicians there is a greater responsibility to be assumed. The patients' interests must come first. As shown in examples given by analysts in this study, patients were often distressed to learn that their analysts had written or even wanted to write about them. As the ethicists all note, there is always a danger that the analysts' ambition to publish may override their ability to remain attuned to their patients' needs. As Goldberg has stressed, self-deception is not unusual even for analysts. Unconscious wishes can influence and even shape what one believes. There is no simple solution for this conundrum.

Discussion with colleagues may be the best way to evaluate whether a contribution is worthwhile, whether disguise or asking consent seems the wisest course, whether a patient may be upset, and whether ruptures are likely to be reparable.

Ethics

There is an intrinsic problem for people to report what they have been told when the relationship to the person who has done the telling is valued. A conflict is stirred if one wants to write to inform oneself and others and simultaneously wants to protect the sources. The protection is not only to maintain their anonymity but also to preserve respectful appreciation of them and their trust. To some extent deception, at least in terms of omission of information, becomes necessary and this is weighted against the responsibility of truthfully reporting. Every analyst is confronted by this dilemma when writing about patients. And I as the author of this book have struggled with the same dilemma. I addressed this issue early in the book and return to it now for fuller consideration. Those who provided information for this book understand my constraint because most experience similar expectations of themselves in relation to their writing about patients.

In agreement with Goldberg (2004c), the narrative does belong to the patient or, in this case, the analysts and patients who related their attitudes, practices, and reactions. They all knew at the outset that what they told me would be published. In this respect, my situation differs from clinicians who have to decide whether to ask for this permission. For me, there would have been no continuing contact, at least around this topic, if they said no. Except when I have indicated otherwise, I have reported all that I was told. The reader therefore has almost as much information as I do about these analysts.

In contrast, when analysts report clinical examples, they are selective in what they relate. The material is chosen to make certain points and other material is excluded so readers are not privy to a great deal that analysts know. While readers certainly form opinions of their own, they do so with a limited data base and might change their views if they knew more as the analyst does; readers of this book are in a better position to judge this material for themselves. In this way, the situation is somewhat different. But what is the same is concern for the sensitivities of my respondents.

I have learned so much from the analysts and patients who volunteered to talk with me. I am grateful to them; without their participation there would be no book. In most instances, the examples did not require extensive commentary, but there were occasions when to not comment I would seem to naively accept explanations that could be seen as rationalizations. But in just those moments I am in the same position as the clinician publishing about a patient who will read it— or worse because I do not offer anything to those who volunteered as the analyst does to the patient.

Most often people agree to participate in research because they believe it is worthwhile to increase our base of knowledge. Undoubtedly, there are other personal, less altruistic motives here too. I believe that it is important to the field to know what analysts believe and actually do but this ideal serves less admirable motivations for me as well. I am less troubled by this when I am reporting things I admire in others, but when my eye becomes critical and what I want to write might cause offense to someone who has generously offered to participate, then I am tugged internally, as is a writing clinician, between wanting to fully state my views and my concern about their impact. Which value wins out? When is one being self-justifying or self-condemning? This is the ethical conundrum.

As I have stated previously, the most troublesome finding in this study was that some analysts, who were strongly committed to positions of either only disguising their patients or always asking their consent, turned away from evaluating the situation for the specific patient, and avoided struggling with conflicting ideas and feelings in favor of an uncontested belief. I have tried to bring these instances to the readers' attention. But my concerns are twofold: first, that I am appropriating something told to me for one purpose to make a point that the person offering the narrative did not intend, and second that when I highlight an aspect of a narrative that I have viewed as unreflective, I am exposing something of which the reporting analyst was previously unaware. The experience of exposure can be a narcissistic injury, an experience of being shamed. It is similar to patients' reactions when they read their analysts' referring to something about them as pathology. It reveals that the listener held a view of what was reported that had not been shared and that may be experienced as objectifying and unflattering.

Since, like analysts who write about patients after termination, I do not have ongoing relationships with most of the respondents, I do not know how they have reacted to what I have written. I do not have an opportunity to clarify to them or them to me what may have been misunderstood. As writers we all take certain risks when we write about others. When is it worth it? I do not believe that reading about oneself must be narcissistically injurious or experienced as detrimental, but there is always a chance that it may be.

Ethicists would like to find a standard that could be applied invariably. So would clinicians. There is no clear commonsense view that applies to all cases. Guidelines can provide minimum, essential requirements such as preservation of confidentiality and truthfulness in the aspects of the data that support the clinical and theoretical points of the author. But since individuals and treatment situations vary, there is no substitute for the judgment of the individual clinician. Undoubtedly once the decision to write is made, an analyst's preference for employing only disguise or asking for consent as well is influenced by character and conflicts that make a solution more comfortable for each analyst. The fact that analysts' motives for writing are also personal is to be assumed. The issue is not whether analysts benefit from writing but whether they have taken into consideration the potential impact on their patients when or if they read the publication.

Clifford's ethical precepts (1845–1879) do not provide guidelines that tell analysts what to do, but they propose the questions that should be asked. Analysts cannot know in advance the consequences of patients' reading material about themselves whether in the context of asking consent or of accidental discovery. But analysts do have information about their patients that furnish evidence to support a belief that makes it reasonable to proceed in a particular manner. Analysts are applying this principle when they state that certain character pathology, such as paranoia, masochism or exhibitionism, or a transference state of intense love or hate, makes it inadvisable to ask certain patients. Still in some specific cases, there might be more leeway given the complexity of each individual. But there are more subtle data that can also be considered, such as difficulty in expressing negative feelings or disagreement with one's analyst, that would also make it inadvisable to involve patients in requests about use of their material.

In contrast, when patients have an appreciation of the importance of contributions to the psychoanalytic field, are able to think of the analyst's writing as being both about them and something other than about them, and negative reactions can be displayed and productively explored, then analysts have evidence that makes it reasonable to consider asking the patient's consent for use of the clinical material. Under these circumstances, even a propensity to shame and difficulty in tolerating ambivalence might not ultimately prove impediments if the dyad is able to analytically process these reactions. A caveat is necessary. When patients rationally accept analysts' wishes to publish, analysts need to be alert that reasonableness not sequester other less rational parts of their patients. One can feel more confident that a patient is not being taken advantage of when the patient is able to explore and express how he or she may in part feel that this or other kinds of misuse is occurring.

It should be added that an analyst might decide not to ask and not to write about a patient because intuitively it does not feel advisable. Specifications of the factors that contribute to that intuition are not always possible, but the reluctance is palpable. The analyst's intuitive sense that it is inadvisable comes from an affective attunement to some aspect of the patient, or engagement with the patient that may not yet, or may never be, conceptualized. This unformulated reluctance to write about a patient who is believed by an analyst to meet all the criteria that "should" make it permissible to ask and increase the likelihood of patient agreement, may come from a preconscious attunement to a narcissistic sensitivity not yet understood, or when treatment has ended, possibly never actualized in the analysis. Analysts' responsiveness to intuitive, ephemeral knowing should be respected.

Sometimes decisions worked well and other times not. Clifford points out that it is not only the consequence of an action that makes it correct. While it is much more comfortable to be certain what to do, strongly held beliefs, when they are not open for reexamination, likely have ramifications beyond the outcome of any particular decision.

Some analysts in this study broadened their thinking and had a new understanding of feelings about intrusion, exposure, betrayal, and disrespect learned from their patients' reactions to the analyst's decision in relation to a publication about them. In these instances, patients have provided perspectives that challenged the analyst's belief after the fact. Most often when analysts were able to grasp the patient's point of view, empathize with it, and apologize for the distress they inadvertently caused, patients responded favorably. Likely, they appreciated their analyst's non-defensiveness, respectfulness, and openness to reconsideration of ideas. They undoubtedly took some pleasure in seeing that they have had an impact on the analyst. Treatments may prosper from such interactions. Clifford's point is that one should try to consider a point of view that opposes one's own prior to making a decision. Doubts should be not only raised, but also actively pursued by trying to find evidence to support them. This is a taxing enterprise since one's beliefs inevitably lead to biases in selection of data and limit perception of contradictory evidence. Nonetheless, the enterprise is worth undertaking.

Knowing what is normative behavior for the professional community provides a perspective against which one can compare one's own decisions. At present, however, since the professional community is almost equally divided in its views, this source of information does not advance one's deliberations. But even when community standards more clearly incline in one direction, it would not substitute for thinking through decisions for the particular situation. If it did there would never be new views or intellectual innovations. Received wisdom needs to be questioned. Consultation, however, does become a way to explore one's thinking about the effect of a decision in the particular instance. While as I have previously said, there is always the likelihood that one chooses someone whose views will probably support one's own, nonetheless an external observer most often raises considerations that expose some area that one's own being too close to the process has obscured. Ultimately, each clinician needs to weigh the input from others against his or her own careful self-scrutiny to make a judgment. It seems the closest thing to a guideline that we can meaningfully have.

Factors in Decision Making

Analysts struggle with questions of what can and cannot be worked through. On one side, they may overemphasize the extent of their impact and blanketly rule out writing clinical examples if they think their papers will be read by their patients. On the other side, they may treat asking and reading as being of so little import that they fail to carefully attend to the process that follows. The question of the clinical impact of asking or not asking is a central consideration for analysts. The interweaving of judgment, ethics, and clinical consequences is not easy to disentangle. A consideration not often made explicit is the analyst's ability to both repair injuries when they occur and use these experiences for deepening analytic work with the specific patient.

Commitment to different theoretical conceptions of psychoanalysis also affects analysts' decisions. Those analysts who believe that affects and transference should spontaneously emerge with as little stirring by the analyst as possible will be disinclined to ask. They will want to minimize the impact of interactions. But many analysts now view abstinence as having its own effect on the process. Those analysts who think of analysis more as an intersubjective engagement will be less reluctant to stimulate the transference and probably less conflicted about introducing a request about writing. Analysts of each theoretical persuasion are equally convinced of the benefit of their model. Anecdotal accounts can provide support for each perspective. We have no definitive data. Again, it probably depends on the particular patient, particular analyst, and their interaction.

Meaning of Awareness of Readers

When analysts consider writing or presenting material about patients, they become aware of the potential presence of an outside observer. The effect of imagining this other in connection with the dyad has variable meanings. Some non-writing analysts contend that an awareness of "a third" is an intrusion, but at least one analyst contested this opinion as a rationalization for never exposing analytic work. While writing analysts often have more positive views of outside observers, the meaning of the awareness of readers is in no way uniform. As stated previously, analysts have viewed it as providing a sense of containment and safety because the wider professional community is informed about the analytic interchanges (Pizer 2000), facilitating a sense of separateness by interrupting the dyad's enmeshment (Friedlander 1995), or stimulating of primal scene fantasies and offering a developmental push toward triangulation for the patient (Gerson 2000). Many analysts, however, remain much more conflicted about this topic and continually struggle between concern about the potential disruption that patients may experience when they know others will read about them and a belief that clinical illustrations are essential for the health and progress of psychoanalysis as a field. Knowing that others will read, however, also pushes analysts to more clearly define their thinking and try to cogently present their point of view. It often sharpens the analyst's awareness about aspects of the patient, the treatment, and oneself that may benefit the patient.

THE IMPACT OF DECISIONS ON THE PATIENT AND THE CLINICAL PROCESS

To Disguise Alone or Ask Consent

Analysts interviewed for this project have provided material that demonstrates that neither asking permission nor having patients discover they have been written about without permission necessarily disrupts or is permanently detrimental to the analysis or the patients' view of the analyst. In both instances, there is no formula for what makes it understandable and acceptable to the patient. As it has repeatedly been stressed, it depends on the characteristics of the particular patient and the nature and quality of the relationship with the analyst.

In contrast, both finding material when analysts have not asked permission and the process of asking permission and its ramifications were each, at times, very disruptive. In certain instances, the experience interfered with the patients' ability to make further beneficial use of their analysis. Often, though not always in these latter cases, boundary crossings, not related to writing about the patient, were involved.

Nonetheless, usually when analysts decide to ask permission, most of them are extremely sensitive as to which patients they ask and how they do it. The assumption that patients will feel compelled to consent is not always warranted. Some patients do refuse; the influence of the transference is not the only factor in patients' decisions.

Patients' reactions of pain or pleasure not only may change over time, they also are not the criteria for assessing the effect of these decisions on the treatment. The overarching question is what the patient can usefully assimilate that facilitates integration, healing, and growth.

Therapeutic Benefits from Patients' Reading about Themselves

As previously stated, Joffe (2003) believes that sharing written material with patients can bring patients and therapists together to jointly consider and review aspects of their work. Halpern (2003) points out that reading what therapists write can validate patients' perceptions. Howe adds that patients' reactions to what is written provide therapists with opportunities to learn from their patients. It allows therapists to see patients' negative feelings more clearly and to search for them when they may be less apparent in other material. The discussion also provides an opportunity for the therapist to be empathic and make amends if the patient has felt hurt.

As I have also previously described, when analysts believe that the material they wish to write about can be shared with the patient for potential benefit in the treatment, they are less reluctant to ask permission. Many analysts who showed their patients what they wrote found that both the request and the patients' reactions evoked material that was central to their patients' difficulties. As we learned, some analysts even introduced a request for permission to publish the material with a focus on what the request and the reading of the paper would stimulate in analysis. While over the years many analysts have become more interactive with their patients, analysts whose theoretical perspective inclines them to the relational school of thought tend to believe interactive engagement is the vehicle for expressing and exposing the deepest layers of the self. As such, the active interchanges and greater exposure of the analyst's more personal self that are likely to occur around negotiations about writing do not pose as great an obstacle as they do for some more classically oriented analysts. However, there is a much greater overlap among these different theoretical groups than might be expected. The long-term clinical consequences of self-disclosure are still unknown.

Inevitable Problems

There are some problems that cannot be avoided. One danger is that the analyst's view of the patient may substitute for the patient's view of himself. Another is that while countertransference responses that have been explored in the treatment are more palatable, they are often upsetting to revisit. In fact, even when material has been well explored and understood, there is often a painful reliving of past experiences and of seeing oneself as one once was despite all the concomitant pleasure in recognizing how one has changed. As noted earlier, Howe (2003) also points out that even when clinicians are tactful in how they write, some patients may be prone to reading in a negative judgment. Still another concern is that once the impressions of the patient and analyst are in print, they are frozen and preserved in this form forever; patients may then feel trapped in unmodifiable constructions of themselves and relationships with their analysts.

There are some patients who should not be written about. As stated previously, some analysts believe that patients who are paranoid, masochistic, compliant, or exhibitionistic should be excluded as subjects. However, masochism, compliance, and exhibitionism are likely to be some part of many people's characters and would not seem reason to exclude them unless these issues could not become the topic of analytic scrutiny. But there are issues that analysts do need to avoid to protect their patients. The specific content that needs to be avoided varies from patient to patient and treatment to treatment.

I will repeat what I have previously stated because it is important to stress, both in terms of clinical caution and its implications for psychoanalytic knowledge: some material is too private for publication. This material is likely to be shame producing, hurtful, or frightening, such as most intense countertransference reactions. Such exclusions mean that what is presented in the literature is skewed. Readers of analytic publications need to keep in mind that all that goes on in treatment may not be being told. The priority is to protect the patient and the treatment.

EFFECT ON THE PROFESSIONAL COMMUNITY

Conflict of Loyalties

This brings us to a conflict central to psychoanalysis that I have tried to elucidate throughout this book. Analysts need to protect their patients by writing in a respectful, non-shaming way. They also need to be truthful in what they write for the professional community. Being truthful does not mean that "everything" must be written. But, at times, it might provide perspective if readers were informed that analysts were choosing not to expand a topic or not to address some areas because of consideration of patients' privacy. Analysts also need to be humble in their claims. Humility is important for both the professional community and the patient. This observation returns us to the point that however well informed the therapist's view is, it is not the only one, nor necessarily the most accurate.

Accountability is limited by inevitable subjectivity and unconscious biases, conflicts, and self-interests. In addition, what is thought to be acceptable is influenced by cultural values of particular historical times. As I have said, two and a half decades ago it was viewed as expected by many analysts that they would write about their patients without asking permission. Cultural attitudes were more hierarchical. Currently, the pendulum has swung; individual rights and autonomy are considered in a different light. It is, therefore, not surprising that it is increasingly common that patients are asked for their permission before articles are published. It is also to be expected in professional communities that what is common practice influences and ultimately shapes the attitudes and behaviors of members in the group. There is a danger, though, of losing the larger perspective that analyst-authors do have dual responsibilities. The importance of representative published clinical reports may be insufficiently appreciated.

While analyst-authors can remain sensitive in tone and respectful in attitude, not everything they wish to write will be acceptable to their patients. If analysts cannot write about paranoid, masochistic, compliant, or exhibitionistic patients, does this mean accounts about these difficulties will no longer appear in the literature? If shameful and private material is to be avoided in papers, how will knowledge about these difficulties and how to work with them analytically be communicated and our current understanding be preserved historically? While it is understandable and usually clinically wise that analysts are reluctant to ask patients who are in negative states of emotion, if such examples are no longer published analysts whose patients are in these negative states may come to feel incompetent, ashamed, and possibly reluctant to discuss such experiences with colleagues. They may believe these difficulties to be more unique and personal to their skill than they actually are. In order to keep a balance of clinical experiences in the psychoanalytic literature, we have to hope that some analysts will continue to find ways of disguising patients that both preserve confidentiality and do not distort the material in order that negative and difficult experiences can be part of the psychoanalytic literature. The needs of the individual patient must come first, but in this era of egalitarianism, there still is a need for an accurate representation of analytic work in the literature.

Budd (1997) makes a similar point in her concern that if the current trend to write primarily about process dominates the psychoanalytic literature, readers may come to define the field in this fashion. In the instances she describes, only the patient can recognize the material since biographical details are omitted rather than disguise added. Many analysts believe that under these circumstances often patients themselves do not recognize the examples as their own, or at least are unclear if this is so. Other patients believe the examples are about them when they are not.[2] The difficulty with this method is not for the patient, but for the psychoanalytic field. Since overarching narratives are usually not included in these accounts, many important aspects of analytic thinking are neglected. Therefore, what is published may begin to shape readers' ideas about what analysis is, and thereby change theory itself.

---

2. Of course, both patients and clinicians listening to or reading any clinical examples may also erroneously believe they have identified a patient.

Need for Awareness of Inevitable Subjectivity

While throughout this book I have emphasized the unavoidable skewing that comes from subjectivity, I could not have a concluding chapter that did not return to this topic and repeat some of what has been previously stated. Joffe (2003) points out that it is inevitable that the person recounting a narrative does so from his or her own point of view. He also notes that readers will be likely to privilege the analyst's account since the analyst will be perceived as the authority. A follow-up study of the outcome of psychoanalysis (Kantrowitz 1987) compared analysts' views, patients' views, and pre-analysis and post-analysis psychological test results. It was found that there were significant discrepancies not only between the analysts' and patients' perceptions but also between each of their views and the psychological test results' assessment of change. Considerations of what transpires during treatment or its outcome cannot be judged against any one evaluative source. While the scientific community may be inclined to take the analyst's view and the psychological test results as more objective measures, each is an evaluation from a specific purview.[3] When analysts have patients read what they have written about them, it is incumbent on analysts to include the patient's perspective if it is different from their own. This does not mean that it supersedes the analyst's view, but that readers know that such a disagreement exists. I am not suggesting that it is necessary for analysts to invite their patients to contribute their

---

3. An analyst's view that change has occurred, when a patient feels no change in distress, may be considered subjectively biased, but that does not necessarily mean they are incorrect—though of course, they may be. Comparisons of pre- and post-analysis psychological test results that show change are more objective measures of such change. In other words, it may be true that a patient changes in some dimensions, at the same time that it is also true that the patient does not feel less distress. The relationship between analytic change and therapeutic benefit remains complex. How a patient feels during or after treatment, while not the only valid way of assessing what occurred, is ultimately the only meaningful view of the success of the treatment process from the patient's point of view. By this, I do not mean that the patient necessarily has to like the analyst or, as Halpern indicates, be free of pain, but that in some experiential way the patient needs to believe there has been a benefit in participating in the therapeutic process. The discrepancy between the analyst's and the patient's post-treatment evaluation is a matter for scientific inquiry. We should seek to understand this discrepancy over time.

views to publications, as Stoller (1988) did, nor even that the patient needs to be informed if the analyst believes the patient will not read it. What I am proposing is that analysts should include the information they have about the differing views in the publication. I am also alerting readers to be aware of unavoidable skewing of material because of the author's subjectivity.

REASONS FOR WRITING CLINICAL EXAMPLES

Given all the problems that writing about patients may cause, unless there is therapeutic benefit for the patient why should it be done? The arguments for the need to have written clinical material are manifold.

New Ideas and Historical Record

Writing introduces new ideas into the field. In addition, we need a record of the history of psychoanalysis, both in theory and technique. Ideas and practices change over time. We need to appreciate what is thought at a particular historical moment and how this is influenced, not only by what was previously thought but also by the historical context itself. Often this kind of understanding is clear only in retrospect. Ideas that are passing fancies compared with those that withstand the test of time often cannot be assessed when they are initially presented. Ideas rejected for many decades may also then resurface and be viewed as having been erroneously dismissed. Freud's seduction hypothesis is such an example (Breuer and Freud 1895).

Dissemination of Current Thinking

Published material also provides a wider dissemination of current thinking than supervision or local seminars can. People trained in the same communities often tend to share similar ideas. Published papers allow readers to become aware of what is thought and being done in other geographical locations. It keeps analysts from becoming parochial.

Illustrations of Theory and Technique

What also needs to be emphasized, however, is that clinical material is offered to illustrate a concept, theory, or technique. Clinical examples can never prove anything about the particular patient. Papers are written with certain perspectives in mind and intend to transmit certain points. The material presented is unavoidably shaped by the analyst's vantage point. As previously stated, the analyst's subjectivity places limits on selection and perception of data. And even were the patient's account added, the presentation would still be restricted to some particular focus and to the conscious layers of the minds of participants. In this respect, clinical examples are never only about a particular patient, though the reader needs to trust that the account is accurate to the analyst's conscious knowledge. Examples both provide recognition of clinical phenomena and may circumvent misunderstandings of abstract concepts. They make theoretical ideas come alive. Clinical illustrations can never be used to prove something is "true" but they can sometimes at least show what is not true. Even one illustration that contradicts a given assumption means that the assumption must be reconsidered.

Models for Clinical Practice

Furthermore, analysts need to report what they do. They need to do so, not only to learn from each other but also to keep what is done as something that is known in the community. The analytic relationship is a private one, filled with all the possible danger that such privacy can create. By writing, analysts keep what they do open to the community's scrutiny. Appropriate professional sharing shields the relationship from self-deluding practices that may be harmful to patients. Writing does not prevent secret and suspect activities from occurring in the name of therapy; but it provides some models for what are and are not acceptable practices, or at least opens debate about which practices are and are not acceptable.

Analysts who believe negative countertransference reactions should be written about stress the importance of including an examination of these negative reactions and their reverberations in the treatment in the psychoanalytic literature. As proposed earlier, other analysts need to know that such reactions occur and not feel so ashamed or isolated in feeling negatively toward a patient that they try to deny this reaction or fail to seek consultation should this be desirable.

Aid in Self-Scrutiny

It is my contention that both clinical contributions to the psychoanalytic literature from which new insights can be gleaned and psychoanalytic research that challenges long-held theoretical assumptions can help analysts to overcome resistance to scanning certain parts of the relationship in which there are particular sensitivities and vulnerabilities. The implications of avoidances of self-scrutiny are broader than decisions about methods for preserving confidentiality. Every analysis is likely to have limitations due to areas in both the patient's and the analyst's individual conflicts and covert areas in the relationship that remain shielded by narcissism and intractable privacy. These untouchable areas may be unique to each dyad and may relate to the frequency of second analyses. Analysts aim to expand the purview of touchable topics within the dyad, a purview that always has blind spots specific to each treatment. Supervision and consultation are aids in this process; publications of clinical material that illuminates impasses or areas in patient–analyst engagement that remain unfathomable or aspects of analysts' struggles to overcome blind spots also serve to stimulate intellectual curiosity and psychological growth.

SUMMARY

There are no easy answers about how to write, when to write, or who and what to write about. Simple rules will not work. There are principles that can be learned from the examples provided by the analysts in this study that inform clinician-authors about what not to do. But there is no substitute for the individualizing in which each clinician carefully considers the characteristics of the patient, and the nature of their relationship at any given time. Clinicians must remain vigilant about being self-serving. Publications are valuable, but nothing is more important than the protection of the patient. There is no way around the case-by-case approach.

In conclusion, analysts need to write for the benefit of the field, their patients, and often themselves. At the same, analysts must continue to struggle with concerns about potential harm to their patients from being written about. There are patients for whom it is damaging. The examples in this book show that analysts are not always aware which patients will feel injured or what aspect of the writing they will experience as injurious. Patients do not always tell their analysts or sometimes even know themselves until a later time that they have felt hurt or experienced other adverse consequences from having their analysts write about them. There is no perfect solution. Not sharing clinical material is not an acceptable answer. All analysts can do is to try to be sensitive in their requests and in their writings, and alert to the ramifications of their decisions.

Appendix

PART I: ANALYST'S DECISION TO WRITE ABOUT A PATIENT

1. What leads you to decide to write about a particular patient?
   —the particular problem area the patient struggles with becomes an area of interest
   —your own interest in an area that the patient's material illuminates or illustrates
   —an internal conflict that the patient stirs
   —a transference–countertransference interaction that leads you to new understanding
   —an internal conflict that work with the patient helps you understand or work on
   —other
2. When you decide to write about a patient with the intent of publication, do you inform him or her?
   If not, how do you deal with their material?
   If so, what do you say to the patient about this?
3. Timing: When do you bring this up?
   —at the beginning of treatment as a general possibility?

—after termination?

If so, how long after and what is your thinking that determines this decision?

—during the course of the treatment?

If so, at what point and what is your thinking that determines this decision?

4. Is there a difference in your attitude about writing for publication about someone who is a member of the mental health community and someone who is not? Explain.

5. Is there a difference if this is an adult or a child? If it is a child, do you request permission from the parents? Do they read what you have written? Is the child informed? Does the decision to inform the child relate to the child's age? If so, at what age would you do so? Explain.

PART II: PATIENT'S DECISIONS AND EFFECT ON ANALYST'S THINKING AND TREATMENT

1. Have you ever had a patient refuse to give you permission to use their material?

During what phase of the treatment?

What, intrapsychic consequences did this have for you?

What, if any, manifestations or overt reactions occurred from the patient?

How was this worked on?

Were there long-term ramifications to your having made this request?

If so, to what extent were they resolved? With what degree of satisfactory closure on the patient part? On your part?

2. Have you ever had a patient give you permission and then rescind it?

If so, why did this change of mind come about?

Did the patient explain it? Did you think you understood the reason(s)?

What intrapsychic consequences did this have for you?

What, if any, manifestations or overt reactions occurred from the patient?

If this occurred during treatment, how was this worked on? Were there long-term ramifications of the patient's withdrawal of permission? If so, to what extent were they resolved? With what degree of satisfactory closure on the patient part? On your part?

If this occurred after termination, how have you handled it? Did the patient want to discuss it further? Did this result in further work together? If this was a patient who had kept in touch after terminating, did this change?

> Why did this change of mind come about?
>
> Did the patient explain it? Did you think you understood the reason(s)?

3. If it was agreeable to the patient that you write about him or her, do you show the patient what you have written?

> If so, how did your patient react to reading about himself or herself and the things it revealed about your thinking or feeling about the patient and your work together?
>
> How did you discuss and process this?

A. *After termination*: If this occurred after termination, did you send the patient the material?

> Did you invite the patient to come in and discuss his or her reaction to what you wrote with you? If so, did you charge the patient?
>
> If the patient and not you requested the meeting, did you charge for it?
>
> If the patient wanted you to change, leave out, or modify some part of what was written, how did you respond? Overtly? What were your internal thoughts and feelings about the request? Have you ever had a patient object to the disguise provided for confidentiality? If so, how have you handled this? Exploring with the hope of both understanding and helping the patient learn something but without changing it? Modifying and then checking with the patient again? Collaboratively creating a disguise acceptable to the patient? Describe.

B. *During treatment:* If you ask a patient about writing about him or her during the course of the treatment,

> what, if any, manifestations or overt reactions occurred from the patient?

how was this worked on?

Were there long-term ramifications to your having made this request?

If so, to what extent were they resolved? With what degree of satisfactory closure on the patient part? On your part?

Can you provide an example.

4. In the specific instance of your writing about a patient in the article in————Journal, can you address the questions above?

5. Has anything in your experience related to writing about patients changed your view about any aspect of the process of writing about patients or even the decision about writing about them at all?

If so, what and in what way: Result in not using patient examples? To only conceal and never ask patients? To always inform patients? To conceal or request permission under specific circumstances? If so, describe. To write about patients only after termination? Describe.

PART III: OTHER ISSUES RELATED TO ANALYSTS' REFLECTION ON USING CLINICAL MATERIAL

1. Do you think your thinking about any of these issues related to writing about patients has changed over time? If so, in what way? For how long have you held this different view? What led you to change your views?

2. Do some patients come to treatment telling you that they have a specific knowledge that you write? Have they chosen you in part because of this? Do they spontaneously offer themselves as material? How do you respond? Do they request that you not write about them? Is this different for patients in the mental health community and those who are not?

3. Have you ever used material about yourself and disguised it as being from a patient?

4. To your knowledge, were you ever written about when you were a patient? If so, did you read? What were your reactions? Did you discuss it with your analyst? Would you describe the process and your thoughts about it over time?

5. If you don't ask permission of patients to use their material, would you elaborate on the reasons for this and what your concerns are about its impact on them, the treatment, why you think it would not be analyzable, and so on. If you have had any patients read what you've written with your consent or due to their finding it, would you detail what occurred, how you worked with it, what you thought and felt about it, and the long-range consequences (of the patient reading about himself) as fully as possible.

References

Aron, L. (2000). Ethical considerations in the writing of case histories. *Psychoanalytic Dialogues* 10:231–245.

Beebe, B. (2004). Faces in relation: a case study. *Psychoanalytic Dialogues* 14:1–51.

Berman, E. (1995). On analyzing colleagues. *Contemporary Psychoanalysis* 31:521–539.

Berman, J. (1985). Philip Roth's psychoanalysts in *The Talking Cure: Literary Representations of Psychoanalysis*, pp. 239–269. New York, London: New York University Press.

—— (2001). Book review of *Tales from the Couch: Writers on Therapy*, ed. J. Shinder. *Psychoanalytic Psychology* 18:743–755.

Bernstein, R. (1983). *Beyond Objectivism and Relativism*. Philadelphia: University of Pennsylvania Press.

Brendel, D. H. (2002). Case report: I see dead people: overcoming psychic numbness. *Harvard Review of Psychiatry* 10:165–170.

—— (2003). Complications to consent. *Journal of Clinical Ethics* 14:90–94.

Brenner, I. (in press). Termination of analysis and September 11th. *Psychoanalysis Quarterly*.

Breuer, J., and Freud, S. (1895). Studies on hysteria. *Standard Edition* 2.

Bridges, N. (2003). *Clinical writing about patients: negotiating the impact on patients and their treatment*. Unpublished paper.

Budd, S. (1997). "Ask me no questions and I'll tell you no lies: the social organization of secrets." In *The Presentation of Case Material in Clinical Discourse*, ed. I. Ward. London: Freud Museum Publication distributed by H. Karnac (books) Ltd.

"Carter, J." (2003). Looking into a distorted mirror. *Journal of Clinical Ethics* 14:95–100.

Casement, P. (1985). *On Learning from the Patient*. London: Tavistock.

Chused, J. F. (1992). The patient's perception of the analyst: the hidden transference. *Psychoanalytic Quarterly* 61:161–184.

Clifford, W. K. (1845–1879). The ethics of belief. In *Introductory Readings in Philosophy*, ed. M. G. Singer and R. R. Ammerman, pp. 94–100. New York: Scribner's Sons, 1962.

Clifft, M. A. (1986). Writing about psychiatric patients. *Bulletin of the Menninger Clinic* 50:511–524.

Cocks, G. (1994). *The Curve of Life: Correspondence of Heinz Kohut 1923–1981*. Chicago: University of Chicago Press.

Crastnopol, M. (1999). The analyst's professional self as a third influence on the dyad: when the analyst writes about the treatment. *Psychoanalytic Dialogues* 9:445–470.

Deutsch, H. (1921). On the pathological lie (pseudologia phantastica). *Journal of the American Academy of Psychoanalysis* 10:369–386, 1982.

——— (1973). *Confrontations with Myself*. New York: W. W. Norton.

Ehrenberg, D. (1992). *The Intimate Edge*. New York: W. W. Norton.

Eifferman, R. R. (1987). "Germany," "the Germans": acting out fantasies, and their discovery in self-analysis. *International Review of Psychoanalysis* 14:245–264.

Feiner, A. (1996). Bewitched, bothered and bewildered: some core issues in interpersonal psychoanalysis. *Contemporary Psychoanalysis* 32:411–425.

Freud, A. (1922). Beating fantasies and daydreams. In *The Writings of Anna Freud* I, pp. 137–157. New York: International Universities Press.

Freud, S. (1899). Screen memories. *Standard Edition* 3:301–322.

——— (1905). Fragments of an analysis of a case of hysteria. *Standard Edition* 7:3–122.

Friedlander, S. (1995). The "third" party in psychoanalysis: Lacan, the signifier, and the symbolic order. *Clinical Studies International Journal of Psychoanalysis* 1:17–31.

Furlong, A. (1998). Should we or shouldn't we? Some aspects of confidentiality of clinical reporting and dossier access. *International Journal of Psychoanalysis* 79:727–739.

——— (2004). *Discussion of Kantrowitz, J. L., Writing about patients II: pa tients' reading about themselves and their analysts' perceptions of its effect.* American Psychoanalytic Association, Winter Meetings.

———— (in press). To ask or not ask for consent in clinical writing. *International Journal of Psychoanalysis.*

Gabbard, G. O. (1997). Case histories and confidentiality (letter to the editor). *International Journal of Psychoanalysis.*87:820–821.

———— (2000). Disguise or consent?: problems and recommendations concerning the publication and presentation of clinical material. *International Journal of Psychoanalysis* 81:1071–1086.

Gabbard, G. O., and Lester, E. P. (1995). *Boundaries and Boundary Violations in Psychoanalysis.* New York: Basic Books.

Gabbard, G., and Williams, P. (2001). Preserving confidentiality in the writing of case reports. *International Journal of Psychoanalysis* 82:1067–1068.

Galatzer-Levy, R. (2003). Psychoanalytic research and confidentiality: dilemmas. In *Confidentiality: Ethical Perspectives and Clinical Dilemmas,* ed. C. Levin, A. Furlong, and M. K. O'Neil, pp. 85–106. Hillsdale, NJ: Analytic Press.

Gardner, R. (1983). *Self-Inquiry.* Hillsdale, NJ: Analytic Press.

Gedo, J. (2002). Book review: *Heinz Kohut: The Making of an Analyst,* by Charles B. Stozier. *American Imago* 59:91–102.

Gerson, S. (2000). Therapeutic action of writing about patients: commentary on papers by Lewis Aron and by Stuart A. Pizer. *Psychoanalytic Dialogues* 10:261–266.

Goldberg, A. (1997). Writing case histories. *International Journal of Psychoanalysis* 78:435–438.

———— (2004a). Who owns the countertransference? *Psychoanalytic Quarterly* 73:517–523.

———— (2004b). A risk of confidentiality. *International Journal of Psychoanalysis* 85:301–310.

———— (2004c). Psychoanalysis and the problem of ownership: an effort at resolution. Unpublished paper.

———— (2005). *Panel presentation: In strictest confidence: reporting clinical material.* American Psychoanalytic Association, Winter Meetings.

Gopnik, A. (1998). Annals of psychoanalysis: Amana goes to see a doctor. *The New Yorker.* August 24 and 31, pp. 114–121.

Guntrip, H. (1975). My experience of analysis with Fairbairn and Winnicott. *International Review of Psychoanalysis* 2:145–156.

Halpern, J. (2003). Beyond wishful thinking: facing the harm that psychotherapists can do by writing about their patients. *Journal of Clinical Ethics* 14:118–136.

Howe, E. G. (2003). Lessons from "Jay Carter." *Journal of Clinical Ethics* 14: 109–117.

Hurwitz, M. (1986). The analyst, his theory, and the psychoanalytic process. *Psychoanalytic Study of the Child* 41:439–466.

Jacobs, T. (1991). *The Use of the Self.* Madison, CT: International Universities Press.

Joffe, S. (2003). Public dialogue and the boundaries of moral community. *Journal of Clinical Ethics* 14:101–108.

Kantrowitz, J. L. (1986). The role of the patient–analyst "match" in the outcome of psychoanalysis. *Annual of Psychoanalysis* 14:273–297.

——— (1987). Suitability for psychoanalysis. *Yearbook of Psychoanalysis and Psychotherapy* 2:273–297.

——— (1996). *The Patient's Impact on the Analyst.* Hillsdale, NJ: Analytic Press.

——— (2003). Tell me your theory. Where is it bred? A lesson from clinical approaches to dreams. *Journal of Clinical Psychoanalysis* 12:151–178.

Kantrowitz, J. L., Katz, A. L., Paolitto, F., et al. (1987). Changes in the level and quality of object relations in psychoanalysis: follow-up of a longitudinal prospective study. *Journal of the American Psychoanalytic Association* 35:25–46.

Kantrowitz, J. L., Paolitto, F., Sashin, J., et al. (1986). Affect and availability, tolerance, complexity, and modulation in psychoanalysis: follow-up of a longitudinal study. *Journal of the American Psychoanalytic Association* 34:529–559.

Karme, L. (1988). A mother dies, a child denies: the reparative psychoanalytic process, a case study. *Psychoanalytic Review* 75: 263–281.

Kleinschmidt, H. J. (1967). The angry act: the role of aggression in creativity. *American Imago* 24:98–128.

Klumpner, G. H., and Frank, A. (1991). On methods of reporting clinical material. *Journal of the American Psychoanalytic Association* 39:537–551.

Kohut, H. (1979). The two analyses of Mr. Z. *International Journal of Psychoanalysis* 60:3–27.

Lafarge, L. (2000). Interpretation and containment. *International Journal of Psychoanalysis* 81:67–84.

Lear, J. (2003). Confidentiality as a virtue. In *Confidentiality: Ethical Perspectives and Clinical Dilemmas,* ed. C. Levin, A. Furlong, M. K. O'Neil, pp. 3–17. Hillsdale, NJ: The Analytic Press.

Levin, C. (2003). Civic confidentiality and psychoanalytic confidentiality in *Confidentiality: Ethical Perspectives and Clinical Dilemmas,* ed. C. Levin, A. Furlong, and M. K. O'Neil, pp. 51–74. Hillsdale, NJ: Analytic Press.

Lipson, C. (2003). *Kohut and Mr. Z.* Unpublished paper.

Lipton, E. L. (1991). The analyst's use of clinical data and other issues of confidentiality. *Journal of the American Psychoanalytic Association* 39:967–985.

Little, M. (1981). *Transference Neurosis and Transference Psychosis*. New York: Jason Aronson.

Loewald, H. (1960). On the therapeutic action of psychoanalysis. *International Journal of Psychoanalysis* 41:16–33.

Mahony, P. (1984). *Cries of the Wolf Man*. New York: International Universities Press.

———(1986). *Freud and the Rat Man*. New Haven, CT: Yale University Press.

Mauger, J. (2003). Public, private . . . In *Confidential Relationships: Psychoanalytic, Ethical, and Legal Contexts*, ed. C. Koggel, A. Furlong, and C. Levin, pp. 53–60. Amsterdam and New York: Editions Rodopi.

McLaughlin, J. T. (1981). Transference, psychic reality, and countertransference. *Psychoanalytic Quarterly* 50:637–664.

Michels, R. (2000). The case history. *Journal of the American Psychoanalytic Association* 48:354–375.

Person, E. S. (1983). Women in therapy: therapist gender as a variable. *International Review of Psychiatry* 10:193–204.

Pfeffer, A. (1961). Follow-up study of a satisfactory psychoanalysis. *Journal of the American Psychoanalytic Association* 9:698–718.

———(1963). Meaning of analyst after analysis. *Journal of the American Psychoanalytic Association* 11:229–244.

Pine, F. (1990). *Drive, Ego, and Self*. Madison, CT: Basic Books.

Pizer, S. A. (1992). The negotiation of paradox in the analytic process. *Psychoanalytic Dialogues* 2:215–240.

———(2000). A gift in return: the clinical use of writing about a patient. *Psychoanalytic Dialogues* 10:247–259.

Popkin, R. H., and Stroll, A. (1969). Ethics. In *Philosophy Made Simple*, pp. 1–55. London: W. H. Allen.

Rangell, L. (2002). The theory of psychoanalysis: vicissitudes of its evolution. *Journal of the American Psychoanalytic Association* 75:1245–1250.

Reed, G. (1993). On the value of explicit reconstruction. *Psychoanalytic Quarterly* 62:52–73.

Reiser, L. W. (2000). "The write stuff." *Journal of the American Psychoanalytic Association* 48:351–354.

Renik, O. (1994). Publications of clinical facts. *International Journal of Psychoanalysis* 75:1245–1250.

Ringstrom, P. (1998). Therapeutic impasses in contemporary psychoanalytic treatment: revisiting the double-blind hypothesis. *Psychoanalytic Dialogues* 8:297–315.

Roazen, P. (1982). Introduction to Helene Deutsch 1921 paper "On the Pathological Lie (pseudologia phantastica)." *Journal of the American Academy of Psychoanalysis* 10:369–386.

Roth, P. (1969). *Portnoy's Complaint*. New York: Random House.

———— (1970). *My Life as a Man*. New York, Chicago, San Francisco: Holt, Rinehart & Winston.

Scharff, J. S. (2000). Writing from clinical experience. *Journal of the American Psychoanalytic Association* 48:421–427.

Schlessinger, N., and Robbins, F. (1974). Assessment and follow-up in psychoanalysis. *Journal of the American Psychoanalytic Association* 22:542–567.

Schwaber, E. A. (1992). Countertransference: the analyst's retreat from the patient's vantage point. *International Journal of Psychoanalysis* 3:349–362.

———— (1997). *Discussion: Ethical issues in clinical case reporting*. Discussion group, chairs S. Behnke and E. Wallwork, American Psychoanalytic Association, Winter Meeting, New York.

Shapiro, T. (1994). Psychoanalytic facts: from the editor's desk. *International Journal of Psychoanalysis* 75:1225—1232.

Silber, A. (1996). Analysis, re-analysis, and self-analysis. *Journal of the American Psychoanalytic Association* 44:491–509.

Simon, B. (1993). In search of psychoanalytic technique: perspectives from on the couch and behind the couch. *Journal of the American Psychoanalytic Association* 41:1051–1062.

Smith, H. (2001). Hearing voices. *Journal of the American Psychoanalytic Association* 49:781–812.

Smith, R. (1995). Publishing information about patients: time to change from guarding anonymity to getting consent. *British Medical Journal* 311:1240–1241.

Sonnenberg, S. M. (1991). The analyst's self-analysis and its impact on clinical work: a comment on the source of personal insight. *Journal of the American Psychoanalytic Association* 39:687–704.

Spence, D. P. (1991). Discussion of "The Troubled Standing of the Case Study." Panel of presentation of clinical experience, reported by R. Galatzer-Levy. *Journal of the American Psychoanalytic Association* 39:727–740.

Spezzano, C. (1998). The triangle of clinical judgment. *Journal of the American Psychoanalytic Association* 46:365–388.

Spillius, E. (1994). On formulating clinical fact to a patient. *International Journal of Psychoanalysis* 75:112–1132.

Stein, M. H. (1981). The unobjectionable part of the transference. *Journal of the American Psychoanalytic Association* 29:869–892.

———(1988a). Writing about psychoanalysis: I. Analysts who write and those who do not. *Journal of the American Psychoanalytic Association* 36:105–124.

——— (1988b). Writing about psychoanalysis: II. Analysts who write, patients who read. *Journal of the American Psychoanalytic Association* 36:393–408.

Stein, R. (2000). "False love—why not?" Fragments of an analysis. *Study in Gender and Sexuality* 1:167–190.

Stern, S. (2002). The self as a relational structure: a dialogue with multiple-self theory. *Psychoanalytic Dialogues* 12:693–714.

Stoller, R. J. (1988). Patients' response to their own case report. *Journal of the American Psychoanalytic Association* 36:371–391.

Strozier, C. (2001). *Heinz Kohut: The Making of an Analyst*. New York: Farrar, Straus and Giroux.

Szecsody, I. (2000). Commentary on Robert Michels's paper, "The Case History." *Journal of the American Psychoanalytic Association* 48:397–403.

Tessman, L. H. (2003). *The Analyst's Analyst Within*. Hillsdale, NJ: Analytic Press.

Tuckett, D. (1993). Some thoughts on the presentation and discussion of the clinical case material of psychoanalysis. *International Journal of Psychoanalysis* 74:1175–1190.

——— (1998). Evaluating psychoanalytic papers: towards the development of common standards. *International Journal of Psychoanalysis* 79:431–448.

——— (2000a). Commentary on Robert Michels's paper, "The Case History." *Journal of the American Psychoanalytic Association* 48:403–411.

——— (2000b). Editorial: reporting clinical events in the journal: toward the construction of a special case. *International Journal of Psychoanalysis* 81:1065–1069.

Wallwork, E. (2005). Discussion of Judy L. Kantrowitz's paper, "Writing about Patients V: Analysts' Read about Themselves." American Psychoanalytic Association, Winter Meetings.

Yanof, J. (1996). Language, communication and transference in child analysis I: the medium is the message. *Journal of the American Psychoanalytic Association* 44:79–116.

Index